# Underwater Potholer

## Whittles Dive Series

editor Rod Macdonald

The Whittles Dive Series is a collection of cutting edge books dealing with every aspect of diving – from exploring lost shipwrecks to cave diving, technical mixed gas and rebreather diving. The Series is edited by internationally acclaimed diving author Rod Macdonald, noted for works such as *Dive Scapa Flow* and *Dive Truk Lagoon*.

# Underwater Potholer

## A cave diver's memoirs

### Duncan Price

Whittles Publishing

Published by
**Whittles Publishing Ltd.,**
Dunbeath,
Caithness, KW6 6EG,
Scotland, UK

www.whittlespublishing.com

© 2015 Duncan Price

*All rights reserved. No part of this publication may be reproduced, stored in a retrieval system, or transmitted, in any form or by any means, electronic, mechanical, recording or otherwise without prior permission of the publishers.*

ISBN 978-184995-158-6

Printed by

Latimer Trend & Company Ltd., Plymouth

**Also by Duncan Price:**

*Cave Diving Group, Welsh Sump Index (2005)*

*Cave Diving Group, Somerset Sump Index (with Michael McDonald, 2008)*

*The Cave Diving Group Manual (with Andrew Ward, Colin Hayward, David Brock, John Cordingley, Rupert Skorupka, Richard Stanton, Mike Thomas, John Volanthen and Clive Westlake, 2008)*

*WOOKEY HOLE: 75 years of cave diving and exploration (with James Hanwell and Richard Witcombe, 2010)*

www.underwater-potholer.com

DISCLAIMER:

Cave diving is dangerous – do **not** do it. *Remember I told you so.* Everything else I say is bollocks!

Duncan learned to snorkel on a family holiday to Majorca aged 8. At 17 he took up scuba diving with a local BSAC club but never completed his training before he went to university. A school friend introduced him to caving and further scuppered his chances of ever getting a diving qualification. Despite this, Duncan progressed to cave diving and has been involved in many discoveries, including helping establish a new British cave diving depth record at Wookey Hole Caves, in 2005. He has co-authored a number of books about cave diving, including the current **Cave Diving Group Manual** and the award-winning **WOOKEY HOLE: 75 years of cave diving & exploration**.

When Duncan is not underground, he lives in Wells, Somerset, and masquerades as a chemical engineer in the semiconductor industry. He still hasn't 'officially' learned to dive.

www.underwater-potholer.com

### *Cover photographs*

*Front: Duncan Price in the shaft at the start of Sump 2, Emergence de Crégols, France. (photo: Liz Rogers)*

*Back: Duncan Price in Chamber 9, Wookey Hole Caves, UK, at the end of nine hours' exploration: cold, tired, smelly – and grumpy! (photo: Martyn Farr)*

## Contents

Foreword .................................................................................... ix
Maps ........................................................................................ xi

1  Duncan the Diver .................................................................. 1
2  Night of the Drunken Caver ................................................. 10
3  The Gothic Diggers ............................................................... 17
4  In Remembrance ................................................................... 28
5  Nightmare in Elm Hole ......................................................... 36
6  Down in the Clydach at Midnight ....................................... 48
7  Coming to America ............................................................... 54
8  Pilgrim's Progress .................................................................. 61
9  Lesser Welsh Caves ............................................................... 68
10 The C-word ........................................................................... 75
11 Saturday Night at the Movies ............................................... 84
12 An Unwelcome Guest ........................................................... 92
13 Dodgy Devices ...................................................................... 100
14 A Close Shave ....................................................................... 110
15 In Search of Chamber 26 ..................................................... 120
16 Veteran Cave Diver ............................................................... 129
17 'And then the Donkey Stood on my Foot!' ........................ 141
18 An Unfortunate Series of Events ......................................... 154

| | | |
|---|---|---|
| 19 | Deepest Mendip | 160 |
| 20 | No Picnic at Ilam Park | 171 |
| | Acknowledgments | 175 |
| | Glossary | 177 |

# Foreword

This is something to reflect on … I'm the best part of a mile into the multi-sump Old Cottage Cave (in New Zealand) and on my own. It wouldn't be so bad if I was just exploring a dry cave – but here I am, the other side of three dives, each separated by varying lengths of dry passage. It's over 500 metres from Sump 3, which I've just swum through, to the undived, unexplored, Sump 4 that I'm facing next. Granted, my cylinders are small – only 5 litres apiece – but with reels, spares, food and photo equipment, the entire load weighs in at over 20 kg. I have reached my destination, Llyn Glas, the Blue Lake, the furthest point I'd reached a year ago, also on a solo mission. At this point I decide to leave my photo equipment behind, as when it comes to exploration I can't afford to be distracted.

Once again, I run through all my equipment checks; everything's working exactly the way I'd like it to. I relax for a couple of minutes, then take a good deep breath … just what I'll find next is anyone's guess. This is the exciting thing about cave diving!

I slip gently beneath the surface and my line reel slowly unwinds as I move along the spacious tunnel. The visibility is at least 4 metres and the depth is much the same, for which I'm extremely grateful. My thoughts are focused totally on the here and now: nothing else intrudes. Then amazingly at 85 metres into the dive I surface to air – and better still, the sound of a thunderous free-flowing river somewhere close ahead. Any new ground is exciting stuff, but when it comes to a discovery like this I know I'm onto something big. I de-kit yet again, but this time it's the dive equipment that I leave safely stowed on a ledge; for the time being it seems as though I won't need it. Liberated from all encumbrances, I stride off up the waterway. Nothing else in life is as exciting as this …

There is no simple, logical explanation for an activity that voluntarily takes one away from the comfort of daylight and into a world of darkness and deprivation. The sport of caving involves little glamour: it's cold, damp and dirty; it involves great physical effort, isolation; and without question there are real dangers. To see a caver emerge after several hours or more from the confines of some hole in the ground, plastered in mud from head to foot, with a suit perhaps torn or shredded beyond redemption – naturally there are questions, not least concerning sanity. Why on earth should anyone subject themselves to such an experience?

But see the smile on that face, listen to the tales of camaraderie and feel the sense of achievement. Caving – indeed all subterranean activity – is generally misunderstood, and those participating are often considered more than a little strange. By comparison, climbing and mountaineering are perceived as acceptable. The armchair explorer can see the rationale; they can see that getting to the top of something is a goal worthy of challenge and risk.

But let's reflect that there are far more accidents in these 'acceptable' pursuits – not forgetting others, such as horse riding and rugby, which are statistically far more dangerous than those involving activities underground. Caving is an esoteric pursuit that's generally misunderstood and shrouded in mystery. This is understandable, perhaps, when we consider that nowhere are there mysteries greater than those below the surface of the earth. We can see mountains; we can lower cameras into the deepest oceans and we can view distant places such as the moon or Mars. But we're still ignorant of much of what lies below our feet. There will always be people with an insatiable appetite for knowledge and for whom overcoming problems is a challenge. Combine the quest with darkness, the physical nature of the activity – climbing, crawling, squeezing through low or narrow clefts, sheer drops, roof falls, unstable terrain, and last but not least water – and we have all the ingredients for a real adventure.

Cavers come in different forms. They may be scientists, environmentalists or simply individuals keen to embark on a sporting challenge. Despite the common impression to the contrary there is great beauty underground, and this attracts photographers, artists, and poets. Water is a major part of caving; it is nearly always water which is responsible for cave formation, and for sculpting and decorating, and ultimately it is water that presents the greatest difficulty for exploration.

Caving attracts a very special breed of person. This will become apparent as you submerge yourself in the pages of this book. You will be amazed, enthralled and amused by the tales Duncan recounts. You will raise an eyebrow or two (more than once!). While he and I are very different people, you will gain a fair insight into the commitment, dedication, determination and eccentricity of the participants. Most importantly, you will gain a unique insight into contemporary exploration. Let the entertainment begin …

*Martyn Farr*

# Maps

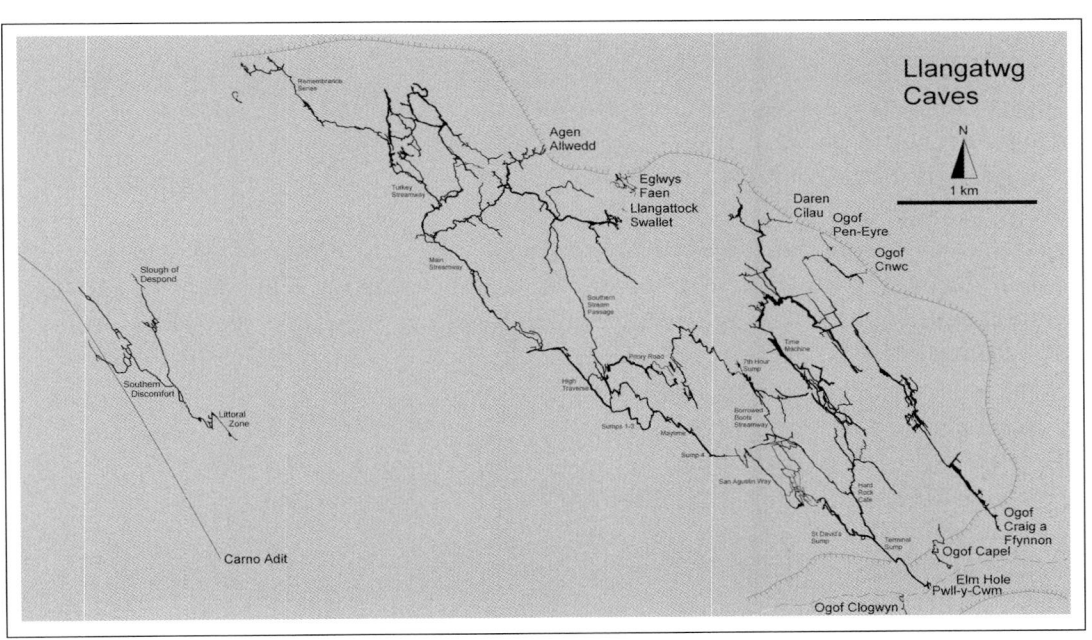

## Underwater Potholer

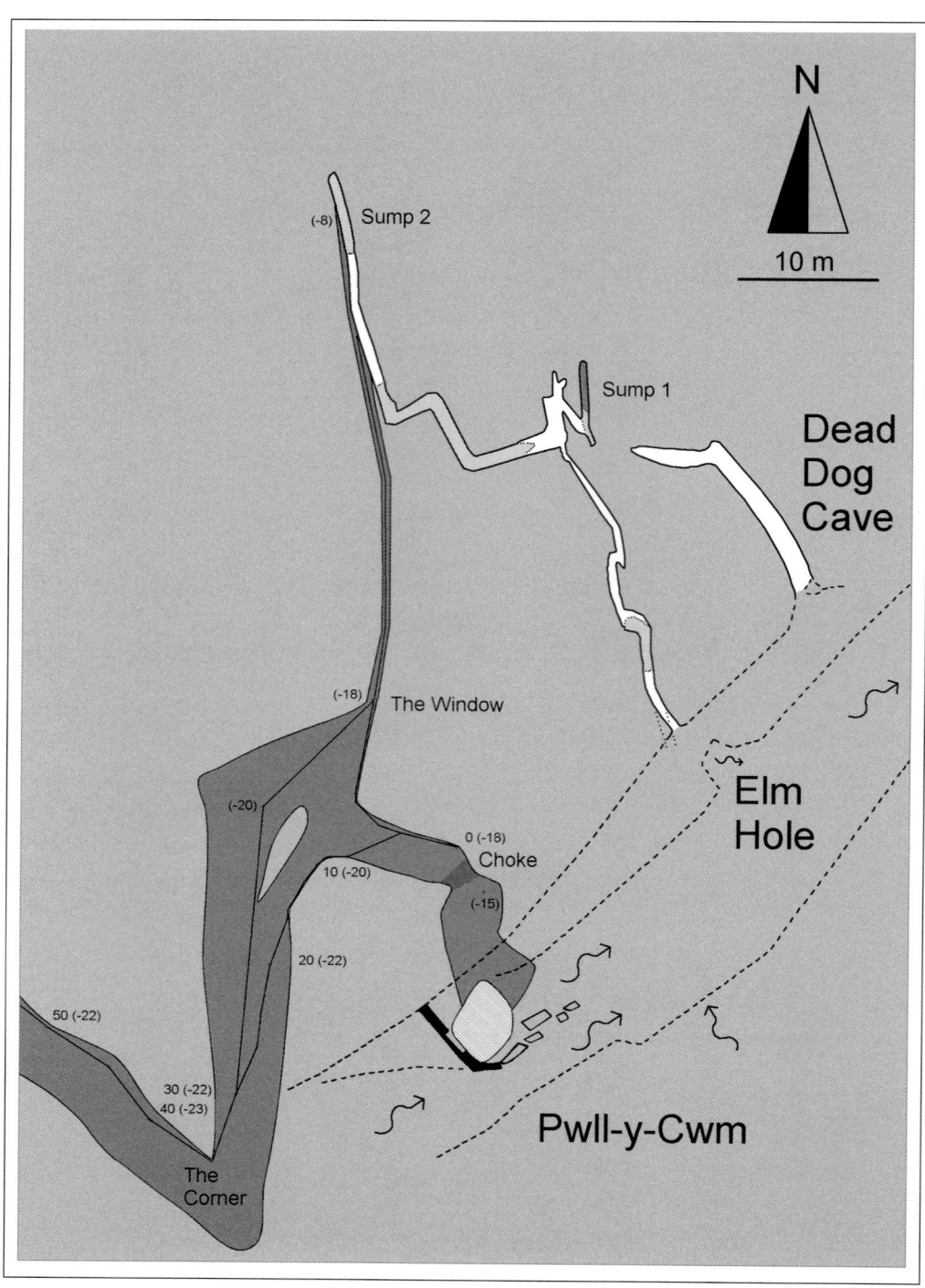

XII

*Maps*

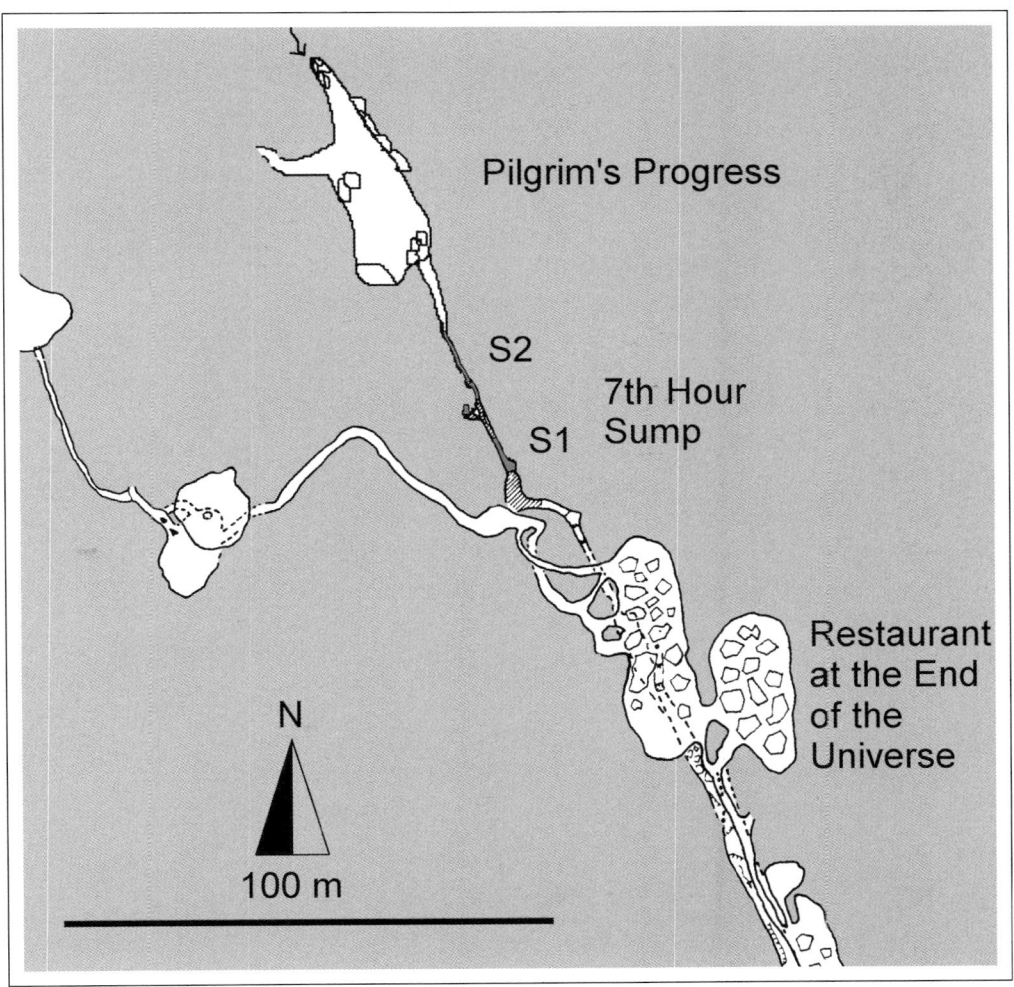

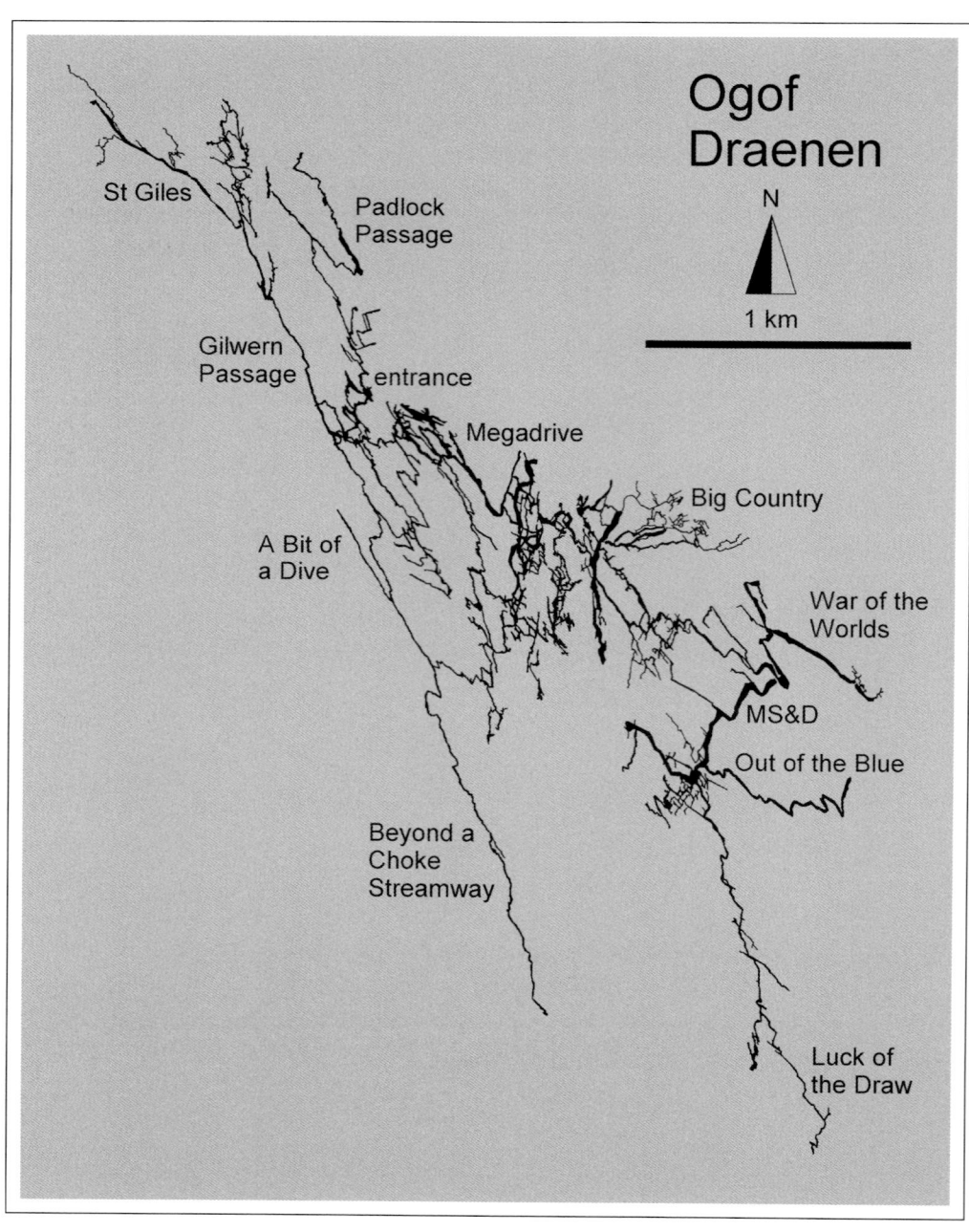

# Maps

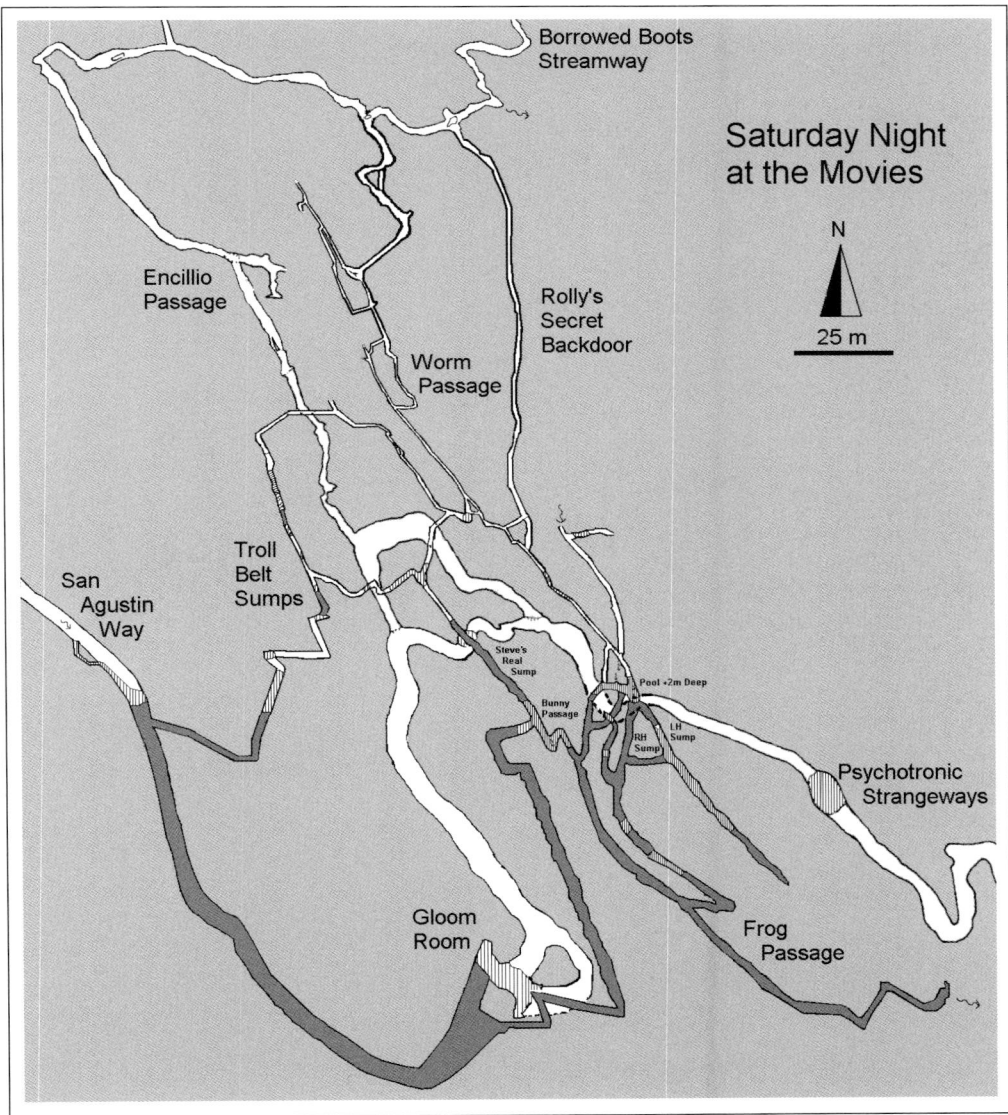

Linley Caverns
N
100 m
E
E
Hole in
the Wall

Caves of Chapel-le-Dale
N
100 m
Chapman's
Rising
Meregill
Skit
Aquaflash Pot
Joint Hole
Midge Hole
Hurtle
Pot
Jingle Pot
Weathercote
Cave

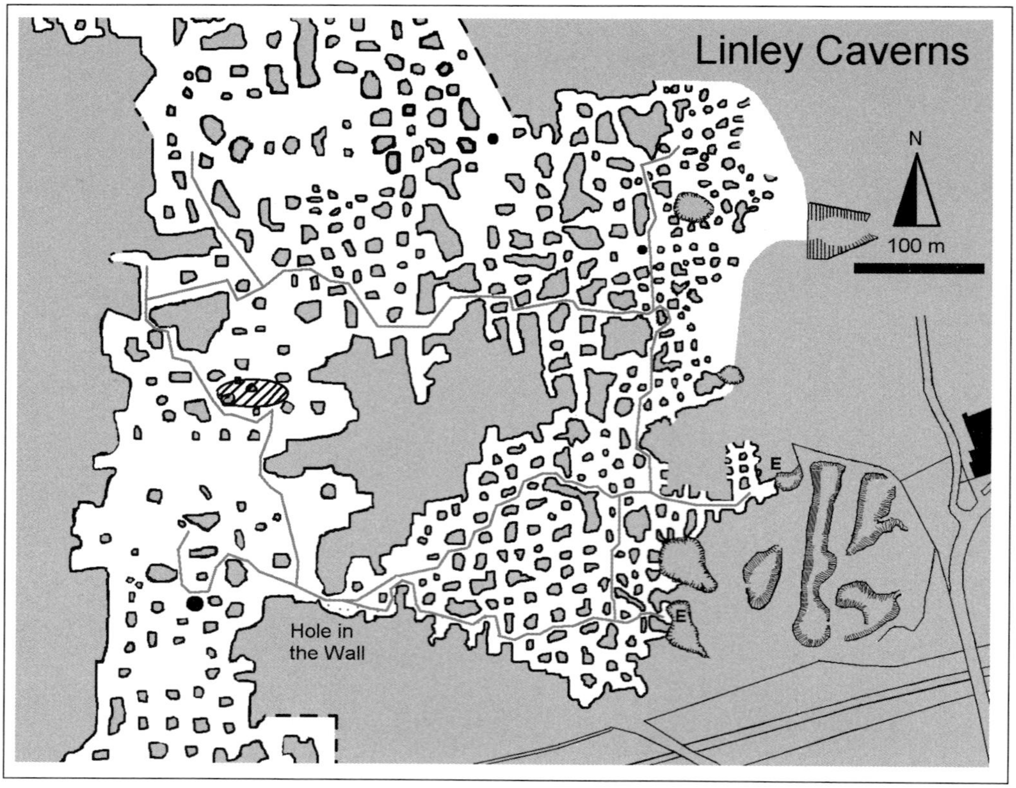

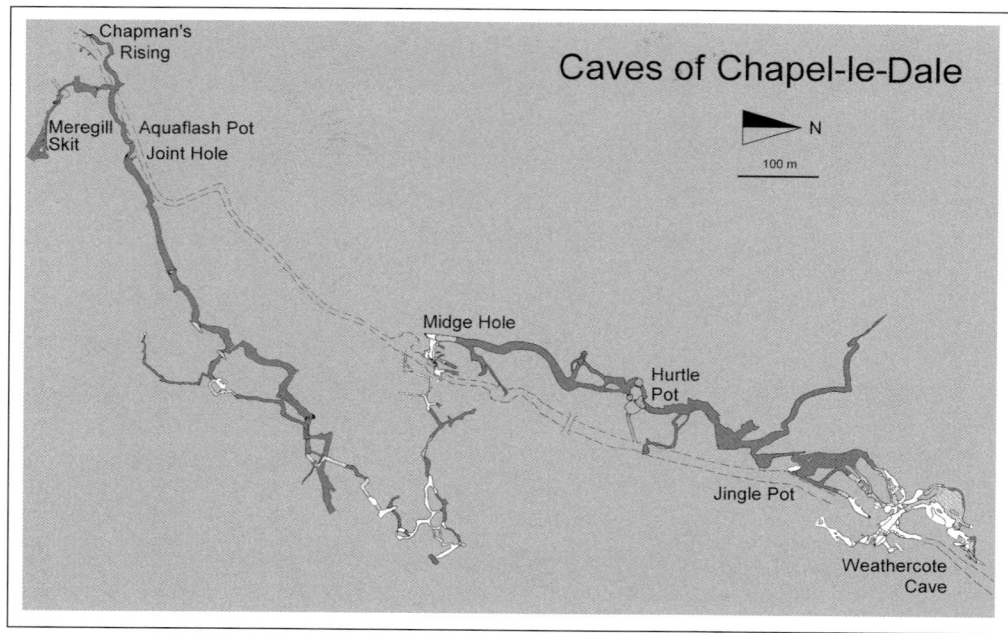

*Maps*

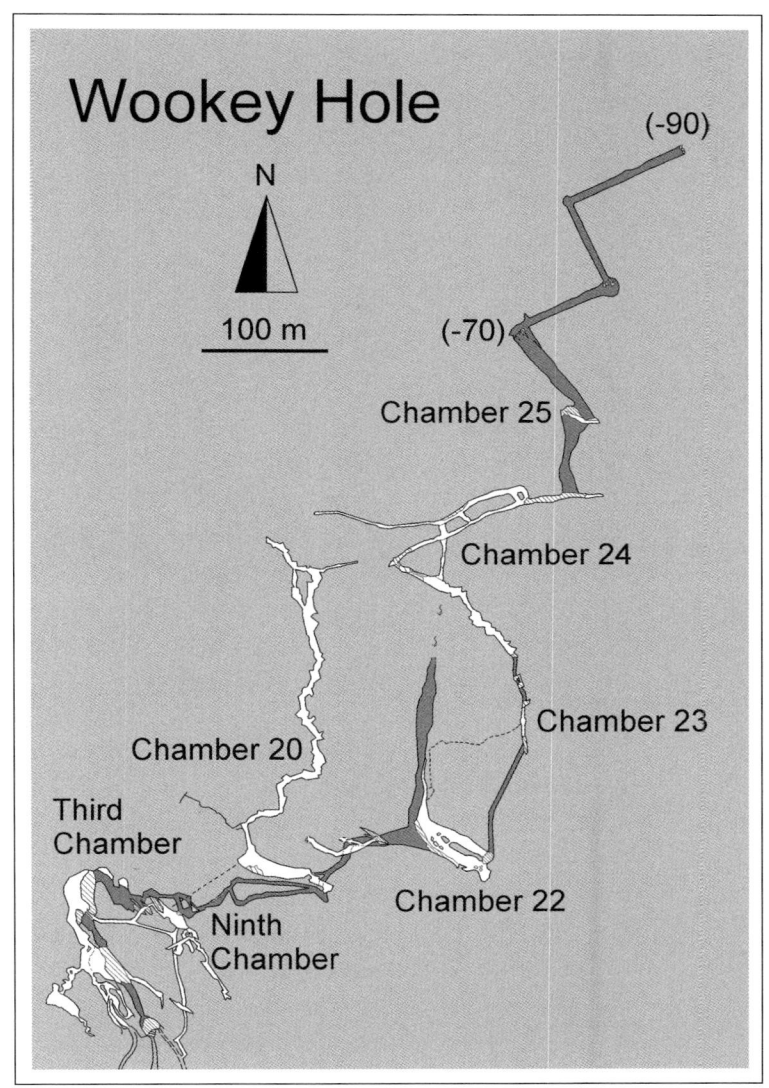

# Underwater Potholer

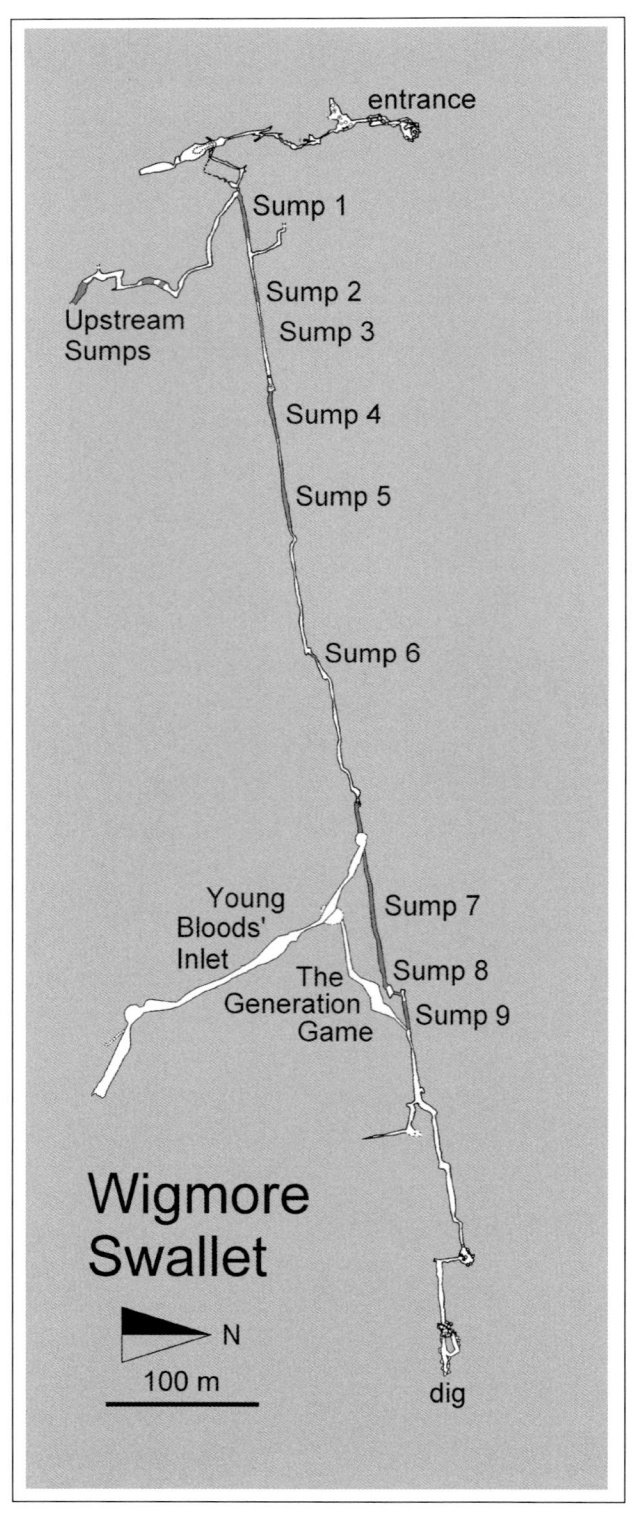

*Maps*

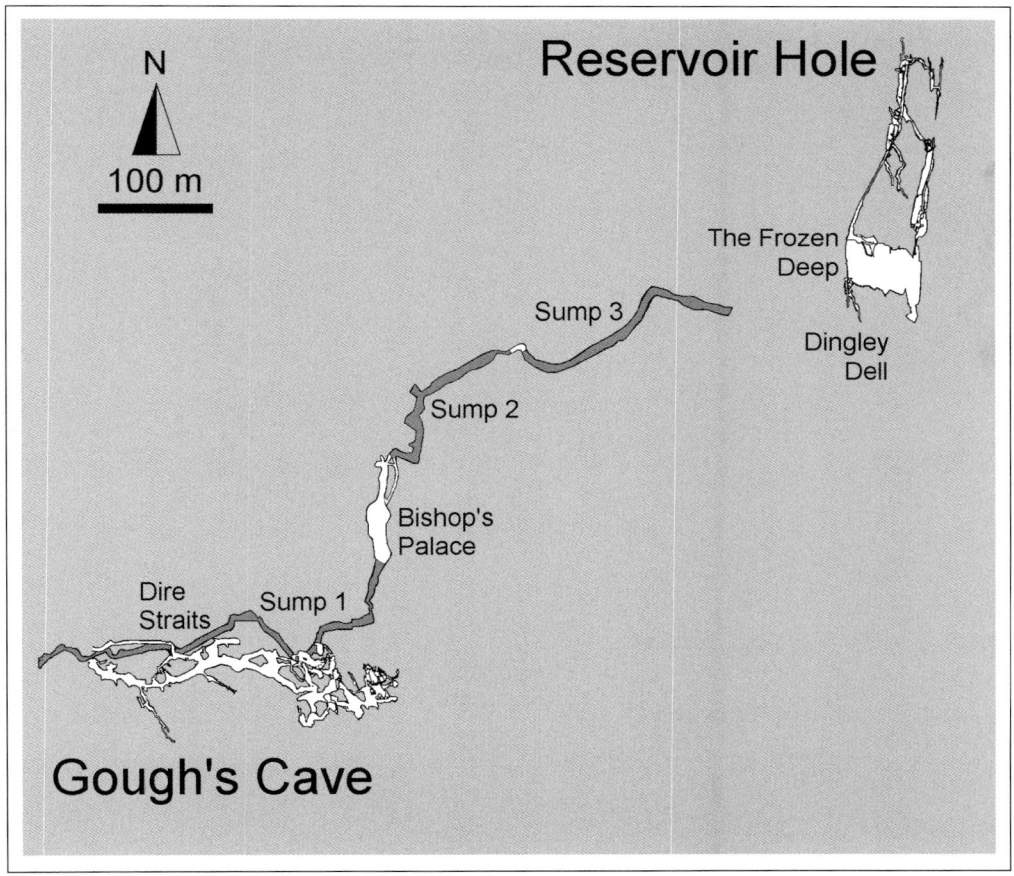

# 1

# Duncan the Diver

I'd really done it this time; I was completely stuck. I couldn't move forward and I couldn't move back. My body tensed up as I fought off a rising urge to panic. I tried to relax and think clearly – not easy considering the narcotic effect of the gas mixture I was breathing. Trying to stay calm, I reached behind me and unclipped one of my diving cylinders. Then I was able to turn around somehow, and get free. My chances of survival had only marginally improved: I was still lost, deep in an underwater cave and a long way from the surface.

Although it might not be everybody's idea of fun, caving and cave diving is an activity which has dominated my adult life for over 30 years. It's not so much a hobby but, as this book will show you, more of a way of life. Although the characters that appear on these pages have different motivations for pursuing these madcap activities, we all share an innate curiosity about our environment which drives us to explore some of the most inhospitable environments known to mankind, and unites us in unbreakable bonds of friendship.

Let me explain how I got into my predicament …

As a child, I wasn't particularly good at competitive sports, but I was an adequate swimmer and I enjoyed being in the water – or rather underwater. When I was eight years old, my parents had bought me a snorkelling set during a family holiday to Mallorca, and I'd been shown how to use it efficiently by another holidaymaker in the hotel pool *(see colour section)*. Back at home in rural Somerset, I looked forward to trips to the Devon coast to float around in rock pools bothering crabs and the like.

When I was 16 years old, a new leisure centre was opened close to where I lived. I could be found there on Sunday mornings when I used to hang out in the deep end and try to impress girls by swimming a couple of lengths of the pool underwater. My activities were not lost on one of the male swimmers, who asked me if I'd like to join a diving club that was being formed to use the pool for training. I thought at first that he was talking about high board diving, but it turned out to be a scuba diving club under the auspices of the British Sub-Aqua Club (BSAC), Branch Number 1212 *(see colour section)*.

My parents were very supportive of my new interest and provided a taxi service for me on club nights. I felt very grown-up calling the adults in the club by their first names, whereas my father addressed them as 'Mr Sawyer' or 'Mr Thompson'. Lectures on diving physiology, underwater navigation, boat handing, tides etc were delivered after the pool sessions at the nearby United Services Club.

But my tuition progressed slowly. Because of my youth, I was not seen as a high priority for scuba training, so I spent a lot of time practising my snorkelling skills. I helped to raise money for the RNLI by taking part in a sponsored swim around Bristol docks; I needed to buy a wetsuit for this, so my dad took me shopping in Bristol, where I struggled in and out of a two-piece neoprene wetsuit in a very small curtained-off cubicle. The wetsuit trousers got stuck on my ankles, and my dad had to pull at the legs to release me … It must have been quite a sight to witness the commotion coming from the cubicle. In order to finance my dive training, I got a job helping the village butcher deliver meat on Saturday mornings, and by the time I was 18, I owned everything I needed except for a compressed air cylinder.

My best friend at secondary school was one Michael Wright, who was no more athletic than me. I would attribute this more to laziness than inaptitude. Mike could run, but preferred not to – unless pub closing time was approaching. We decided that we would start Somerset's own space programme using homemade rockets fuelled by a mixture of sugar and weed killer. I lived in a small village and the bottom of my parents' property overlooked nothing but a cow pasture, which made the garden a convenient proving ground for our missiles. Using a length of drainpipe as a launch pad, we became increasing ambitious until one day we decided to construct a two-stage rocket by simply placing one of our rockets on top of another. This plan backfired (quite literally), as the contraption sailed through the air over the field, went out, spun around and reignited. This propelled the second stage like a warhead into the garden next door, where it detonated with a loud bang. To make matters worse, my neighbour (already exasperated by living next door to a warzone) was tending his vegetable patch at the time, and gave us a dressing down over the garden fence. Worse, the unburned propellants dispersed by the explosion meant that he couldn't get anything to grow in the impact crater for the next six months.

A more serious incident occurred a few months before my 18th birthday in the summer of 1982. I managed to set fire to myself. I'd poured some petrol into the disused septic tank in my parents' garden to dispose of some leaves and other garden detritus that had accumulated there. A lighted match followed the accelerant, and when nothing happened I peered down the hole. Flames shot out and blackened my face like something out of a *Tom & Jerry* cartoon. I summoned my mother by telephone and went next door for help. I immersed my head in the kitchen sink, full of cold water. Then my long-suffering neighbour fetched my snorkel so that I could keep my face underwater to cool my skin. My mum turned up and took me to hospital to be patched up. With my head swathed in bandages, I looked like a cross between *The Mummy* and *The Invisible Man*.

I was in the middle of my A-level exams at the time, and a day or two later I arrived at school for my first chemistry paper, still smelling like a bonfire. This didn't seem to have any effect on my grades, though I can't speak for the other students in the exam hall. I left the room with an imprint of the windows bleached onto my face due to silver salts in the ointment on my exposed skin acting as a photographic emulsion.

*Duncan the Diver*

These exploits pointed to a career in chemistry, so at the beginning of October 1985 I left home to study the subject at Exeter University. The only evidence of my pyromania was a slightly wonky haircut and the lasting inability to grow a full beard. I joined the university sub-aqua club, but since I was already ahead of the new intake of members in terms of the training I'd already done, I had to bide my time while they underwent their basic pool training.

*Duncan at Meadfoot Beach, Torquay, Devon, 1983 (Helen Pressman)*

During the early 1980s hardly anyone owned a drysuit; they were simply too expensive for mere mortals, and if you happened to have one you would be treated like a Dive God. As a consequence, we all wore wetsuits and horse-collar-style Adjustable Buoyancy Life Jackets (or ABLJs). Diving watches, too, were rare and costly – I used an early digital watch that was not rated for swimming, let alone diving. Depth gauges were of the mechanical variety, the cheapest ones being little more than a pipe with an air bubble of air trapped in a pipe which got smaller as you went deeper.

By the following spring, we were all ready to take our BSAC Third Class Diver theory paper before the start of the diving season. As part of the exam we were asked questions on decompression theory and dive tables. A few questions required the candidate to plan dives using the Royal Navy Physiological Laboratory tables then in favour with the BSAC. Long, cold underwater stops were to be avoided at all costs, so most of the scenarios involved 'no-stop' dives; when presented with a dive profile which went to the very limit of the need to decompress, the correct answer would have been to ascend directly to the surface. My responses were more conservative; I inserted a minimal decompression stop of five minutes at five metres. This was not the expected answer, and it contributed to me failing my theory paper – though in retrospect I can claim to have invented the safety stop.

I was interviewed by the club's diving officer after the exam and I explained my reasoning: I could not always trust my watch or depth gauge and had added a stop just to be certain. He encouraged me to revise my paper so that my answers aligned with the required response, and after I'd done that I was allowed to go diving in the sea with the club. But it was a little late in the season by then, so I didn't get a chance to complete the required number of dives at university to obtain my BSAC Third Class Diver qualification (equivalent to Sports Diver in modern parlance) before the long summer break.

So at the end of my first year at Exeter, I went home and got a summer job nearby with a local printing ink company. Meanwhile, Mike Wright had also gone home for the summer and was labouring on a building site in Bath. He had gone to Birmingham University to study metallurgy and had joined the university caving club. He had previously organised a trip to an easy cave on the Mendips for our school friends over the Christmas break, but my parents had refused to allow me to go – maybe they weren't keen on me going caving or maybe I'd been grounded for some indiscretion. Mike was still keen to take me underground, but I was sure that my parents would object. But an opportunity arose when they went on holiday to the Isle of Wight for their silver wedding anniversary; their 19-year-old son was now home alone with the keys to his mum's car. On the morning of Saturday 10 September 1983, Mike collected me, and in the company of another friend we headed over to the nearby village of Priddy.

At the village green we climbed a very rickety set of steps into the loft of an old barn which also served as a dovecote (in retrospect, this was probably the most dangerous part of the trip). I squeezed into my two-piece diving wetsuit and put on a thick pair of woollen socks and an old pair of army boots. Mike presented me with a lead-acid miner's light and building site helmet. I used my diving weight belt (minus the weights) to secure the heavy battery pack around my middle, plus a Tupperware box containing my camera and flash gun. It was a bit ambitious to carry my expensive camera and flashgun in this way, but both survived the trip.

We walked up the road and across several fields to a strange round stone tower at the corner of a watercress bed. A metal plaque announced that this was Swildon's Hole and in the event of an emergency one was to dial 999 and ask for Cave Rescue. An opening in the floor of this folly led into the cave. A cold stream coursed down several cascades to the top of a more substantial drop, known as a pitch – a term borrowed from mountaineering – where Mike uncoiled a wire ladder. With a rope tied around my middle, I climbed the ladder down the waterfall, getting drenched. This particular climb was known as The Twenty, due to the length (in feet) of the descent. We then faced a couple of deep pools, which I just about managed to skirt around without getting a second baptism. At one point we climbed up above the stream through a series of pretty stalagmite-covered grottos and then back down to the river again.

We stopped at an ominous-looking pool of water known as a sump – where the cave continued underwater. Mike told me that this particular section was very short and that I could pass through it by taking a deep breath and pulling myself through on the thick rope that disappeared down into the water. I watched as Mike and his mate plunged in. They convinced me that they were not dead by sticking their legs back through the underwater archway and wiggling them around. But despite my diving experience and even though I was wearing a warm wetsuit, there was no way I was going to follow them, so they returned and we retraced our route back to daylight.

My parents found out about my subterranean adventure, but as they were more concerned about the fact that I'd managed to dent the wing of my mum's car when I was driving back from a shopping expedition to Bath, I believe this served to convince them that being down a cave was less risky than getting there. When I returned to university I enrolled in two clubs: the sub-aqua club and the caving club, Exeter University Speleological Society (EUSS).

At the start of the academic year, new university students are conned into joining a lot of clubs and societies which they will never take an active part in. In October 1983

## Duncan the Diver

I was starting my second year as an undergraduate and wise to such tactics, spurned most entreaties . But as university caving clubs often have great difficulty recruiting new members, it must have been a little odd when a keen chap rolled up and announced that he'd like to sign up without any coercion whatsoever.

'I'm Duncan!' I said. 'I've been caving and I'd like to join your club!'

'I'm a diver,' I added – but didn't let slip that my only caving experience to date had been a trip down Swildon's Hole when despite being the best-equipped member of the party I'd refused point-blank to pass Sump 1.

Since I had been caving once before, I was spared the beginners' trip. I was taken on another outing, to Swildon's Hole, with the more experienced members of club. It had been raining heavily and the cave was in flood. We went down the streamway as far as Sump 2. I had no problems free-diving through Sump 1 – indeed, I had no choice, as once I'd entered the froth-covered pool the force of the water practically blew me down through the sump.

In the caving club I soon fell in with a bunch of regulars that included Mark Sewards, Piers Leonard and Mike Hobbs. Mike was a year above me at Exeter and also studying chemistry – I used to borrow his notes to help me with my coursework, but I don't think it did me any good. Mark and Piers were both in their first year; Mark had never been caving before, but Piers had taken up the sport while at school. As he had a car, he and I were to do a lot of caving together.

*Piers Leonard in The Green Canal, Dan-yr-Ogof (Duncan Price)*

I soon progressed to doing more advanced caving excursions, such as the 'Short Round Trip' in Swildon's Hole. This is a circular route within the cave system, and it involves getting through several sections very nearly full of water, known as ducks ; you can negotiate these by lying on your back and slipping through slowly head-first to stop the water going up your nose.

We made another visit to Swildon's Hole during the Christmas holidays with Mike Wright and some of his Birmingham friends. A feature of my early caving experiences was the unreliability of the club headlights, relics of Britain's declining coal mining industry. This trip was no exception, and on my journey out from Sump 1 I had to rely on the other cavers for illumination. I don't think anyone carried back-up lights in those days and we often found that one of the bulbs in our headset (either the main bulb or pilot bulb) had blown. Times have changed since then: today, most cavers use LED lighting and carry at least one backup torch.

Another highlight of university life at Exeter was the Rag Week every February when students organised various madcap events in order to raise money for charity. EUSS was no exception to this, and our contribution was a sponsored 48-hour occupation of a cave called Baker's Pit in Buckfastleigh, Devon. The advertised Weekend Underground turned out to be 22 hours from closing time in the Waterman's Arms on the Saturday night till shortly before Last Orders on Sunday. Our activities underground comprised eating, drinking, sleeping and listening to Radio 1 (the cave is on a hill and reception was actually quite good).

In May 1984 we visited Stoke Lane Slocker at the eastern end of the Mendip Hills. This was my second trip into this cave; my previous hopes of exploring it had been thwarted by fears of flooding after taking the guidebook description too cautiously; Mike Wright and I had turned back, having convinced ourselves that (despite the clear skies we'd seen outside) the water was rising in the cave and we could be drowned any minute. But on returning to daylight, we found that the stream flowing into the cave was if anything lower than it had been when we'd gone underground. This second time round, however, we were sure that the weather was stable and we'd be able to safely visit the well-decorated chambers which lay beyond a short, free-diveable sump.

The route to Sump 1 was low, uninspiring and narrow in places; the fact that one particular tight squeeze between the roof and the floor is known as The Nutmeg Grater should give you the general idea. This ended up at a dirty pool frequently covered in bits of flotsam which sometimes bear more than a passing resemblance to dog turds. An awkward duck-under through the sump, so short that it didn't have a guideline in it, gave access to a fine stream passage with large high-level chambers well decorated with stalagmites. Everything was going well until we returned to go out back through Sump 1; I swam too far, passing right under the scum-covered airspace above me, and found myself trapped under a solid rock roof. I reversed, got stuck, on the verge of panic for what seemed like hours, and was finally pulled out by my feet. My diary records 'Almost my last sump!'

That trip can't have been too traumatic, though, as my logbook shows that my next caving trip was also down Stoke Lane Slocker, followed the next day by a visit to Swildon's

Hole, where I free-dived Sump 2. This sump is a much more serious proposition than Sump 1, as it's 7 metres long, with a couple of small off-route airbells part-way through. Like Sump 1, it has a thick guideline through the underwater passage for cavers to pull on. At the upstream end there was a cache of lead weights, left there to save others having to carry them from the surface. I strapped on a couple of the weights, then dived the sump on my own as a practice for going further into the cave on a future visit.

At the beginning of November a party of us visited the cave, and I repeated the free dive, this time with Mark Sewards; I went first, remembering to duck under a bulge in the roof just before surfacing in Swildon's Three. This part of the cave has two large airbells in waist-deep water, separated by a short duck, followed by Sump 3. I gave three tugs on the line to show that I was through, and Mark returned the signal to indicate that he was about to dive. The rope went taut as he pulled himself along, while I counted the time under my breath. Reaching 10, I expected Mark to surface at any moment. But as I reached 30 the line went slack, and I began to wonder what was happening. After what seemed like an age, there was movement on the rope – and then nothing. Receiving no signal from base, I steeled myself for the return, fully expecting to have to negotiate a dead body in the sump. But no sooner had I submerged than I was dragged back and out of the water by a very-much-alive Mark.

Realising that we were now in one of the smaller airbells in the middle of the sump, I was also aware that Mark had used up most of the oxygen in it. It transpired that he'd hit his head on a rock near the end of the sump, and had reversed into the little airspace where I'd found him. At that point he'd dropped the line and had tried kicking around with his feet in order to recover it. So, thrusting the rope into his hands, I told him to get going and give me a signal when he was out. As soon as I received his tugs, I dragged a lungful of the foul air and followed (thinking that I was going back to Swildon's Three). The next thing I remember was being pulled from the water, surrounded by a sea of worried faces in … Swildon's Two. Somewhat disorientated, I set off out of the cave, coughing, spluttering and cursing loudly. What a cock-up! Then by the time I'd gone some distance up the passage, I found I'd forgotten to remove my weights. Fortunately someone kindly returned them for me, as I wanted to have nothing to do with the neighbourhood of Sump 2 ever again.

I had tried with little success to interest my girlfriend, Tricia, in taking up caving. We had met when I'd enrolled on a course at university to earn my Royal Life Saving Society Bronze Medallion at the college swimming pool. Tricia had worked as a lifeguard at the swimming baths close to her home town of Bradford, West Yorkshire, before going to university. I'd taken her underground once, not very far into Swildon's Hole, and she had enjoyed the experience but didn't share my obsession. We got engaged during our third year at university, and Mike Wright came down from Birmingham on his motorbike for the celebrations. Tricia and I didn't set a date to get married, though, as we wanted to finish our studies first.

My final year as an undergraduate was notable owing to the success that EUSS had in recruiting new members and our consequent failure to deter them after we'd extracted their membership fees. One of the reasons I'd applied to Exeter was because it had more female students than male, and this happy (for me, at least) state of affairs was reflected in the gender balance of the caving club.

Until then, my activities had been limited to the caves and mines of the Mendip Hills in Somerset and a few sites in Devon. But in January 1985, my horizons were broadened by a club trip to the Brecon Beacons; we stayed at the South Wales Caving Club HQ at Penwyllt and made excursions into Ogof Ffynnon Ddu and Dan-yr-Ogof. Then over the Easter break, I was treated to another trip to the area, on the back of Mike Wright's motorbike. Turning up on the side of a windy hillside overlooking the Usk valley, we waited for one of Mike's friends from Birmingham, John Hunt (looking the part of an absent-minded professor) to arrive in his beat-up green Land Rover, to go down Ogof Daren Cilau. But Mike decided that the hostelries of Crickhowell were more attractive than going underground, so we went caving without him.

Daren Cilau had a fearsome reputation for possessing a strenuous entrance crawl, over half a kilometre long, which took fit cavers more than an hour to pass (some people called it 'Darn near killed I'). Until 1984, there had been little more to the place than this tight passage, ending at some infrequently visited chambers beyond, but members of the London-based Chelsea Speleological Society had discovered major extensions which made a trip worthwhile. But John and I ran out of time, and we had to leave without taking in its full extent. My only footwear was my caving boots, and I had to endure the bike ride back to Somerset still wearing them; by the time I reached home I had very cold feet.

At the end of April 1985 (when I should really have been revising for my finals), I secured a trip to the Yorkshire Dales with a guy who lived in Exeter. Howard Price wasn't a student, but had a real job and owned a Ford Escort XR3i which expedited the journey north. We did several trips but my lasting memory was when we came across some divers preparing to set off the major resurgence of Keld Head and were about to dive into the underwater cave. This sight must have made an impact on me, as the next weekend I made my first proper cave dive, as against free-diving through ducks and short sumps *(see colour section)*.

It transpired that Howard not only had a flash car, but also was an aspiring cave diver. A week after our Yorkshire trip we drove up to the Mendips in the hope of getting to Sump 12 in Swildon's Hole. Howard had borrowed a diving cylinder and regulator for me to use, since several of the sumps *en route* were too long to free-dive. But after late start, it was apparent that our objective was a little ambitious, given that we wanted to be out again in time for a party at the Hunters' Lodge Inn in the evening; we only managed to reach Sump 6 before turning back.

This aborted outing could be seen as the augury of the consequence of an argument I'd had with my fiancée before leaving Exeter. We'd both been studying hard for our finals and were tense, and I should probably have stayed behind to resolve matters and swot for my exams rather than go cave diving. After the weekend I returned to university to discover that I was now single.

*Duncan the Diver*

Unlike the previous two years, in 1985 I spent the summer in Exeter, working as a lifeguard at the university's open-air swimming pool. This curtailed my speleological activities somewhat, until Kate, one of my fellow lifeguards, expressed an interest in going caving with me. The fact that she had access to her mother's car clinched the deal. In the company of a couple of friends, she and I did an evening trip to Dog Hole, near Buckfastleigh. But despite the joys of caving, the highlight of the excursion was an inebriated midnight dip in the university pool as we'd unwisely been entrusted with the keys overnight.

Despite the best efforts of Howard in particular (and the rest of the caving world in general), I managed to get my degree and was awarded a place at Birmingham University to do a PhD. I invested the money I'd been given for my 21st birthday in some SRT gear (for vertical caving), and Mike Wright showed me how to use it in some Mendip caves. Then I packed my bags to head north.

# 2

# Night of the Drunken Caver

At the end of September 1985 I arrived into a ready-made circle of friends in the Birmingham University Speleological Society, plus a girlfriend who shared my interest in the underground and an attic flat in Edgbaston. Birmingham being centrally located in England, the major caving regions in England and Wales were within easy reach of our club trips. We also had a number of members with their own cars, and subsidised access to the geology department's minibus.

Once the new recruits had been introduced to caving with an easy trip around Ogof Ffynnon Ddu in the Brecon Beacons, the club organised a weekend in the Yorkshire Dales. We stayed in the Red Rose Cave & Pothole Club's headquarters at Bull Pot Farm. This bleak spot is on top of the periphery of Britain's longest known cave network, which extends for over 100 kilometres of passages beneath three counties: Lancashire, Cumbria and North Yorkshire.

After a beginners' trip to Sunset Hole, the more experienced members were keen to do something more challenging. Mike Wright, Pat Hall, Steve Tooms and I split up from the rest of the group and trudged up Ingleborough Hill above the village of Clapham, intending to descend Wade's Entrance to the Gaping Gill system. But another group had already put their ropes down the first pitch, laying claim to the cave, so we went over to the entrance to Gaping Gill. This well-known pothole has the distinction of containing Britain's highest waterfall, the river disappearing down the open chasm to the floor of the Main Chamber 100 metres below. We didn't have a long enough rope to descend the full length of the shaft in one go, but we thought that if we tied our two longest ropes together we could do it. Steve, Mike and I went down the shaft as far as a large shelf 60 metres down, where we tied another rope onto an eyebolt set into the wall, to get to the bottom. Steve climbed back up the rope, using mechanical ascenders, to join Pat on the surface, while Mike and I were to carry on down. Once Mike had landed on the floor of the enormous Main Chamber, I undid the rope from the re-belay on the ledge and started off over the edge. Even with my descender tight up against the knot joining the two ropes, there was a fair amount of slack, which was taken up all of a sudden when I slipped on the wet rock and fell off the ledge; for a few seconds I carried out an unplanned bungee jump before continuing to abseil in a more controlled manner to the bottom. Mike and I left the cave via another entrance – Bar Pot – which we found already rigged and full of novices from another university club. Meanwhile, Steve and Pat, having pulled our rope up, came around to meet us on the surface *(see colour section)*.

The only damage at Gaping Gill was to my pride; but a more serious episode occurred in January 1986 when Mike, Kate and I decided to do a grand tour of the Easegill system via the Wretched Rabbit entrance. We didn't have permits for the cave and we shouldn't really have been there. We didn't know where we were going, and neither did anyone else. Predictably, we got lost and ended up going around in circles. To cap it all, I was just helping Kate down a difficult climb when the mud bank I was standing on collapsed, sending me flying down a 5-metre slope and twisting my right leg. Trying to put on a brave face, I told Kate that I was just winded, and suggested that she should go back a different way. In the meantime the pain in my right knee was getting worse and it was obvious to me that I'd done myself a serious injury. We decided that a cave rescue callout would not be popular, so I had to hobble out with assistance from Mike and Kate. I was glad to put my leg in the stream to kill the pain. Walking across the icy fell was a nightmare and we were relieved to get to the warmth of Bull Pot Farm. A trip to hospital when we returned to Birmingham showed that I had a torn cartilage and I was put on crutches for a couple of weeks …

… but no sooner was I able to walk than I was back caving again. This time I was staying at the Chelsea Speleological Society's cottage, Whitewalls, on the Llangatwg hillside above Crickhowell. But there was nowhere for me to sleep, so I made myself comfortable on the floor beneath a bunk in the back bedroom. A major expedition to survey the cave beyond St. David's Sump in Daren Cilau was being undertaken by some cave divers at the time, and so three of us were persuaded to carry some camping gear into the cave for them. My companions had to turn back after one of them fell off a climb, so I joined another team making their way to the sump. Daren Cilau is notable for the largest cave passage in Britain, the Time Machine, in places the width of a motorway, with boulders easily the size of a small house. With my knee still troubling me a bit, I was unable to keep up the pace, so I passed my load to someone else and asked the divers to go on without me. Now on my own, I sat down to rest before contemplating the solo trip out. Fortunately, a light in the distance heralded the arrival of Peter Bolt from the University of Cardiff caving club, and we shared some food before he escorted me out. My morale was further raised when I met some familiar faces from the Bristol Exploration Club (BEC) *en route*, and we all exited together. I can't have been too fazed, though, by my second aborted trip into Daren Cilau, because I returned the next day with another group of students.

Then the club resumed caving in Yorkshire. In fact we spent so much time up in the Dales that we were known to all the shopkeepers in Ingleton; many of them saw us so regularly that they thought we lived there.

In June, I paid another visit to Whitewalls and spent a day on the surface with John Hunt and Simon Abbott, excavating the side of a shake hole close to the Ordnance Survey triangulation point on Llangynidr Moor. Of all of John's circle of friends, Simon was the most tenacious cave digger, even if he didn't always share John's optimism. Despite a phenomenal draught of air between the rocks suggesting that an open passage lay beyond, we dubbed the site another of John's Futile Digs (JFD 4 or 5, I think). On our return to the cottage, we were befriended by one of the explorers of Daren Cilau, Steve Allen, who was trying to encourage us to join him on a trip into the cave on the following weekend.

So, a week later Mike Wright, Pat Hall and I arrived at Whitewalls intending to spend two days underground and get to the further reaches of Daren Cilau. Pat had never been down this cave before, and I was the only one who had been down the Time Machine and as far as Hard Rock Café (an underground campsite set up in order to enable longer working trips to be carried out in the farther reaches of the cave in relative comfort). It took us over two hours just to get through the entrance series, and we arrived at our destination seven hours later. But the contents of Pat's tackle sack, including his sleeping bag, were wet through. Fortunately we were soon joined by Steve Allen and another digger, Mark Lumley, who had covered the same terrain in less than half our time. Steve lent Pat his sleeping back, and went off digging with Mark, while Pat, Mike and I took a much-needed sleep.

We got up at midday, to be joined for breakfast by the diggers. They had entered a passage full of sharp needles they'd named Acupuncture Passage. Their discovery was encouraging, as it headed towards a known section of the cave that could at the time only be reached by cave divers. Without time to rest, Steve and Mark headed out to the Chelsea Speleological Society barbecue at Whitewalls, while Pat, Mike and I set off up the further reaches of the cave before spending a second night underground. Forty-six hours after entering the cave, we were back in daylight, resolving to do more camping and to join in the exploration of this cave system.

In the summer of 1986, Mike and I took part in an expedition to the caving area surrounding the village of Matienzo in Cantabria, northern Spain. The inspiration for this came about at the wake held in memory of Oliver Lloyd in November 1985 at the Hunters' Lodge Inn. Oliver had played a major part in the organisation of cave diving in Britain for over 40 years, although neither of us appreciated it at the wake. Over the free beer (which was probably the reason we were there), Mike and I struck up a conversation with Tony and Roz Williams, who talked us into going to Spain. We wrote to the expedition organiser, Juan Corrin, and eventually received an invitation to join in.

Being students, we did everything on a shoestring budget, including transport. So Mike and I set off from outside his parents' house in Midsomer Norton just after lunch on the afternoon of Tuesday 29 July to hitchhike to Plymouth, and almost immediately a car pulled up, driven by an out-of-work actor who announced that he was going there. Arriving on Plymouth Hoe somewhat earlier than anticipated, we spent the afternoon in several pubs before calling at the ferry terminal. We hid our bags, then set off in search of something to eat. At closing time, we returned to the terminal to discover four dejected French kids sitting on the steps: their belongings were locked inside the building. Mike made them a hot drink while we shared their takeaway meal before climbing into our sleeping bags beneath the stars.

## Night of the Drunken Caver

At dawn the next day we were rudely woken by rain and a growing queue of people waiting to enter the terminal building. After we'd spent a couple of hours in the cafeteria eating an indigestible full English breakfast, we saw more cavers beginning to appear – mostly going to Treviso, another caving area in northern Spain. We boarded the ferry and watched England disappear into the drizzle. Our evening meal consisted of leftovers abandoned by a group of seasick Spanish school exchange students, and we bedded down for the night on cushions from the canteen seating area as we crossed the Bay of Biscay.

Nearing Santander, the ship's complement of cavers got up early to be first to get breakfast. We commandeered a large table and ate as much as we could; rather than going to the buffet individually for drinks, we brought jugs of fruit juice back to our table, much to the dismay of the waiters. Mike was absent as he felt a little tender, but he wasn't actually sick until after the boat had docked in Spain. We shared a taxi from Santander to Matienzo with a pair of cavers, Jim Davies and Andy Hall, who were also on our expedition. Once we had arrived at the small village in the mountains, we were introduced to the rest of the group and learnt sufficient bar Spanish to get by.

*Mike Wright and Duncan, Spain (Roz Williams)*

Our first full day of caving started on 1 August. We pitched our two-man tent in a pleasant oak orchard in an open area of the expedition campsite. At 8 am we discovered why no-one had picked our spot – a stampede of cows almost demolished our tent *en route* to their grazing. Mike and I then set off in the company of three other expedition members to survey and explore the cave of Riaño I. We descended a couple of new pitches, but the passage became too narrow to follow.

A late start the next day saw the entire expedition disappear into three caves in the Four Valleys system, with the object of finding a connection between them. The expedition leader, Juan Corrin, was videoing the proceedings. One group went into Cueva Llueva to let off a smoke bomb at the end of a crawling height passage where there was a strong draught of air, while other teams went into Cueva Uzeuka (Cueva de la Hoyuca) and Cueva de Carcavueso to wait for the gas to come through – the ends of the caves were quite close, and hopes of a connection were high. Mike and I were lucky enough to go down Carcavueso, the shortest of all three caves and conveniently close to the campsite, but we spent three hours sitting around with the only strange smell being that of the beer on our breath. Meanwhile back in Uzeuka, 'Talking' Terry Whittaker was heard doing just that by the party in Llueva, and a connection was forged; much celebration ensued!

The next day, as Mike and I were the only people fit enough to go caving, we were dispatched back into Carcavueso to survey a new chamber that Andy and Jim had found a few days before. A tight climb up through loose boulders brought us into a sizable cavity, which we mapped. But somehow I managed to read the 30-metre tape measure as longer than 30 metres, and we weren't allowed to do any more surveying on our own again. What we did achieve, though, was to find a promising lead, which we marked with an arrow; when the next group in explored it the following day, this yielded no less than 2.7 kilometres of cave passage. The day after that, Carcavueso was connected to Llueva, and more celebrations ensued.

Our next trip was down Carcavueso again, with Talking Terry and Keith Lewis. Keith made specialist lights for the caving world and so he always had the most reliable one. He was a good person to be on a trip with, as you were unlikely to be left in the dark. We enlarged the connection with Llueva sufficiently to get Keith's claret-barrel chest through.

*Mike Wright surveying in Cueva de Carcavueso (Duncan Price)*

(On the way out, though, Mike and I got lost in the original breakthrough point we had found in Carcavueso. In 1987, Phil Gazard and Mike went on an expedition to the same place, and had a sense of déjà vu:

Mike: We're lost!
Phil: Are you sure?

## Night of the Drunken Caver

Mike: Duncan and I were lost here last year.
Phil: How do you know that?

Mike reached into a mud bank and removed a small crowbar: 'Here's Duncan's crowbar, which he dropped when we were lost here last year.' I still have the crowbar, which Mike brought back from Spain and returned to me as a birthday present.

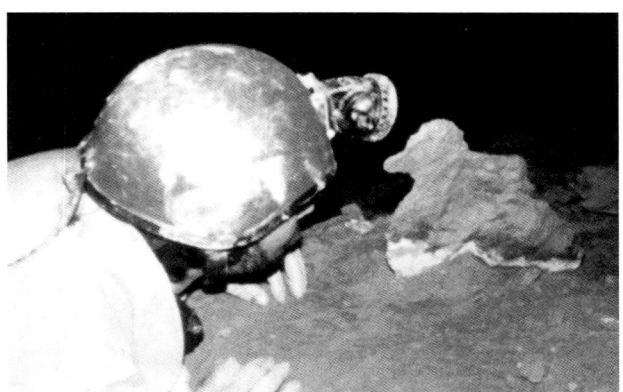

*Pete Seed admires 'The Duck' in Duck Passage, Cueva de Carcavueso (Duncan Price)*

The highlight of the trip proved to be not the caving but the night of the expedition banquet at Bar Thomas. Perhaps because of our youth, we tended to be mothered by the more mature female members of the expedition like Roz Williams and a caver from the Yorkshire Dales that everyone called Big Jane. After the meal, Mike and I retired to our tent only to be rudely awoken by Big Jane who crawled in to join us. Perhaps due to a surfeit of alcohol, Jane had mistaken our tent for her own and was quickly followed by four more people. As our tent was rather small, Mike and I had only erected the flysheet so we were able to escape under the open sides. With its new occupants now trying to stand up, the tent rapidly collapsed, adding to the confusion. Big Jane wandered off into a field, put her arm around a cow and fell asleep.

When we awoke the next morning, it seemed difficult to believe what had gone on, except that our tent appeared to have moved by a couple of feet overnight. Also, Roz Williams was walking with a limp. So instead of caving we went to the beach to practise for that evening's football international against the villagers. The final score was Spain 7, England 4 (plus one goal scored by Jim Davies' wellington boot flying off); two of the cavers were injured, one with torn ligaments and another with a bloody knee.

It was time to go home. Andy, Jim, Mike and I were given a lift to the ferry terminal in Santander where we encountered the returning Treviso team in a nearby bar. They had been there since 7 am and were in good spirits. A calm crossing ensued, and another large breakfast saw us back in sunny Plymouth. The Treviso mob was first off of the ferry and immediately intercepted by UK Customs & Excise. By the time I caught up with them, all of their gear was unpacked and their sleeping bags were being poked about in. I was called aside and also faced detention until Andy explained that I was not part of the same group and that we'd been to a different part of Spain.

British caving resumed at the end of August, with a weekend in the Yorkshire Dales followed by the usual round of beginners' trips for the new intake of student cavers at the university. In the middle of October I spent another weekend camping underground in Daren Cilau with fellow student Rich Panes. We travelled down from Birmingham on his motorbike and were underground for 42 hours looking at various places to dig in order to extend the cave.

We followed this up with two more extended visits to Daren Cilau, but these did not yield much new ground. Due to my increasing affiliation with the diggers at Hard Rock Café – the underground camp in Daren Cilau – I joined the Bristol Exploration Club (BEC) which, along with students from Cardiff University, was the main force behind the efforts to extend the cave.

The BEC had its headquarters on the Mendips, and over the weekend of 9–11 January 1987 I was due to be in Somerset to go caving with them. But a telephone call from John Hunt changed all of that, and I was lured to south Wales instead, to another of his 'futile' digs …

*For many years it was considered that extracting an injured person from Daren Cilau would be impossible, so this toy gun – labelled 'Daren Cilau Rescue Kit' – was hung above the door to Whitewalls (Duncan Price)*

# 3

# The Gothic Diggers

In January 1987 I was about halfway through my research for my chemistry PhD at Birmingham. My girlfriend had moved to Oxford to train as a primary school teacher and I now shared my draughty garret with another chemistry postgraduate. I had no transport of my own, save my own two legs: on foot or pedalling a bicycle. I didn't have access to a telephone, either, unless I waited until after hours and used my supervisor's office telephone on campus.

It was by this means that I received a call from John Hunt inviting me on a digging trip down Agen Allwedd. John had packed in his physics course at Birmingham and had gone to Cardiff University to study geology instead. The site was described as 'draughting' (i.e. there was a flow of air filtering through the rocks which indicated that more open cave passage lay beyond), and reports from other Birmingham University Speleological Society members said that the passage looked just like Daren Cilau. This was very encouraging, as the two caves were not far apart; there was there was a fair amount of rivalry between cavers to be the first to establish a connection between them. I took up the offer of a lift down from Birmingham, and headed down to Crickhowell squashed into a Ford Fiesta with some fellow cavers from Birmingham, Jim Arundale, Rob Murgatroyd and Steve Tooms, for a heavy night in the pub *(see colour section)*.

At midday on Saturday 10 January, we finally went underground – the four of us from Birmingham, John Hunt and an interloper called Spanners. His real name was John Stevens;[1] he was a former Leeds University student who had just joined the Chelsea Speleological Society.

Most of us had not been very far in Agen Allwedd before; certainly not down the character-building Southern Stream Passage which seemed to go on forever. It is debatable whether this was worse than the notorious entrance crawl to Daren Cilau nearby. After getting lost numerous times, we reached a short climb up into Gothic Passage and a T-junction where we took a right turn to where the passage was full of rocks and sand.

---

[1] The derivation of his nickname is unknown: one plausible reason involves the floor of his student flat always being covered in tools used to repair his motorbike. Another explanation was that his anorexic frame gave him the appearance of a bag of spanners.

*The dig face in Gothic Passage (Duncan Price)*

We weren't the only digging team in the cave that day: another group from the Gloucester Speleological Society (GSS) were making their third or fourth visit to the end of the other passage that went off to the left at the T-junction. Since we had plenty of manpower, Spanners went off to see how the GSS team were getting on. After 15 minutes' digging at our own site, we had opened up a route through a localised roof collapse and gained 20 metres of open passage to another blockage. A member of the other team came back to see how we were getting on, only to be demoralised by our rapid success when they had made little progress themselves. We continued removing rocks and building a dry stone wall with the spoil until 6 pm. Then, when we were starting to head out to the pub, Spanners went back down to inspect our handiwork. The rest of us decided to wait for him by the climb down into Southern Stream Passage.

When Spanners didn't return, we gradually drifted back in, to find him excavating a flat out upwardly sloping sand-filled passage at the end of the dig. 'It opens out ahead,' said Spanners. 'I think I might be able to turn around.' One by one, we squirmed up into the passage beyond. A low, wide, sand-floored tunnel stretched across the point of entry, with a 15-metre-high chimney – known to cavers as an aven – rising above us. We ran around in circles jumping for joy! Then we followed the eastern end of the passage until it became choked with sand (unknown to us, the GSS had also broken through their dig and they were the other side of the blockage, exploring over 100 metres of virgin passage). The western end of our passage led to another large aven and a pile of white calcite surrounded by a mud dam (which we dubbed The Snow Boat). Opposite our point of entry into this east–west trunk route, we noted another low, wide crawlway heading south. We scampered along until our progress was barred by a major rock fall, then we spotted a rift nearby and investigated it until it became too tight. We dubbed it Absent Friends Rift, in recognition of all the people who had helped on many of John's Futile Digs but had missed out on the one that actually 'went'. I balanced my camera on a rock and set the timer to take a team photo. Tired and excited, we headed out to celebrate *(see colour section)*.

The next weekend, a big turnout of cavers descended upon the new discovery, braving the snow outside to get to the cave entrance. This included Clive Gardener, who had played a major part in the discovery of Daren Cilau – it seemed that if anyone was going to make a connection between the two caves, he wanted to be in on it!

While the others were marking off vulnerable mud banks with flagging tape and surveying the new finds, Spanners and I sneaked off to the end of Resurrection Passage (as the southerly route had been named since it signified a renewal of interest in the cave) to make a start on the blockage where we'd turned back on our breakthrough trip the week before. Using a crowbar and tape slings, we pulled out blocks until we could get through into the continuation.

But we had not gone far when we were stopped by another loose ramp of boulders with limited headroom. Spanners took the lead and made short work of the obstacle. The passage increased in dimensions and we were left standing in a railway-tunnel-sized passage with gypsum crystals growing in the rippled mud floor. Stopping on a sandbank, and gazing longingly down the passage to a corner in the distance, we summoned the rest of the party.

We set off *en masse* along a wide ledge beside a trench in the floor. At the corner, we turned south across a rock bridge into the continuing route, dead straight, as far as our lights could penetrate. But inevitably our luck ran out; the roof lowered to close to the sandy floor, forcing us to wriggle along like eels. Eventually we had to dig to make progress – but as we didn't have a pull-back rope for the plastic drum we used to move the spoil, most of the party decided to head out, until we were left with Clive Gardener at the front and the rest of the group lying in a line behind him, sending the empty container back to him to fill and pass back. Our efforts were rewarded by the discovery of another short section of open passage, before we were frustrated by another sand-choked section.

We would need to make more trips to pass the next obstacle, and we were informed by our reinforcements that the GSS diggers had found 5,000 feet of walking-sized passage. Although it was nearly midnight, Clive, Spanners and I elected to see if this was true while the others went out. We knew that our finds were heading broadly south-east, towards a section of the cave called Maytime which had been found in 1974 by Martyn Farr. Martyn had dived through three long sumps to get to this majestic section of river cave which had been described by more recent visitors as a 'digger's paradise'. We hoped to find a dry way there – perhaps intercepting other significant cave passages on the way. The GSS extensions, on the other hand, represented an easterly continuation of our large east–west passage (which we'd named Synchronicity owing to the simultaneous nature of the breakthroughs) that we had first entered the week before. This was significant, as it was heading straight for Daren Cilau.

The three of us set of to explore; crawling up over a series of tight squeezes into a high chamber which the GSS had called The Ribbed Vault on account of its rock fluting. Following the right-hand wall of the passage, I soon left Clive and Spanners behind. All at once, the route opened out into the promised roomy tunnel. Rounding a bend, the cave continued in the same manner. I returned to fetch the other two (who were taking more time to look around – not believing that there was bigger stuff ahead), and then we romped off in delight to the end of the passage, where another sand-filled tube marked a temporary halt to progress. By this point we were totally knackered – but Clive (ever the enthusiast) wanted to survey the way back. But the problem was that although we had a compass and could easily estimate the distance, we had no means of recording the course of the zigzag route we'd followed. Clive suggested that we memorise several survey legs each, to reconstruct a map when we got out, but Spanners and I would have none of this. We were so tired!

Slowly we made our way out of the cave, reaching the surface at 4:30 am. Staggering through the door at Whitewalls after walking back through the snow, we found everyone still up, waiting for us. My caving diary records that it was my 200th caving trip. Out of deference to the organisation which owned this cosy little cottage on the flanks of the Llangatwg escarpment overlooking Crickhowell, I applied to join the Chelsea Speleological Society (CSS). This club, founded by cavers living in London in 1956, had bought the building, derelict, in 1963 and rebuilt it as a bunkhouse for its members. As the years passed, CSS had gradually migrated from its traditional power base in the capital city to a club with its caving interests centred on its accommodation in the Brecon Beacons.

Exploration of the Gothic Passage extensions continued apace. The GSS discovery (called Priory Road after the place where the club met on Wednesday nights) yielded a further chamber, Glevum Hall, before degenerating into a series of immature sand-filled tubes (Severn Beach) and the boulder mayhem of Birthday Surprise. Further advances were made here over the following years, closing the gap between Agen Allwedd and Daren Cilau (which itself yielded more cave passages in the right direction) but at the time of writing the link still remains elusive *(see colour section)*.

Meanwhile, our group team toiled away at a couple of promising leads: the sand-filled dig heading towards Maytime, and the westerly continuation of Synchronicity (which ended at a low passage with a hard, compacted mud floor that required enlarging for us to make any progress). This site was promising, as it headed into a large blank area of limestone bounded by the Grand Circle trip down the Mainstream Passage and back up Southern Stream Passage. In mid-February, Spanners and Henry Bennett, from CSS, re-discovered High Traverse Passage when they pulled away a few loose rocks from the side of Synchronicity near the start of Resurrection Passage. High Traverse had first been entered in 1962 through Main Stream Passage; the letters C.S.S. were still visible, written in soot from the discoverers' carbide lights, on the rock that had blocked the end of the passage and which Henry and Spanners had moved to forge the link between the two cave passages *(see colour section)*.

A month later, our dig by the Snow Boat formation had gained a low chamber with no airspace leading off. As this site was muddy and tight, we resolved to abandon it, and instead made our way to the end of Resurrection Passage, to continue shifting sand there. A group of Leeds University cavers turned up to help us as we encountered rocks cemented together by hard-packed mud. Digging progressed until we were able to work our way upwards into a large echoing chamber which we dubbed Reverberation Aven, but 30 metres further on, the route became blocked with sand again.

At the end of March, Ian Rolland, a young corporal based at the RAF base in St Athan, climbed in the roof above the Snow Boat and entered a tube which dropped down into a further 30 metres of passage. He was a member of CSS and not only a good climber but also an accomplished cave diver; although he was only a few months older than me, he had already established a name for himself by supporting Rob Parker on his British cave diving depth record at Wookey Hole Caves in 1985. Ian had also been involved with various 'dry' discoveries in Agen Allwedd and Daren Cilau, as well as making notable extensions to the latter cave by exploring the passages beyond St David's Sump at the far reaches of the system. He had a particular interest in our activities as he was diving in Sump 4 at the end of Maytime. It was known that the combined waters from the two caves emerged from a flooded pothole (Pwll-y-Cwm) in the base of the River Clydach. This was blocked by boulders, but Martyn Farr had dived from the neighbouring cave of Elm Hole into a large underwater tunnel which terminated beneath the rubble-filled shaft. in his subsequent exploration, Martyn had followed the river passage upstream, to establish an underwater connection with the terminal sump in Daren Cilau. If a way on downstream from Agen Allwedd could be found, then a connection with Daren Cilau could be on the cards.

In early April, Simon Abbott, Mike Wright and I climbed up above the Snow Boat using the ladder that Ian had left *in situ*. We removed the ladder and dropped it down the other side into the low-level continuation. From there, delighted to find that we could see the end of our abandoned dig, we soon forced a route through. Over the Easter weekend, Spanners and I took sleeping bags down the cave and spent most of the weekend digging at Reverberation Aven. While we were on our way out of the cave after 50 hours underground, we met a party of cavers carrying diving gear for Ian Rolland and his co-diver, Phil Rust, who were bringing up the rear. Ian and Phil dived through to Maytime later that day, but they deferred their assault on the final sump until the water conditions improved. Instead, the pair tackled various climbs in the section of river cave between Sump 3 and Sump 4.

In retrospect, Reverberation Aven had been a poor choice of bivouac, as there was no running water nearby and all liquids had to be carried there. The end of High Traverse was a more suitable spot, as it overlooked the main stream and was more strategically placed for accessing the multiple sites that we were investigating in the southerly extremities of Agen Allwedd. Sleeping bags, hammocks, stoves etc were ferried here and a campsite established; this became our base of operations from July 1987. Even if one did not feel like sleeping

*Simon Witt and Simon Abbott at camp (Duncan Price)*

underground, it made a convenient place to prepare a hot meal – frequently sourced from the army ration packs left behind at Whitewalls by Ian and his services mates.

Slowly we cleared a path through the sand fill at the end of Resurrection Passage. But with over 30 metres' pull-back on the container used to ferry sand and rocks between the dig face and the growing spoil heap, the rate of progress slowed. Then we encountered a wall of boulders buried in the sand. We attacked them until finally we chiselled our way up through to a point where we could peer into an enlargement – from the gap issued a perceptible draught, and we could hear the sound of dripping water beyond. Just after Christmas, a charge of high explosives was set off at the end, with the intention of turning the final blockage into gravel. This was fired from a safe distance and the place left alone for a couple of days for the blast fumes to clear.

Just before New Year 1988, after a nine-month campaign, the dig finally surrendered; a Gloucester caver, Mike Green, Simon Abbott and I removed the last few rocks and crawled through to find another section of spacious passage, even a few cave formations. Hot on our heels was another team, bringing the cave survey to the end. The way on was blocked by a slope of boulders glued together by calcite, which didn't look that promising.

In early January 1988, Spanners and I were tempted back to the site. By following an undercut in the left-hand wall, we edged forward until the shelter of the sloping wall ran out. At this point, things became decidedly dangerous; boulders kept dropping out of the roof and threatening to squash us. Since Spanners had used up all of his adrenalin for the time being, I squeezed to the end. I could see open passage ahead and was determined to be first through into the new stuff this time, as Spanners had always beaten me to it in the past. But at that precise moment I felt a large rock settle onto my back; I seemed to be supporting it with my shoulder, so I called back to Spanners to see if he could reach in and wedge it up. No go – he couldn't even reach my feet to pull me out.

I tensed up, then breathed out and managed to slide out backwards at high speed, relieved that the boulder didn't drop any further. But the gap was now very narrow and we had to excavate the floor to get through. An hour or so later, Spanners cautiously slid under the same rock, to emerge at the top of a calcite ramp. I passed food and a crowbar through to him, and I waited on the other side for him to stabilise the route. Together, we explored over a hundred metres of gently descending roomy passage containing some very nice stalagmite and stalactite formations which were out of keeping with the rest of the cave. Beyond these, the roof came down to meet the sand floor again, so we went back to camp to get some sleep – I'd been underground for three days – before celebrating in the pub on Sunday lunchtime.

On the following Saturday (15 January 1988) Spanners and I were joined by another club member, Geoff Newton, to go back down in order to photograph the latest discovery. The boulder choke that had threatened to squash me had settled since our previous visit, but was now shored up, and we recorded the formations on film. Deciding to make a start on the end, we cleared a trench down until the roof began to level out. A small crack in the side of the passage was taking quite an air current, but we couldn't enlarge it. Satisfied with our efforts, we started heading out. At Reverberation Aven, we encountered Simon and Rob who persuaded me to stay while the others continued to the surface; Geoff's light was dying, and Spanners didn't fancy staying on to camp underground as we had suggested.

On returning to the dig face, Simon inserted himself at the sharp end while Rob and I cleared the spoil. Swinging the entrenching tool to the left, Simon discovered that the roof rose immediately under a flake, and he soon hit a substantial airspace. After knocking down more sand, we quickly enlarged the hole and popped up into the floor of a roomy passage. But then, on regrouping the other side of the breakthrough, I spotted footprints in our 'virgin' cave. Virtually at a sprint, we rushed along, following the trail: 50 metres from our point of entry the route ended at a balcony overlooking a majestic river flowing in a large tunnel easily 4 metres wide by 5 or 6 metres high. This could only be the continuation of the main stream passage that flows through Agen Allwedd. We weren't the first people there – others had dived three long sumps to get here – but we were the first to come the dry way to … MAYTIME! *(See colour section).*

This was totally unexpected, as the divers' surveys showed the end of our dig to be at least 400 metres away from this sector. (It later turned out that the survey data was accurate … except that the conversion of the underwater measurements from imperial to metric had been omitted.) Leaving Rob and Simon to enlarge the connection, I hurried back to Reverberation Aven to collect my camera, as nobody would believe us unless we had the evidence. On our return to the river, we found the 3-metre climb down into the river a little slippery and I took a photograph of Rob in the knee-deep water before we set off downstream. Just behind us lay Sump 3; ahead the river gained in depth and we had to traverse on slippery ledges in order to keep dry. At last, at midnight, we reached the start of the dive line disappearing into Sump 4. I took more photos on the way out, and we stopped to have a drink at a stream inlet before struggling back to High Traverse, where we opened the bottle of champagne we'd kept for the occasion.

'Guess where we've been?' I said to Clive Gardener, as he sleepily opened one eye as I was about to climb into my bunk at 5 am. A broad smile filled his face when I broke the news – but Spanners and Geoff were less happy, since they had still been in the cave when we'd reached Sump 4, so they went back the following weekend without me.

The weather had been bad, with blizzards almost preventing me from going to visit my girlfriend, who had just started a teaching post in Devon. With snow still lying on the ground in Wales, only Spanners and Geoff went down Agen Allwedd. As the temperature climbed outside, the snow melted and they were trapped in Maytime. It was a close call, as the profile of this section of the cave is very shallow and the water level rose by over 4 metres, forcing them to sit out the flood on ledges above the raging torrent for over 24 hours until the torrent subsided. They were just making their way out when a search party reached them with ropes to help them across the fast-flowing river.

I went back to Maytime at the end of the month; it was the day of the CSS annual dinner. I claimed that we were always reluctant to go underground before midday, because we never came out before midnight: if we started any earlier we'd just spend longer in the cave. But on this occasion, we had to make a prompt start in order to be out in time for the meal that evening. Part of our objective was to clean up after Spanners and Geoff's epic the previous weekend, as a large rescue callout had ensued and there was still equipment scattered *en route*. Another task for us was to rig handlines across some of the river crossings in Maytime, to provide security in high water conditions.

When we were coming out, we met a large party of cavers with diving cylinders going in via the new dry route to Maytime. In July 1987 Ian Rolland had passed Sump 4 to an air chamber dubbed Against All Odds; he had found this after he had dived though to Maytime with only one working regulator and had borrowed a regulator from his support diver, Phil Rust, to dive into the final sump. This party of divers were now taking advantage of the sump bypass to continue their explorations.

Over the next few months, several visits were made to Maytime, but the only sites with significant potential for further exploration were the heavily calcited stream inlet and a muddy U-tube close to Sump 4. The flooding incident involving Spanners and Geoff now discouraged visitors unless the weather was particularly dry and stable, which is what was needed for diving Sump 4. So, after spending the morning in a pub while a new cave management committee was elected, I was in a suitable mood to help Ian dive Sump 4 to look for the way on beyond the air chamber he had reached on his previous visit. Simon Abbott and Martyn Farr were also recruited to help. Martyn had discovered Maytime in 1974; he had been the first to dive Sump 4, in the company of Roger Solari, on 15 June of that year. But tragically, Roger had not returned from the dive. His body stayed in the sump, not to be found until October 1986.

# The Gothic Diggers

*Maytime (Clive Westlake)*

*Rob Murgatroyd manhandles a diving cylinder through
the breakthrough into Maytime (Clive Westlake)*

Perhaps spurred on by the ale we'd consumed at the meeting, we made good time reaching Sump 4. Ian set off ahead, while the rest of us decided to try to enter some high-level passages off the main route; this involved forming a human pyramid with me (the lightest) at the top. After an hour, Ian reappeared with the news that the underwater passage beyond Against All Odds was blocked by boulders. Furthermore, he informed us that he and Phil Rust had already been into the passages that we'd been trying to get into and they didn't go anywhere. This was a bitter disappointment, but in retrospect it was this trip, with two of the country's most proficient cave divers, that began to sow the seeds of my own ambitions.

# 4

# In Remembrance

During the summer of 1988 there was a gradual decline in my digging activities in Agen Allwedd. I was coming to the end of my postgraduate studies and about to start a job as an industrial research chemist in Coventry, but before starting work I spent the weekend at Whitewalls.

On Monday 26 September 1988, Rob Murgatroyd and I each made a dive to the bottom of Pwll-y-Cwm, a pothole in the bed of the River Clydach, where the water from the Llangatwg caves finally reaches daylight. A retaining wall had been built upstream of the shaft to divert stream debris around it, and an airlift had been pressed into service to excavate the hole (which was now 9 metres deep). The metal A-frame which had been used to support the airlift had been placed down the shaft for safekeeping, but winter floods had disturbed the rubble floor, allowing it to sink into the unstable slope of gravel.

Rob had brought his open water diving gear to Wales for the weekend. This consisted of a single back-mounted 12-litre cylinder and waistcoat-style stab jacket. The reel from Rob's surface marker buoy was pressed into service as a safety line to the surface. Rob donned his gear and dived first. I then had a go with it. I remember little about my dive, apart from breathing like a steam train and being terrified most of the time as the thin line got caught up in the submerged metalwork. I was glad to surface after 10 minutes' immersion, cold and with a nosebleed.

A few weeks later, Rob and I cobbled together two sets of side-mounted 7-litre cylinders for a visit to White Lady Cave. Once more, Rob's SMB reel was pressed into service as we took turns to dive through the sump, to surface in the neighbouring cave of Pwll-y-Rhyd.

After some more practice dives, Rob and I travelled down to the Mendip Hills to have a go at reaching the end of Swildon's Hole. We were teaching ourselves how to cave dive, since commercial cave diving courses were unavailable at the time and would anyhow have been beyond our means. John Cooper (known as JC), the treasurer of CSS, was also secretary of the Welsh Section of the Cave Diving Group at the time. He was very helpful, lending us two 7-litre cylinders to use. Diving with one set each, we reached Sump 12 (the end) without too much difficulty, especially considering that the cylinders were overkill for the length of the sumps (the longest of them was Sump 9 at only 40 metres, and the remainder could be free-dived or bypassed). Even so, using a single cylinder to go cave diving is not advisable, except that we reckoned that we could hold our breath to get through if anything went wrong. But on the way out, Rob knocked the cylinder valve of his tank against a rock, breaking the knob – this could have been serious had it not happened as we were packing up our diving gear on the upstream side of Sump 2.

JC didn't seem too upset with us, though, and encouraged us to join the Cave Diving Group (CDG), presenting us with copies of the CDG manual and the Welsh Sump Index to be getting on with. Martyn Farr and Ian Rolland could see that we were keen, and offered to sponsor our applications for membership.

At the end of November, I managed to borrow a 4-litre cylinder from JC and persuaded Ian Rolland to carry this and my demand valve to Northwest Junction in Agen Allwedd. Mike Hobbs and Simon Witt accompanied me to the upstream end of Turkey Passage; this section of the cave takes its name from a stalactite drapery which resembled a hanging turkey. Turkey Passage ends in a series of sumps leading to a network of dry passages with many potential leads for further exploration. Most of this section of the cave was first entered in November 1970, and had been called Remembrance Series, consistent with other parts of Agen Allwedd being called Summertime, Maytime etc.

*Ian Rolland at the entrance to Agen Allwedd (Duncan Price)*

Several years previously JC and his friends had bypassed Sump 1 by enlarging a tight rift over the top of the sump – but the route was still very awkward, and rocks from the roof of the chamber beyond had fallen into the upstream end of Sump 1 thus blocking access for divers. So the only way to get to Sump 2 was to squeeze up through a wetsuit-shredding crevice, taking care not to drop any more rocks into the passage beyond. On reaching Sump 2, I kitted up and dived through the roomy underwater passage, to surface in the open streamway beyond, while Mike and Simon waited for me. This was a memorable moment – it was the first sump that I had ever dived on my own, and also one that I had not been through before. I removed my diving gear and carefully placed it out of harm's way before scrambling up a sandy ramp into a wide, high-level passage that headed back downstream over Sump 2.

Ahead of me, just beyond a small grotto, the route was blocked by boulders. But a slot in the floor of the passage was interesting, as I could shout through it to my friends on the other side of the sump. I removed a few rocks surrounding the hole and could see a rift continuing downwards for a couple of body-length, but as my excavations caused small pebbles to drop through to the others below, it was clear that it was too loose to enter safely. So back in the stream again, I went up to Sump 3. The line through the sump was broken at the downstream end, so I re-tied this and pulled on it to see if it was secure; it promptly broke! Taking this as an omen to go no further, I dived back through Sump 2 and we left the cave.

This should have been the end of my caving for the weekend – but at 2.30 am we were back underground in search of an overdue pair of cavers who had set out to do the Grand Circle trip. Despite covering the cave as far as North West Junction, we didn't find them, and it was not until much later in the morning that Martyn Farr found them, off-route above Southern Stream Passage, as he was on his way back from searching the cave as far as Maytime. Then another rescue team had to be sent out to locate an earlier search party who had got lost after taking a wrong turn at Gothic Passage; they'd ended up in Priory Road.

Then it was my turn to be rescued from Agen Allwedd, when Ian Rolland and I undertook a trip to tackle some climbs at the end of the Remembrance Series in May 1989. In the interim, I had made a couple of visits as far as the start of Sump 5, first with Ian and then Simon Abbott. We had replaced the lines through Sump 2 and Sump 3 in preparation to go climbing beyond Sump 5. We were underground before noon, and had help for part of the journey to the sumps. As we bid goodbye to our sherpas about halfway to the first sump, we reminded them to leave the key for the padlocked entrance to Agen Allwedd by the gate for us to let ourselves out. Continuing, we struggled through the Sump 1 bypass to kit up at Sump 2. Here Ian discovered a leak in his high-pressure hose, so when we reached Sump 5 I was nominated to go first, since my gear was in better working order.

The diving proved easy by comparison with the journey so far; for once, we had taken fins for the longer sumps ahead. This proved a luxury through the roomy Sump 2, where I was able to swim along rather than continually kicking off against the walls and roof of the sump. Beyond Sump 3 lay a short duck, and then we climbed up into the high level bypass to Sump 4. As we approached Sump 5, we noticed that the streambed was completely dry. At the end we found a steep mud bank with the guideline disappearing into a static pool. Diving head first, I had to struggle to get through a tight gravel squeeze in order to get totally immersed. Once I'd got through that, the passage opened out and I was able to fin happily along, laying out a new line alongside the old.

## In Remembrance

Things were going well until my mask began to fill with water. I cleared this without difficulty, but it continued to flood. After clearing it once more, I felt around the seal and seated it more firmly against my face. Then my demand valve, which had a tendency to free-flow slightly (and had already been releasing small bubbles between breaths), began to deliver a mixture of air and water. I struggled to breathe while trying to drink the sump dry, but at least I could see where I was going. As I'd gone beyond a point of no return, I pushed on, trailing the line, coughing and spluttering until mercifully reaching air after 30 metres. Luckily the water levels were very low, so I was then able to wade along in the stream trailing the line out behind me, until I reached the tie-off of the old line.

I removed my gear and waited for Ian to slosh into view. Securing our diving equipment together just in case the water should rise while we were gone, we strolled off up the passage. We noted a few inlets on a corner, but then the cave appeared to end in a wall of rocks. The stream issued out of a tight sump and there seemed no way on until I noticed a body-sized passage half-full of water going off a few feet back. This tight canal of claustrophobic proportions eventually snaked its way to the base of an impressive aven and the continuation of the stream passage.

Pushing on upstream, we quickly reached the terminal chamber replete with 1981 vintage climbing rope left by the last visitor, Martyn Farr. Wedged on a ledge near the top of the climb, I found that hanging onto that rope served two purposes – firstly to lifeline Ian (who was trying to get onto a rock bridge across the aven) and secondly to stop me falling off. Having completed the horrific traverse, cutting hand and footholds in the fractured rock with a crowbar, Ian found that the aven proved to be a dead end; the only passage of note was a small fissure in the middle of the flat roof, watering the passage below. After we had reunited at the floor of the chamber, Ian packed up his kit while I went off to check out a couple of side passages that we had passed *en route* from the canal.

Two large north–south passages were aligned along a fault and ended abruptly in blank walls. Another inlet was narrow, and I got bored before reaching any definite conclusion. Meanwhile, Ian had decided to climb our last lead – the aven by the canal. I arrived just in time to hold the line as he set off up the first vertical stretch, chipping holds with the bolting hammer as he went. No time for ethics here!

Ian was high above me and nearly on a good ledge when his only good foothold fell off. With no protection in place, and no chance of rescue if he got injured, he frantically scrambled to relative safety. Rather shaken, he tied off the rope before wisely deciding to leave it for another day. A little higher was a passage going off the top, and another parallel shaft lay below with a stream flowing across its base. So, knowing that we'd have to return, we wearily made our way back to the surface. At Sump 2 we let most of the air out of our bottles, making them perceptibly lighter to carry out. We ate the last of our food, except for half a Mars bar that I was saving for the walk back to Whitewalls once we were on the surface.

At midnight we reached the entrance and signed out. But at the gate there was no sign of the padlock key (nowadays the gate can be opened from the inside without a key). We looked high and low for that bloody key – to no avail. We tried taking the gate off its hinges – but despite Ian's expertise in removing the wings from RAF fighter jets, the gate defeated us. So finding a couple of plastic rubbish bags by the logbook, we made ourselves makeshift ponchos to wear over our wetsuit jackets in order to keep the cold at bay. After shivering by the entrance for a while, we retreated further into the cave and huddled together in a sandy side passage (Queer Street – how appropriate!) to await rescue.

Since we'd expected to be out of the cave in the middle of the night when everyone at Whitewalls would be asleep, we had left a call-out time of 7 am on Sunday morning. Hourly we got up and jogged to the First Boulder Choke to warm up. We swapped jokes to keep up morale. At 4 am we ate our remaining food. At 8 am we went to the entrance to be let out, since by then somebody would surely have noticed that we were missing.

Meanwhile, back at Whitewalls, everyone was getting up. Someone peered into my sleeping bag and mistook my teddy bear (really!) for my head and assumed that I was still slumbering. Eventually it was realised that we were still underground; Jack Upsall (one of the guys who had helped carry our gear into the cave) was dispatched with a spare key to check up on us, and a rescue callout was started as a precaution. At 9.30 am Jack reached the entrance, put his hand through the grille, lifted a rock – and lo and behold! – let us out with our own key. Twenty minutes later we arrived back at Whitewalls just as the first battalions of cave rescue turned up …

Rob Murgatroyd and I officially joined the Cave Diving Group at the end of January 1989, although we had been showing up at meetings for many months before this. Rob was admitted as a Trainee Diver since he held a BSAC Sports Diver qualification, but I had to join as a Probationary Trainee Diver since I had not completed my BSAC training. This meant that I had to complete a pool test under the watchful eye of Andrew Ward (the Section's training officer and one of its three examiners). By the end of 1989 we had amassed enough experience to take our practical tests; Rob and I were elected as Qualified Divers at the Section's AGM in January 1990.

By this point, I had moved out of my digs in Birmingham and had taken up residence in Coventry with Kate, who had secured a teaching post in the area. Ian Rolland suggested that I get in touch with a mate of his, Rick Stanton, who also lived in Coventry; the pair had first met on a caving expedition to Peru, and had gone on together to do some exploratory work in the far reaches of Daren Cilau. Their discoveries had significantly increased the chances of making a connection with Agen Allwedd. We pencilled in a return visit to Remembrance Series –

*Rick Stanton and Ian Rolland (Angela Timms)*

## In Remembrance

but before that an easier trip, without Ian, was arranged so that Rick and I could become acquainted.

On 25 March 1990, I answered the door to Rick, clad in combat trousers and a baggy jumper tucked into the waistband – perhaps to hold them up? I climbed into his Land Rover with my gear, and we drove up to the Derbyshire Peak District to visit a cave known as P8. With the help of two of Rick's mates to carry our gear, Rick quickly got ready and set off first, leaving me to fix a leaking O-ring seal in my breathing apparatus before I could follow him through the murk. I went through Sumps 1–3 in quick succession with hardly any airspace between them, and surfaced face to face with Rick's wellington boots. He told me that the water level in Sump 4 was high and the rest of the cave beyond this would be flooded – but I had a quick dive in Sump 4 anyway, only to find it was blocked by gravel. As we were packing our gear to go out, I realised that Rick only had one light on his helmet, whereas mine sported a plethora of diving torches. He explained that when the water was as muddy as this, it didn't matter how many lights you wore, as you couldn't see anything anyway.

The following weekend, Ian, Rick and I made an early start into Agen Allwedd, to tackle the climb beyond the canal that Ian had attempted the year before. Ian and Rick shared a pair of fins, using one each for the longer Sump 5; since I had two fins, it fell to me to carry the bag of climbing gear through the sumps. While the others started the ascent of the aven, I went off for a look around some muddy side passages. When I returned, Rick held the lifeline for me as I climbed up to a ledge 15 metres above the floor. Ian was above him, fixing an expansion bolt into the wall, and above Ian's head lay an inviting open passage with a small stream of water coming out of it and down the shaft. But a band of loose rock was in the way. Rick climbed up to take a look and convinced himself that it wouldn't 'go'. I thought that a rigid climbing pole might get us in (though getting it up there would be another matter). We abseiled back down, and Rick went walkabout while Ian and I packed up. We surfaced after a 13-hour trip, and I remember feeling very tired as we had carried all of our gear in and out of the cave ourselves.

I had kept my cave diving activities under the radar as far as my family were concerned – and Kate in particular. Even though she had given me a copy of Martyn Farr's history of British cave diving (*The Darkness Beckons*) as a Christmas present when we had first got together, she'd told me not to get any ideas from it. The fact that we lived at opposite ends of the country when I had started cave diving helped me maintain the subterfuge. And then by the time Kate moved in with me, I had qualified in the CDG so it was a *fait accompli*. In May 1990 she came down Agen Allwedd with Ian Rolland, a fellow services caver, Syd Yates, and me for what turned out to be Ian's last cave dive there.

Ian arrived at Whitewalls where I had some news for him; Kate and I were engaged to be married, and I asked him if he would be best man; Ian seemed the obvious choice, as I didn't have any siblings, and we were so similar in age and build that we were frequently mistaken for brothers. Ian agreed, and then asked if he could borrow my new diving watch (an engagement present from my fiancée) for the trip, since his diving watch was having a new battery fitted. We headed off down the cave where he was dispatched into Sump 4 in superb diving conditions. 'Give me an hour and then go out,' were his instructions. He didn't want us to wait too long for him – if he found something, he wanted to explore it fully, and if he met with some mishap then there was nothing we could do. We retreated to the equipment dump near Sump 3 to brew up on the stove there. Several cups of tea later I asked Syd the time – I knew that Kate didn't have a caveproof watch, and my timepiece was with Ian. But Syd wasn't wearing a watch either. Just then, Ian sloshed into view, his characteristic boyish grin hiding the disappointment that he'd located no way on underwater. The only option would be a dig though the boulders in Against All Odds.

In the summer of 1990, Ian moved from St Athan in South Wales to Leuchars in Scotland. Being so far away restricted his activities under Llangatwg until a work commitment in the area during November gave us the opportunity we needed. Getting underground late in the afternoon, Ian, Kate and I made slow progress to Synchronicity, where four cylinders, a pair of fins and a crowbar were cached; we left the cave via the Main Stream Passage, thus doing a 5-kilometre circuit around the cave system known as the Grand Circle (mainly for Kate's benefit as she'd not done this trip before) having a grand day out ourselves!

Ian and I went back at the beginning of December to dive Sump 4. We made good progress to our cylinder cache, but it took us a further two hours to get our kit to Maytime – at one point Ian took his gear on ahead (since he had less to carry) and came back to help me. In Maytime, the conditions were

*Ian Rolland and Syd Yates at Sump 4 in Maytime (Duncan Price)*

excellent: the water was clear, though not as low as we had hoped. We decided to put on our cylinders near Sump 3 and walk down to Sump 4, ready to dive. But it transpired that one of Ian's regulators would not work, so we had to call the dive off and reluctantly head out, leaving our cylinders behind in Maytime for another time. Ian admitted to me later that there had actually been nothing wrong with his gear: while he was shuttling our equipment through the cave he'd had a premonition that I would die in Sump 4 and so he'd sabotaged his regulator.

With Ian's job keeping him away from Wales, I eventually recovered my cylinders from Maytime by diving them out one way through Sumps 3–1. I saw that the original line was still in good condition, despite only being secured in three places. Cave diving techniques had certainly moved on since the 1970s, when the absence of snoopy loops and other belays meant that the line had to take the shortest and most direct route through the sump rather than, as now, being routed through the roomiest parts of the passage, so avoiding undercuts and other obstacles. As a consequence, sumps really were shorter in the old days.

## In Remembrance

Two days before Kate and I were married, on Easter Monday 1991, my last cave dive with Ian took place. With just one complete set of gear between us (including just one wetsuit!) we took turns at diving in Pridhamsleigh Cavern in Devon, the paucity of equipment being a feature of Ian's Alpine approach to cave diving.

Sadly, he died three years later, on 28 March 1994 while diving in the San Agustin sump in Sistema Huautla, Mexico, whilst on an expedition attempting to establish a new cave depth record. His body was found a few feet underwater in the second sump, and it is thought that he had been coming out due to some problem. He had recently been diagnosed as diabetic, and it is possible that he had become hypoglycaemic. He was diving with an experimental mixed gas rebreather at the very cutting edge of cave diving exploration in the deepest cave in the western hemisphere. As it was going to be Ian's 30th birthday while he was in Mexico, Kate and I had written a card for him, which had gone out with Rick Stanton; Rick didn't deliver the card, but instead helped bring our friend's body out of the cave. I received the news via a phone call from my other cave diving mentor, Martyn Farr. No sooner had I replaced the handset when Ian's wife, Erica, called to tell me the same story. They had three young children: Leonie, Carly and Connor.

# 5

# Nightmare in Elm Hole

A short way downstream of the rising of Pwll-y-Cwm in the Clydach Gorge is the entrance to Elm Hole. This crevice in the cliff face was first explored in 1961, when it was discovered behind a fallen tree. Twenty-five metres of difficult going along a small tube rimmed with sharp flakes of rock gives way to a T-junction. To the left, a low crawl through two pools with limited airspace gains a narrow rift which ends at a static pool. This tight slot was investigated by Chris Gilmore in November 1966, when he reached the bottom of the rift at a depth of six metres. Roger Solari dived here in March 1974 (three months before his death in Agen Allwedd), making 20 metres of progress in an ongoing small passage. While Roger was caving in Ireland at Easter, Martyn Farr looked at the sump to see if a connection could be made with the bottom of Pwll-y-Cwm nearby. After 40 metres of tight and awkward going, the route joined a large underwater tunnel at The Window, but as he was not wearing fins, Martyn decided it would be best to tackle this section another day.

He made a follow-up dive in Elm Hole a couple of weeks later, equipped with fins and a reserve set of air cylinders. He followed the large conduit downstream to a pile of unstable boulders at the base of Pwll-y-Cwm. Going upstream, he then followed a ledge until it ran out, causing him to undertake an unexpected head-first descent to the floor. Beyond this, the route lay wide open. Shaken by the poor visibility, the large size of the passage and the arduous nature of the approach, Martyn beat a hasty retreat. The cave acquired a bad reputation, and it was not until the 1985 discoveries in Daren Cilau had reached a downstream sump at the same level as the resurgence that Martyn was tempted to go back.

Initially, the putative connection between Daren Cilau and the Clydach Gorge was explored from the Daren Cilau end, despite the difficulties in carrying gear there. In three dives, Martyn progressed over 300 metres into the shallow underwater passage, whereupon the depth increased dramatically. Martyn believed that the route had intercepted the main drain from Agen Allwedd, and that the best option for future progress was from the uninviting downstream end. Beginning in March 1986, he made a series of dives upstream from Elm Hole, finally achieving success on 3 July when he made the connection. Route-finding in the main drain was difficult due to the poor visibility: the best option was to follow the base of the right-hand wall upstream (often in and out of alcoves) so as not to get disorientated. A month later, Martyn made a through trip between Daren Cilau and Elm Hole, and this was made the subject of an HTV Wales documentary.

Rick Stanton and I discussed potential cave diving projects. Following the water downstream from Agen Allwedd to the resurgence at Pwll-y-Cwm seemed difficult, since it involved diving a long way inside the cave – but going the other way seemed easier, especially since Martyn thought that there was an underwater inlet from Agen Allwedd in the large underwater passage reached from Elm Hole. We set aside a weekend in May 1990 to investigate.

It transpired that two cave divers based in Cardiff, Malcolm Stewart and Peter Bolt, were also interested in Elm Hole and had made a couple of dives there to sort the line out. I contacted them, secretly hoping that they'd like us to stay away and thus spare us the unpleasantness of Elm Hole. But Malcolm replied that they had no objections – and by the way the sump was really nasty. The night before our first visit, we met them in Crickhowell after they had just visited the cave. Malcolm had managed to reach The Window into the main underwater passage with the benefit of several dives' experience. I boasted that we were going to dig the downstream choke beneath Pwll-y-Cwm. Rick thought this was a little ambitious, and Peter cautioned me not to try to emulate anything Rick did.

The next morning found Rick and me dressed in wetsuits, waiting in the car park of the Drum and Monkey Inn at Clydach for Rick's friend Barry Suddell to arrive. Eventually, a beat-up car ground to a halt in the nearby lay-by on the opposite side of the Heads of the Valleys' Road. As I was introduced to Barry and his girlfriend, Ceily, I couldn't help but be impressed by the state of his diving equipment, which appeared to be just about to give up the ghost along with the vehicle carrying it. The effect was completed by Barry's ferocious appearance, with his long, curly black hair and matching beard, although this belied the friendly northern personality beneath.

Down in the gorge, Barry donned his drysuit for a dive in Pwll-y-Cwm, while Rick, Ceily and I set off into Elm Hole. Eventually we arrived at the sump pool, where Rick, wearing two wetsuits, kitted up with a couple of 7-litre cylinders and disappeared down the rift. Forty minutes later, the sump started frothing again, heralding his imminent return. As he removed

*Rick Stanton diving in Elm Hole, (Duncan Price)*

his gear, he described the passage and how he'd laid a line from The Window to the base of the Pwll-y-Cwm boulder choke. We were heartened to learn that he had tied a line to a scaffold pole sticking out of the rubble, so the blockage could only be short. In addition, digging the choke from beneath appeared easy, if exciting – particularly when there was a collapse in the loosely compacted pile of boulders. Being able to fin backwards when this happened proved an advantage!

As there was ample air left in Rick's cylinders, I forgot the advice given to me the previous evening and put on Rick's gear for a dive. Wriggling down the tight rift without fins in almost zero visibility, I followed the route by touch as far as The Window. Pausing to turn on Rick's 20-watt dive light, all feeling of claustrophobia disappeared as I practically fell into the main drain. To go any further would have been foolish, so I returned to the surface; I'd been away for only 15 minutes. Back in the gorge, Barry had seen Rick's bubbles rising up through Pwll-y-Cwm. While Rick went for a dip in the resurgence in his drysuit, I took a couple of cylinders into Elm Hole, ready for the next day.

Sunday dawned, and we transported another mound of gear into the cave. Barry wriggled into his drysuit and went to wrestle with the boulders at the base of the Pwll-y-Cwm choke. Unfortunately the rock which appeared to be holding the whole thing up was underpinned by an even bigger boulder, too large for Barry to shift. With much swapping of gear, I took my place in the sump, using one of Barry's partially depleted bottles and a fresh cylinder that I had brought in. I set off upstream from The Window carrying a line reel. Reaching a prominent corner where the route swung north, I tied on my line and swam across the passage to the opposite wall about 4–5 metres away. Turning left, I followed the wall downstream in north-easterly direction and then south to meet the line running from The Window to the choke laid by Rick on the previous day. Tying my empty reel to the other line, I retraced the loop to The Window and swam back past my reel and on to the choke, taking rough notes for a survey. On reaching the surface again, thus ending my first exploratory cave dive, I found that Rick had come in to help us with the gear.

The next Sunday, I made a day trip to Wales in order to retrieve my line reel. Arriving early at Whitewalls, I took cups of tea upstairs to those still slumbering, until I found someone gullible enough to help me. Once in Elm Hole, I headed downstream to the choke, freed my line reel and wound it in to a point opposite The Corner. The visibility was atrocious, less than half a metre, but I did a quick search of the walls to check that the main drain turned through 90 degrees at this point and that there was no passage going straight on. I left the line reel at The Window, then retired to the Drum and Monkey – only to be reprimanded by JC for removing a line that I had not followed on the way in ; if it had turned out that the line had been broken, I would have found myself marooned with no guide to safety. Such a calamity had happened to novice cave diver Paul Esser at Porth-yr-Ogof in 1971; his remains were not recovered until 2010, and there is a memorial plaque to him at the cave.

For the next dive, I took a radiolocation beacon to the choke in order to get a better fix on the position of the blockage. This was difficult, as the contraption was encased in a wooden frame; I had to hold it down with several rocks, while ensuring it was still perfectly horizontal. As it might take some time for its signal to be picked up on the surface, I left it *in situ* to be recovered at a later date by Malcolm Stewart. I found the Elm Hole side of the choke to be at 16 metres true depth, and a metre in from the cliff face.

Since diving in via Elm Hole was not as difficult as we'd expected, Rick, Barry and I were keen to push upstream from The Corner to try to find the Agen Allwedd–Daren Cilau junction, which was reputed to be a little way beyond the connection point of Martyn Farr's dives in 1986. In mid-June I mustered up a large team to help me into the cave. Above water, everything went smoothly and I was efficiently dressed by my assistants. Carrying a disposable line reel (i.e. cheap, homemade and with no rewind handle) containing 100 metres of line, I progressed upstream from The Corner. Swimming along at a depth of around 24 metres in a large tunnel, I found the existing line was in good condition. But 70 metres upstream from The Corner, I found that my pair of 7-litre cylinders were at thirds. Although I'd delayed tidying the line as I went, I didn't wish to push my luck, so I tied off the reel and headed back out. At The Window, I consulted my contents gauges again; although I still had a fair amount of air left I decided to go back up the tight passage to Elm Hole. But then I found that the outline – my way out – had got caught around the pillar valve under my left armpit. No amount of gymnastics was going to free me from the entanglement. So taking a firm hold of the line, I sliced right through it. This freed me. I managed to keep hold of both the ends of the line and knot them firmly together again, then I headed out along it, much relieved.

Nearly a month later, Rick, Barry and I were reunited for another push. (In the meantime, Rick had been further upstream, using three bottles, (two side-mounted and one on his belly), with a novel inner-tube buoyancy compensator to make the third bottle float. However, he had got very cold in his wetsuit, and the further he'd gone up the line the looser it had become, and eventually he had found himself swimming up and down the walls, in and out of alcoves, in fruitless effort. Now Rick had bought a new drysuit and was keen to use it in anger.

It was Barry's turn to dive first, and he struggled to The Corner in his drysuit wearing a 7-litre and a 12-litre cylinder before his dodgy equipment (one of his high-pressure hoses was about to explode) caused him to return. I was due to dive after him, in order to place a stage cylinder for Rick to use the next day. A description of Barry's struggle through the squeeze at the bottom of the rift made me rather reluctant to go, but since Rick's dive depended on it I agreed to give it a try. I left one of my 7-litre cylinders at The Window for Rick, with a regulator attached, ready to go, then spent several exciting minutes digging the choke and bringing down lots more rocks.

The next day, Rick set off, wearing side-mounted 7- and 12-litre cylinders. He collected the bottle I'd dropped, and headed on upstream. Pausing at The Corner to adjust his equipment, he continued up the main line until he passed the connection point of the lines, about 300 metres in. A few metres beyond, the passage seemed to decrease in size, indicating that he'd reached a junction with the major route to Agen Allwedd going off to one side. Tying on our line reel, he laid out ten metres along the wall in what he assumed to be the correct direction towards Agen Allwedd before deciding that as he'd used up a third of his air supply he'd better head out. But turning on the cylinder that he'd picked up *en route*, he discovered that the second stage was supplying air to the sump, not his mouth! With half of his available air supply gone, he quickly retraced his steps, only to realise that he was going up the line to Daren Cilau not Elm Hole … eventually, a very stressed diver reappeared at Elm Hole just three minutes inside his no-stop time according to his new dive computer. While Rick took things easy, we emptied the cave of gear. We were happy that at last we'd made real progress towards a link with Agen Allwedd, even though achieving this had been something of an epic.

I called on Rick a few days later to discover he'd spent the previous day being treated for decompression sickness. On Monday night he'd complained of pins and needles down one side of his body and had gone to his doctor the next morning. The bends was diagnosed, so off he went to a nearby recompression chamber for treatment. But his symptoms returned, and he had to go to the Admiralty Deep Diving Research Centre at Portsmouth for further treatment. He was then forbidden to dive for several months, until he had recovered fully. This incident meant that we had effectively lost our most experienced diver. (One interesting side-effect of his bends, though, was that he went out and bought a new suit – quite uncharacteristic of Rick, who is normally cautious with his money. Although … he did buy it in a charity shop for £5!)

Another push was scheduled for the last weekend in July. On the Saturday, Malcolm Stewart started laying a line up the opposite wall from The Corner, looking for inlets. I aborted a dive at the bottom of the rift when my main light imploded, and decided to save my air for the next day when I'd changed the bulb. One of Rick's friends and a fellow firefighter, Paul Whybro, paid us a visit by going to The Window and back before helping dig Pwll-y-Cwm with the aid of Rick's winch. Barry planned to dive on Sunday using a couple of 12-litre tanks and a drysuit. But his high-pressure hose finally gave up the ghost while he was kitting up – which was fortunate, as it would have been very serious underwater. We had no spare – and to cap it all both bottles fell into the sump as he was undressing …

Two weeks later I was back in Elm Hole with Malcolm Stewart, who had kindly recovered Barry's bottles from the rift where they had lodged six metres down. I strapped them on and wore a part-inflated ABLJ to keep me off the floor of the sump. Slowly I made my way through the narrow, jagged section to The Window, where I put some more air in my ABLJ and set off upstream, intending to sort the line out as I went. After I had passed my previous limit, the line changed from orange to blue, and zigzagged about more often. At one point it crossed the passage to the opposite wall and then back again, taking the shortest route up the huge tunnel; then 100 metres further on, the line changed back to orange and I stopped atop some prominent fallen blocks sticking up into the passage to look ahead before consulting my watch and contents gauges. For once, the visibility underwater was superb and I was tempted to continue, as this was an outstanding experience. But I was close to thirds on my air and already I was feeling cold – it seemed an awfully remote spot. Thinking that this was a good reference point to remember how far I'd come, I turned around and cruised out on automatic pilot whilst trying to not think how chilly I was or how far I had to go. I began to slip into a trance-like state to conserve energy yet remain alert to any problems.[2]

Reaching The Window, I snapped back into full attention for the awkward passage ahead. Quite remarkably, wearing bigger cylinders was an advantage, as their bulk naturally guided me into the path of least resistance. At the bottom of the rift, I stopped for five minutes of boring but essential decompression before I could surface. Then I allowed my emotions to surface, too, and my first comment to Malcolm – who'd been patiently waiting for my return – was: 'Magic!'

I returned Barry's cylinders in exchange for a liquid reward, and for my next dive was fortunate enough to be able to borrow a similar set of large tanks. With a bit of last-minute help above water, I reached the end of the line laid by Rick on his previous dive. I continued to follow the right-hand wall until a familiar pile of boulders came into view. Looking up, I spotted an orange line crossing the passage above my head: evidently I'd done a loop and was now heading downstream. Winding in the line I'd laid back to Rick's limit, I tied off the reel and went back to the main line. I still had a fair amount of air left, so I went up the line towards Daren Cilau for a few metres. The passage appeared to open out again, but I didn't feel like pushing on, so I turned around to spend the seven minutes of my decompression stop watching shrimps at the bottom of the rift.

There was much discussion back in Coventry about whether there was a junction at this point at all … maybe the Agen Allwedd water joined Daren Cilau further upstream beyond the end of the sump? On a tight schedule, I made a day trip into Elm Hole. Unfortunately, my cylinders were less well filled than I would have liked, so there wasn't much time to look around. But as the visibility underwater was superb, at over five metres, I was able to inspect most of the passage as I went upstream. Nearing the tie-on at 300 metres I could even spot our white line going down the opposite wall. A few compass bearings confirmed this, and I wound the reel in and left it attached to the main line before I went out. On the way back, I did my five minutes' decompression in the rift, followed by an hour's recuperation in the Drum and Monkey.

I made another dive in early December 1990. But as my 7-litre cylinders were in Maytime at Agen Allwedd – I had abandoned them there after an aborted dive with Ian Rolland the day before – I had managed to secure the loan of a pair of 10-litre cylinders belonging to the Welsh Section of the CDG. These were delivered to the sump on the Friday evening, and two days later I made a solo trip into the cave with the rest of my gear, carrying a long metal bar to worry the PwII-y-Cwm choke. But at the bottom of the rift one of the tanks fell out of my harness – the thread had stripped in the bolt used to tighten the fastening – so I had to abandon my plans and drag my gear out, leaving the bar behind.

It wasn't until the end of March 1991 that I managed to return to Elm Hole. Under the watchful eye of Ian Rolland – recovering, as I was, from the effects of my stag night the

---

2  In Sports Science, this state of mind is called 'peak flow', or more colloquially 'in the zone'.

evening before – I collected the digging bar from the bottom of the rift and swam down to the choke. Several rocks covered the line, which was still in good condition, although the scaffold pole connected to it was no longer visible. I eased out several boulders (one the size of a coffee table), although the dig was mostly self-clearing. Then I opened up a 20-centimetre-high slot and poking my digging bar through it, managed to wiggle it quite freely, suggesting that the slot widened out beyond.

*Digging and filming at Pwll-y-Cwm  (Duncan Price)*

A concerted digging operation at Pwll-y-Cwm was arranged for the May Bank Holiday weekend, resulting in quite a large turnout of divers. Film cameraman Rob Franklin turned up to record the proceedings, so Rick Stanton and I skulked off into Elm Hole to avoid the media circus unfolding in the Clydach Gorge. Rick dived in a drysuit, and spent nearly an hour excavating his way through the slot I'd noted on my previous dive. He gained entry for his head and shoulders into a small chamber roofed by boulders apparently held back by a length of aluminium I-beam and a couple of lorry tyres. His exhaust bubbles were seen rising through the floor of Pwll-y-Cwm. The next day, it was my turn to have a go. I rolled more rocks from the choke and waved the digging bar at the lorry tyres to some effect; we then thought that a judicious explosive charge would shake up the rocks.

So on Whitsun Bank Holiday Monday, fresh from recovering my tanks from Maytime the day before, I met up with Bill Gascoine, a chemistry teacher from nearby Brynmawr, who had brought the explosives with him. The clarity of the water in Pwll-y-Cwm was amazing – just like a swimming pool – but this was destroyed after I put a pipe bomb at the toe of the risings, to be fired from the surface. I'd had to put a fair amount of trust in Bill, since he was holding the top end of the wire that not only set off the charge but also acted as my guideline back to the surface …

When Bill had gone, I changed into my caving gear and started constructing a wooden platform at the sump in Elm Hole, in order to make getting into and out of our gear easier. A month later, another charge was detonated and more improvements made to the platform over the sump pool. Some hosepipes were also set up to syphon the pools *en route* to the sump, which would make getting there less unpleasant.

I made a dive in Elm Hole using Rick's 15-litre cylinders, which served to demonstrate that it was possible to get even bigger cylinders though the cave and into the main drain, although I had to turn back at The Window due to problems with my buoyancy. At the end of August, Rick swam upstream for over 400 metres wearing the same cylinders, but without finding any evidence of an inlet from Agen Allwedd; a corner 380 metres in had showed some promise, although it was heading in the wrong direction. I followed up this dive with a look for myself, reaching 460 metres and rounding another corner before my air margins were reached; beyond 300 metres the passage felt smaller and was definitely shallower.

Operations were suspended for a few weeks after some divers, unconnected with our activities, had upset the locals with a rather large bang in Pwll-y-Cwm. Meanwhile I acquired a third-hand drysuit from Rob Murgatroyd, and secured the loan of his 12-litre cylinders; until then, I'd done all my dives wearing two wetsuits and an additional vest. It was hard work getting into the cave clad in so much neoprene – but once I was in the water I stayed tolerably warm for an hour or so.

On 25 October 1991, Bill Gascoine released some fluorescent dye into the Agen Allwedd streamway, and I set up my kit for a long-range dive into the sump to look for it. A day later, I took the last of my gear – my drysuit – into the Elm Hole. JC followed empty-handed, on his first visit to the cave. Just after noon I slid into the water and set off upstream; 30 minutes later I surfaced in Daren Cilau, not having seen a hint of the dye all the way. I'd only used about a quarter of my air supply. *En route*, though, I'd had trouble with my buoyancy; the air in my drysuit had migrated to my feet and had pinned me upside down in the roof of the sump. This was only the second time that I had worn a drysuit for diving, and I suppose that I should have done some more practice. Luckily I was able to hold onto the guideline and pull on it to bring myself upright.

Despite this sobering incident, I was excited to have dived through to Daren Cilau, even though there had been no one there to witness it. I took a 15-minute rest stop in Daren Cilau while I contemplated a slight high pressure leak from one of my contents gauges, then dipped back under the water and headed out. On the way back, I checked out the 380-metre corner; the side passage turned out to be an alcove. By the time I reached The Window, most of my lights had gone out; I did the last part of the dive and my 15 minutes' decompression in semi-darkness, before surfacing to meet JC, who'd just come back into the cave to await my return.

Having searched the sump through to Daren Cilau, we shifted the focus of our efforts to opening up a route in from Pwll-y-Cwm. On one dive at the end of November we managed to reopen the slot that had been accessible in the spring. The space beyond seemed to be stable, so I reached in with my right arm intending to move forward – but a rock fell on my elbow, so I backed out at high speed. Meanwhile, Rick was diving in Pwll-y-Cwm, where he arrived at the bottom just in time to see the floor disappearing in a cloud of murk. He half-expected to see me pop through. But at the other side of the blockage, I decided I'd had enough excitement for one day and retired. Back on the surface, Rick had another look in the risings. A metre-deep pit had been produced, thus exposing more of the I-beam.

A few weeks later, I'd summoned up the courage to return to the dig with more air. After 20 minutes tackling the left-hand side, I moved across the choke, to wave the digging bar at a wall of boulders in an ascending rift on the other side of the passage. A well-placed prod saw the whole lot fall in, and I beat a hasty retreat. After a few minutes, when things had appeared to settle down, I returned to the area to find lots of gravel which I scooped out, only for it to be replaced by a continuous avalanche of fresh material. The presence of leaves and twigs suggested that I was close to the bottom of Pwll-y-Cwm – and when I was changing mouthpieces a pea-sized stone lodged in my throat. I coughed my way back through the murk to the surface after a 70-minute dive. Then I put my drysuit back on and went to have a look at the bottom of Pwll-y-Cwm. Two metres of I-beam stuck out of the floor, and a gravel cone funnelled down to an impenetrable arch.

The breakthrough was tantalisingly elusive. Digging trips were soon producing more items that had been washed through from Pwll-y-Cwm: golf balls, bits of wood and sundry metalwork. But then the zip on my cheap drysuit gave up the ghost, so I was forced to return to two wetsuits. Then other projects took precedence – and then in November 1992 all my caving and diving gear was stolen from my garden shed. It took some time to replace everything – but at least the insurance meant I was able to invest in a new drysuit and more reliable gear, so the incident might well have saved my life in the end.

Over Christmas and New Year 1992–93, Rick and I dived Pwll-y-Cwm, half-expecting the blockage to have cleared itself naturally – but no chance. Rick went into Elm Hole in March, reporting that the choke looked little different from when we had first started work there in 1990. Easter 1993 was too wet to dive in Elm Hole, so we got shot-blasted by the gravel blowing out of the choke at the base of Pwll-y-Cwm instead. We relocated the I-beam and, with the aid of a hauling team on the surface, pulled it out; Rick turned the metalwork into a set of ramps for his Land Rover. He wastes nothing, and he still cave dives using a red canoe helmet that I'd given to him after its chin strap had worn out. I have since wised up to Rick's ability to make do and mend: if he offers to dispose of anything I've broken, I realise that it can probably be repaired.

At the beginning of May, while digging the choke I found a plastic toy VW Beetle and brought it out as a souvenir for my wife, who owned a real one. My exit, though, was pretty fraught, as at the last minute a lump of grit had lodged in the exhaust valve of one of my regulators, meaning that I got a lungful of water every time I tried to breathe from it. I was

## Nightmare in Elm Hole

*Above: Rick Stanton at the entrance to Elm Hole (Duncan Price)*

*Below: Pwll-y-Cwm in flood (Duncan Price)*

forced to swim back to Elm Hole using only one of my cylinders. When I surfaced, there was so little air in it that I was able to remove the regulator from it without closing the tap – this would normally be totally impossible, due to the pressure inside the cylinder holding it on. (We had modified our protocols surrounding our air margins, as we spent most of the dive in one place, more or less, and so only allowed ourselves sufficient emergency reserves to exit on a single cylinder. Thus the remaining air could be allocated to digging. This incident, although worrying, did at least show that we had judged it right.)

The next day, it was Rick's turn to dive. Taking advantage of some help, and since much of the gear was already in the cave, I dived in Pwll-y-Cwm at the same time. As soon as Rick's bubbles appeared, I set off, armed with a 3-metre length of plastic pipe. Reaching the bottom, I started poking it through a low arch on the left. Like an underwater chimney sweep I pushed the tubing in and out, in order to clear a route. After several attempts, the pipe slid in cleanly – and it was instantly pulled from my grip. When it came back into my grasp again, Rick gave it couple of tugs as the signal to hold still while we both measured the amount exposed on each side; then we tied off both ends of the tube to the diving lines, forging a physical link between Pwll-y-Cwm and the cave beyond. Next, the visibility dramatically decreased as Rick tried to scrabble a route through the last metre of rubble – but despite digging like a man possessed, he realised that his air reserves demanded he should exit through Elm Hole again, rather than coming up via Pwll-y-Cwm.

Over the summer more digging from Elm Hole exposed a pair of lorry tyres in the base of Pwll-y-Cwm. My exit along the tight underwater rift to Elm Hole was delayed by my harness becoming undone. Once I had attended to this, I discovered that I'd fastened myself to the line. To cap it all, Rick persuaded me to dive in the Pwll-y-Cwm to attach a rope (made up an assortment of car tow ropes borrowed from the audience of interested cavers) to one of the tyres so that we could pull it out. But we found it impossible to budge. Very low on air, I dived again to undo the knot – but I ran out of air and had to make a hasty ascent.

It was not until 26 September 1993 that I made another dive in Elm Hole, this time with Spanners as support. Carrying three bags and two cylinders between us, we set off underground at 11 am. Inside the cave, the effect of the recent heavy rain was obvious: both ducks were full, leaving only a few inches of airspace in places. We quickly transported the equipment through, and then, while Spanners started the siphons that I had installed to drain the ducks, I assembled my gear on the diving stage. This done, I stripped off to change into my dry underclothes, which had been brought into the cave wrapped in bin liners. Seeing me completely naked, Spanners made a wry remark about taking a photograph of me and entering it in the 'Cave Life' section of the annual cave photography competition. Liberal application of body lotion to the wrist seals of my drysuit soon filled the place with fragrance as I was zipped in. After checking my contents gauges, I told my shivering sherpa that I'd be about 40 minutes. Spanners left the cave with a bag containing the wet clothes that I'd worn into the cave, and set up another siphon *en route*.

Meanwhile, beneath his feet I was digging the choke in very poor visibility – less than a metre. A metal bar with a length of cord attached to the main line gave me some security.

## Nightmare in Elm Hole

Recent floods had blown out most of the fine gravel from the dig face, leaving only fist-sized cobbles to move. Working up through the centre and then across to the right, I was able to poke my head into an enlargement: an ascending rift by the wall of the passage where a big block and scaffold pole had once been. But after the pole had shifted, allowing the block to come out, this area had filled up with gravel running in from above. Now it was open, I could make out a black space at the top. When I waved the digging bar about I met no resistance, and I considered leaving it there to collect from the other side. More digging allowed me to feel around the slot with my outstretched arm to see how much room there was, but the letterbox didn't appear to be big enough to admit me. Backing out into a less constricted space to change breathing sets, I could see that I only had another few minutes of air left before I would have to leave. But the next diver would probably get through … so, composing myself, I had one more go at the restriction. I dredged another inch of gravel back, and performed a dogleg move to align my body. As I pushed forward with all my strength, a helmet-scraping squeeze allowed me to look through. Another shove – and I popped out like a cork and glided effortlessly onward.

But where was I? In the poor visibility, it was impossible to tell. Gliding upwards, I found myself under a solid roof and I followed it around to a tight rift. Surely this must be Pwll-y-Cwm? I was beginning to have my doubts. Going back down to the deepest part, I was considering fighting my way back through the slot, when I came across a familiar-looking lorry tyre with a float attached to it. I *was* in Pwll-y-Cwm! Now to find the line.

Meanwhile, on the surface, Spanners was getting rather concerned at the length of my absence. Bubbles were still rising from the pool after 45 minutes, when I should have been on my way back. A mass of air rose to the surface: maybe a free-flow? Trouble? Then the bubbles crossed the pool and disappeared – but there was still no movement on the line. The bubbles reappeared at the usual place and then, like a fisherman, Spanners felt the rope twitch. Up I popped, to embrace his feet as he stood by the water's edge. On removing my mask, I found that I had a slight nosebleed, but I was so I pleased that I didn't care. I did some quick mental arithmetic to check the need for decompression (I'd been down 50 minutes and had made a rather hasty ascent). My gauges told me it had been close … while Spanners went into Elm Hole to collect the rest of the gear I inflated my drysuit and floated on my back contemplating the sky – glad to be alive and pleased that the back door to Daren Cilau was now open.

*Spanners and Duncan in the car park of the Drum & Monkey Inn after the first dive between Elm Hole and Pwll-y-Cwm in September 1993 (Andy Kendall)*

# 6

# Down in the Clydach at Midnight

In September 1993, exactly five years from my first dive in Pwll-y-Cwm (and nearly three and a half years after starting work in Elm Hole) the underwater connection between the two caves had been made. Although only a small amount of new passage had been found, we now had easy access to the bottom of Daren Cilau. We repeated the through trip between Elm Hole and Pwll-y-Cwm a month later, as in a dive in the resurgence I had found a cone of gravel filling the arch I'd passed through earlier. I had left a line to the surface tied to a rock at the bottom of Pwll-y-Cwm and disappeared into Elm Hole the next day to dig my way out. The dive went very smoothly, and 50 minutes later I bobbed up in the Clydach.

The choke was still open on my next visit, and after removing one cylinder I was able to reverse though it and enlarge the way out without having to dive from Elm Hole. The following day, I swam from Pwll-y-Cwm to Daren Cilau and back; the total dive time (including some digging at the base of the pothole on the way back plus decompression) was around two hours.

But over the winter the route became blocked again, and several frustrating dives had to be made from the Elm Hole side to open it. Rick Stanton repeated my dive through to Daren Cilau and went up to St David's Sump, and by using an improved side-mounting system for his cylinders, he didn't even have to remove them to pass the choke. But high water levels and a number of problems with his equipment prevented him going any further. Then in April 1994 he drove down from Coventry, dived into Daren Cilau from Pwll-y-Cwm, continued through St David's Sump and, still wearing his drysuit, carried on up to the Gloom Room where he left our 100-metre line reel which had previously spent three years halfway through the downstream sump. The trip took 12 hours door to door; fortunately his drysuit was fitted with a pee valve.

During another day trip in May, Rick and I ferried some gear into Daren Cilau. We left a small cylinder and some ropes at St David's Sump and cached a bag of emergency provisions containing an oversuit and pair of boots not far from the underground campsite of Hard Rock Café. This seemed a sensible precaution in case one of us became stranded underground – at least we could then leave the cave via the dry route, however unappealing that might seem.

*Down in the Clydach at Midnight*

On 11 June, a line through the archway gave evidence of a visit by Martyn Farr, who'd had to dig his way in. Since the route was still tight, Spanners, who had now taken up cave diving, went into the water first to enlarge the archway before Rick and I went into Daren Cilau, each of us wearing a pair of large tanks strapped to our sides plus a 7-litre bottle and an empty tackle sack on our chests. For the first time, both of us were using the 'American' sidemount system, whereby our cylinders were clipped into our harnesses by karabiners at the waist and elastic cord under our arms. This enabled us to attach them one at a time while we were in the water, which made kitting up far easier. Reaching St David's Sump, I collected the extra bottle that we'd left there, and Rick ferried through the climbing gear.

Making our way up to the Gloom Room in drysuits and carrying a heavy bag each was hard work. We stopped a couple of times to put in a handline on the slippery slope out of a pool of water, and then to hang a short length of ladder on a three-metre vertical climb. The photographs I'd seen of this part of the cave did not do the place justice: it was full of loose rocks, with plenty of scope for ripping open a drysuit. On our arrival at the Gloom Room, we rigged another rope down the steep mud ramp down to the sump, and I helped Rick get ready to dive. Eventually he submerged beneath the murky water and was gone. I waited a few minutes for the twitching of the line to stop before climbing back up the incline to await his return.

Fifty minutes went by and lights in the water heralded his return. 'That's the most dangerous sump in the world!' said Rick as he surfaced. Apparently Martyn Farr's thin old line from his dives in 1985–86 had been washed down the passage and lay draped everywhere. The empty line reel in Rick's hand told another story: he had laid out 100 metres of line, heading directly for Agen Allwedd. The depth at the end of the line was 7 metres, and Rick was confident that on the next dive he would surface.

On 9 July a large group of divers converged on the Clydach. Meanwhile Spanners had soloed into Daren Cilau, intending to rendezvous with Rick and me at noon. Due to problems with crowd control, I didn't enter Pwll-y-Cwm until after midday; then I took just over 30 minutes for the swim through to Daren Cilau, where Spanners had been waiting for 20 minutes. Rick arrived a little later and we set off up to St David's Sump, stopping to borrow a pair of fins from the pile of diving gear that had been brought in by Martyn Farr previously. After we had bumped our way along the roof of St David's Sump, we divided up Rick's gear between us, and we made good progress to the Gloom Room. The empty reel was loaded with 150 metres of new line, then I helped Rick into the water and we watched him depart shortly before 4 pm.

We agreed to give Rick three hours before Spanners and I would start out, although with only one complete set of diving gear, it made sense for Spanners to exit via an alternate but longer dry route, rather than waste time ferrying tanks back from the downstream sump. In view of the difficulties involved in going out ahead of Rick, we decided that we would delay our departure until he was an hour overdue.

Thankfully, bubbles and lights in the water heralded the safe return of our means of easy escape five minutes before Rick's deadline. He tried to convince us that he'd lost the line and had spent the last three hours in an airbell. But the scribbles on his slate told another story. As expected from the profile of the passage, he had surfaced 100 metres from his previous limit in a passage of similar dimensions to that sump (5 metres wide by 2 metres high). This quickly developed into substantial river cave, which he had followed for 400 metres, gaining height rapidly. Then the route changed character abruptly below a roof tube (later found to be an oxbow) and developed into a series of zigzagging rifts, evidently side-stepping across the strata towards Agen Allwedd. After another 250 metres, the way onwards was barred by another sump. This didn't look too promising, but it was the only good lead. Rick had followed various side passages as far as he had dared wearing a drysuit – one northerly-heading tube had ended in low sandy fill, which he thought might yield on digging. The total length of the find was estimated to be over 700 metres. By now, Rick's survey slate was extremely precious and we took great care not to rub off any of his notes.

Full of enthusiasm once more, we made our way back to daylight. Rick and I surfaced around 10 pm, to be greeted by a welcome band of helpers on the banks of the Clydach. Spanners, having almost ended up at the bottom of St David's Lake, stumbled into Whitewalls at midnight, an hour after we'd arrived. Plans were made to go back: Rick and I would dive into the new discovery and Rick would tackle the next sump. In the meantime, I'd accepted a nine-month secondment to work in the USA, starting in October 1994. This, combined with the Rick's plans to go on a caving expedition to Spain, meant that we only had a few weeks to pull off the follow-up trip. So we stashed a pair of wetsuits and a 7-litre cylinder at the bottom of Daren Cilau on 6 August, ferrying them into the cave via Pwll-y-Cwm.

The following Saturday was scheduled as the day for the big push – we had high hopes of making a connection between Daren Cilau and Agen Allwedd. Everyone wanted to be part of the action, with Paul Whybro, Martyn Farr and a third diver, Nick Geh, intending to dive in with us. Spanners would come in via Daren Cilau as before, while non-diver Charles Bailey even agreed to meet us at the Gloom Room via the longer, dry route. Rick, Paul and I assembled in the Clydach Gorge with a strong surface support team. The water was even murkier than the previous week – but someone at least had to dive in to meet Spanners and Charles, who had already gone ahead from the other side of the hill. Martyn Farr rolled up late, without his diving gear; Nick was not coming due to work commitments and now Martyn was withdrawing as well.

In spite of this, Rick set off, amid a barrage of photo calls. Then me. I had just submerged to 3 metres when I met him on his way back – the choke was blocked! Paul Whybro went in to investigate, and kindly offered to try to dig it open again. Once he had achieved this, I'm sure that he was secretly relieved to have too little air to come with us … two hours later than intended, Rick and I groped our way through the sump to meet Spanners in Daren Cilau. He had wisely decided to wait until we arrived, and Charles was still with him. A long discussion ensued, and we eventually adopted Plan J. This entailed leaving one 7-litre tank by St David's Sump and taking two 4-litre tanks back out again. The return journey provided an interesting moment when I reached a tie-off 200 metres into the sump and due to the very poor visibility couldn't find the continuing line. But after searching for what seemed an age, I located the way out and caught up with Rick at The Corner before we surfaced after a rather shorter trip than we'd originally planned.

We were rather demoralised at the failure to do our planned assault on the end of the cave. But due to Rick's forthcoming trip to Spain and my stint in the US, it was important that we should recover at least some of the gear before the end of the month, so we lined up an attempt for the Friday preceding the August Bank Holiday weekend. Frantic mid-week phone calls to Peter Bolt and Charles Bailey to check conditions meant that by Thursday morning our trip was on. The next day saw Rick and me down in the gorge with the usual mound of frogman's apparatus; fortunately we had help with our gear from Arthur Millet – a stocky Welshman with an impressive beard which endowed him with a passing resemblance to a garden gnome. Arthur lived in Crickhowell, working as a plumber, and was always willing to help carry diving gear for us.

By midday, we were both at the bottom of Daren Cilau. On his previous visit to the new passage, Rick had risked tearing his drysuit on razor-sharp rocks on the approach to the final sump; this would have been a disaster, as he would have got very cold on the long dive out again. So on this occasion we had carried in wetsuits; at least if we put a hole in them it would be less serious, as our wetsuits already had a few battle scars anyway. We thus experienced the joys of changing out of our nice, warm drysuits into cold, wet wetsuits. Reaching St David's Sump with a pair of 4-litre tanks, we collected the other cylinders and dived through. We struggled up to the Gloom Room and kitted up at the top of the mud ramp.

As I was unfamiliar with the sump, I was delegated to dive first, in order to take advantage of any visibility. A thin white line disappeared into the pool, passing over glutinous mud banks which, when disturbed, rapidly destroyed the clarity of the water. The route continued under several low shelves, gaining depth as I followed the original line laid by Martyn Farr. Loose line lay draped alongside the one I was following, so I stayed well clear of the floor to avoid any possible entanglement. Martyn's line terminated at a block shaped like a house brick, where our thicker white line led off around a prominent right-hand corner into the main drain. This was the deepest part of the dive, which we had christened Taffy Turnip's Terrible Tangle in mocking reference to the previous explorer. As I was overweighted at this depth, it was a struggle for me to follow the line as it took the shortest route through the undulating passage.

One hundred metres further on, the line changed to the orange polypropylene cord that Rick had deployed on his breakthrough dive. In spite of the length of the sump, I felt surprisingly comfortable in my wetsuit, and was almost disappointed to surface after a 15-minute swim. The above-water passage was a roomy tunnel, and the stream meandered between mud banks as the passage gradually got bigger and bigger. The whole character of the cave had changed, and one could be forgiven for thinking that one had emerged from Sump 4 into Maytime, in Agen Allwedd.

A few minutes later, Rick joined me and we sorted out a set of gear to tackle the next sump. We had called the passage the San Agustin Way as a tribute to Ian Rolland; other parts of the cave had been named in reference to a trip to Peru on which Ian and Rick had first met, so we considered it appropriate to commemorate Ian by naming our discovery after the cave where they had said farewell *(see colour section)*.

This trip was certainly going to be in Ian's style, employing an Alpine assault rather than siege tactics. Pausing at a pile of rocks in the passage, we topped up the line reel left from the last visit, and looked into a short oxbow that carried the stream. A little way further on, we spent several minutes chasing round another series of oxbows where the stream cut down rapidly through the limestone. Vertical chert banding in the rocks produced several small cascades as we reached a 4-metre climb up into a roof tube *(see colour section)*.

But we chose to ignore this, and followed a stream which emerged from a narrow rift. We traversed along this until we reached a prominent left-hand corner, where we parked the diving gear and scrambled up into the other end of the roof tube. A sandbank ahead denoted the northernmost extremity of the passage, and I was prompted to have a poke around to see if it continued; we had no tools, so I simply shifted the stuff by hand. A body-length of progress was enough to show me that we'd need a shovel to go any further, but there did seem to be a way on, over the low muddy fill. The roof tube turned back southwards, to end overlooking the stream at the top of the 4-metre climb. The high-level passage was littered with fallen blocks and gypsum crystals, suggesting that it predated the existing river passage.

Continuing on our way upstream, we reached another corner with a stream inlet which turned out to be a short oxbow. Our progress became more difficult beyond this, as we followed the water along a rift, squeezing sideways, up to our necks in the river. A couple of zigzags later, we reached an enlargement leading to the final sump. While Rick prepared to dive, I swam along the passage to find somewhere to tie off the line. At 5 pm, Rick entered the water saying that he'd be no longer than an hour and a half, and probably only 30 minutes. When he had gone, I did some step-ups on a convenient ledge to try to keep warm and pass the time.

Ninety minutes later the sound of bubbles and a dull glow in the water heralded Rick's safe return. We were both relieved to see one another. Diving into the sump, Rick had followed the right-hand wall to a corner beyond a small airbell. After 55 metres underwater, the passage surfaced in 130 metres of streamway, ending in another sump. Rick had dived this for a further 65 metres along a rift until, with a few turns of line left on the reel and feeling out on a limb, he reached a convenient block where he tied the line off at a depth of 6 metres. He thought that this must surely be near the point reached by Ian Rolland on his last dive downstream in Agen Allwedd in May 1990 – the connection appeared to be close.

But with no equipment or inclination to explore further, it was now time to for us head out. We reached the upstream end of the Gloom Room Sump without difficulty, and Rick beat me into the water. Following him through diminished visibility was not a problem, although I saw nothing for the final part of the dive. But disaster struck when I lost a fin on surfacing. As I clambered up the handline behind Rick, I found that didn't have the strength to get to the top, and ended up having to pass my gear up to him before returning to search for my lost equipment. Several duck-dives in nil-visibility water later, I found my fin, and we staggered on to St David's Sump, leaving a full 4-litre tank by the Gloom Room for another time. Wisely, we remained in our diving gear for the swim across St David's Lake as we struggled to stay afloat – and then, once we were back into our drysuits we had the opposite problem, unable to submerge as we tried to attain the correct trim to dive out.

Midnight in the Clydach: two tackle sacks bobbed to the surface, followed by two very tired cave divers. Four pairs of wellington boots surrounded us, and we were whisked back to the cars by Millet's Removals … unbeknown to us, Arthur had rung around to find out who was coming down for the weekend and arranged some help. Everyone had been waiting since 11 pm. The next morning dawned sunny and bright; as I drove along the escarpment away from Whitewalls; I reflected that I was leaving for some time …I was pleased by the success that we had achieved in Daren Cilau, but also anxious about what I might miss out on while I was away.

# 7

# Coming to America

At the beginning of October 1994, I crossed the Atlantic for a nine-month secondment in the USA. I went to work for a subsidiary to the chemical company that employed me in the UK. The site manufactured self-adhesive, solar-control window tint film for cars and buildings, the sort of stuff that's used to obscure the interiors of posh limousines and boy-racer hatchbacks. Amongst the factory's products was a flexible printed circuit material made from a thin sheet of copper glued to heat-resistant plastic film, and due to a change in raw materials the adhesive required reformulation in order to maintain its performance. As a consequence of market requirements, it turned out that the recipe I'd come up with had other uses. One of these was sticking the laminate lining onto the walls of the toilets in commercial aircraft; as some passengers would use the toilets to try to smoke, the décor needed to be especially fire retardant. Not only was my adhesive designed for bonding metals to plastic – it was also heat resistant and non-flammable. So the next time you relieve yourself on a Boeing jet, you can feel safe in the knowledge that I invented the glue that holds the wallpaper up!

Having rented out our house in Coventry, Kate and I found ourselves living in a basement apartment in the town of Martinsville, Virginia, about 10 miles north of the state line with North Carolina and around 50 miles from the Blue Ridge Mountains. We had shipped a small amount of caving gear to the US, and we made contact with a local caving club (or grotto as they are called) affiliated to the National Speleological Society. But our requests for information about the nearest caves that we could visit were politely but firmly ignored. We discovered that American cavers are very secretive about cave locations, in order to protect them from vandalism. But I had more luck when I contacted a Virginian cave diver called Ron Simmons who lived in Charlottesville; he invited me on a couple of exploration trips to a cave in the Blue Ridge Mountains which he and his friends had established as the longest cave in the area. This was also kept secret, and since I'd travelled to and from the cave entrance in the back of Ron's truck, I couldn't possibly give anyone directions to it.

I was keen to do some cave diving while I was in the US, so we made plans to spend ten days visiting the Florida springs in early December. Rick Stanton flew out to join us, and early the next morning we set off from Martinsville for the 10-hour drive south. We arrived in High Springs around 4 pm and, with plenty of time to kill before checking into our motel, decided to visit Ginnie Springs nearby. After reporting to the dive shop, we went snorkelling, and spent an hour free-diving around boulders at the cavern entrance. The shop itself was a real eye-opener in terms of the diving goodies that were on display. At the time, British cave divers had to make their own equipment (primary lights, harnesses, line reels etc.), but here it was all made by Dive-Rite. The store also sold cold beer, which no doubt helped to lubricate the flow of money from our wallets into the cash register.

We spent the next morning exploring the antique shops in High Springs before returning to Ginnie Springs to meet up with two local cave divers, Tom Morris and John Moseley. Tom had met British cave divers before – Peter Bolt had dived with him in 1992, and had adopted the configuration used by Tom and other American sidemount divers, subsequently importing it into the UK. When Rick dived with Peter at Otter Hole, he had been so impressed by its ease of use over the traditional British method of wearing cylinders on a belt around the waist that he (and then I) had adopted it *(see colour section)*.

While I dived sidemount, Rick used a back-mounted twinset configuration with integral wing (a buoyancy compensator) typical of the native cave divers. In addition, Tom had loaned us some nice bright diving lights to supplement the dim glow of our helmet-mounted diving torches. Once in the water, Tom asked us if we were going to do a buddy check. Rick and I looked at one another in a confused sort of way:

Duncan to Rick: Are you ready?
Rick: Yep!
Duncan: So am I. Let's go!

The Americans laughed, and we set off into the Devil's Eye/Ear cave system for our first experience of what the Floridian aquifer had to offer us.

Devil's Eye is an oval gash located up a short tributary of the Santa Fe River; it is linked to Devil's Ear by a short tunnel. The Ear is much bigger and, situated in the middle of the river, is characterised by an area of cool, clear water in the tannic river water. Many Florida springs are like this, and in times of flood are known to reverse their flow and fill with brown river water. The Devils Eye/Ear system is unusual, however, in that it generally has a strong outward current and very rarely reverses direction.

Descending into the cave, we found the flow to be quite strong and we had to swim close to the walls of the large passage to stay out of the full force of the water. We picked up the permanent line a short way in, and followed in single file to a constriction known as The Lips, which proved difficult to negotiate without pulling on the rock (frowned on in conservation-minded US cave diving circles). Up to this point the cave walls had been scoured white by careless divers, but now the route was coated with goethite. We turned off the main tunnel and down a large side passage which took us on a circuit back into the main drag. Heading a little further into the system, we swam over a series of sandbanks which gave us the impression of being on a rollercoaster. Eventually we turned around and followed the main line back to the start, our exit being aided by the current. We did our 20 minutes' decompression sitting astride a tree trunk jammed inside the entrance.

The next day was to be a break from diving, so we went to Ichetuknee Springs to go canoeing instead. The site is a nature reserve where several springs discharge crystal-clear water to form a river which joins the Santa Fe. The place is very popular with tourists, who hire large rubber rings (inner tubes) and float downstream in the current. We were more ambitious, and decided to hire a Canadian canoe. We were also overly optimistic about the time it would take for us to drift down the Ichetuknee and along the Santa Fe. The first stretch of our journey went smoothly and we diverted up a few inlets to see where they went. There were lots of turtles basking on fallen trees – and fortunately no alligators. We made good time to the confluence with the dark waters of the Santa Fe – but there we lost the current and had to paddle like a Polynesian war canoe to meet our pickup on time.

Sunday saw a change of scene: we moved to the Steamboat Dive Inn at Branford on the banks of the Suwannee River. Upon entering our accommodation, we discovered that 'dive' was indeed the operative word – especially as it was on a busy road which kept us awake at night with the sound of trucks pulling up to the State Inspection post just up the road. We dropped off our luggage and went to Peacock Springs for a dive; this is one of the most extensive underwater caves in Florida, and boasts a number of traverses between several sinks and the head spring. Kitting up on some nice wooden steps was quite a luxury. Rick and I almost reached Challenge Sink before having to turn back … unbeknown to us, we had stopped just short of an opening where we would have been able to surface, recalculate our air margins and continue to another exit at Orange Grove Sink, thus completing a traverse.

Regaining the entrance, we met a couple of American cave divers who had just done a long traverse using scooters. These devices (more properly known as diver propulsion vehicles) are essentially battery-powered torpedoes that pull you through the water. The offer to try one was just too tempting, and first Rick sped off into the depths, then I had a ride, zooming around the cavern zone while keeping an eye on daylight filtering in from the surface so that I didn't get lost.

The next day, we set off early to Crystal River to go swimming with manatees. *En route* we stopped at Manatee Springs (another major spring with a major underwater cave behind it) before reaching Crystal River for lunch. Here we met Bill and Diana Oestereich (both cave divers) and, after fitting Kate out with a wetsuit, we went out into the bay with Diana. Manatees don't normally come so close to the shore at this time of the year, but we were lucky when we spotted a group while cruising up an inlet. After carefully entering the water so as not to disturb them, we spent an hour with the extraordinary creatures; it was a captivating experience for us, and especially so for Kate.

After two nights at the Dive Inn, we'd had enough of being kept awake by road traffic in the early hours. As we prepared to check out, Tom and John turned up to meet us for another dive … it was funny how the proprietor's indifferent attitude towards us changed when he realised that we were mixing with the likes of Tom. We drove in convoy to Duckweed Sink, a site which had been explored by Tom and his friends for a long way in the direction of the resurgence at Ichetuknee. Unlike our previous dives, this was a 'wild' cave, not frequented by tourist cave divers.

The entrance to Duckweed was in a large circular pond, usually covered by vegetation. An impressive gash in the bottom led into the cave with upstream and downstream routes. We swam downstream for about 500 metres to a depth of 42 metres before turning for home. We lolled around in the entrance pool for an hour's decompression, looking for artefacts (shotgun pellets, fossils and fishing lures) amongst the silt. As I used up my air, I became more buoyant and I finished the dive carrying everyone's light batteries as ballast.

After we spent a comfortable night with Tom and family in Gainesville, Rick was keen to do a long scooter dive with Tom back at Ginnie Springs. Meanwhile, Kate and I went to a nearby dive shop to purchase some cheap diving tanks for me to use while I was in the country, as I'd left my cylinders in the UK. After another night in the Morris household, entertained and impressed by Tom's knowledge of the Florida caves and its fauna, we drove to Orlando to put Rick on a flight back to the UK. Resisting the temptation to visit Disney World, Kate and I took a little more time off and drove across to Cape Canaveral to see some rockets before heading north to the oldest town in the US – San Augustine, founded by the Spanish. Here we located an English pub where I scoffed a plate of steak and kidney pie with chips, washed down by a couple of pints of imported British ale. Luxury!

In February 1995, Kate and I took advantage of a cheap flight from the US to Mexico in order to visit the cenotes of the Yucatán peninsula. We arrived at Charlotte airport to be told by the check-in staff that if we ever wanted to see our diving gear again we'd better carry it on as hand luggage, since the baggage handlers in Cancún were not to be trusted with expensive sports equipment … somehow we managed to fit four large rucksacks into the overhead lockers on the plane.

We were met in Mexico by Tony and Nancy DeRosa from the Aquatech Dive Center with whom we'd arranged our trip. At the DeRosas' apartments in Akumal, we met up with Rick Stanton and Paul Whybro; they had arrived a week ahead of us and had settled into a routine of daily cave diving. Part of the whole cenote experience is to make use of the services of a guide to find the caves and show you around. Normally the package comprises a morning dive, lunch and then another dive in the afternoon. But Rick and Paul preferred to do one big dive (often with stage tanks), have a late lunch and then enjoy what was left of the day fettling their gear, followed by some relaxation in the rooftop bar of our accommodation.

When we arrived Rick and Paul already had a few amusing experiences to tell us about; for example, before one dive, Rick had discovered problems with his rechargeable diving light and had taken it apart to investigate. Paul was having similar problems, and attributed it to the dubious quality of the Mexican power supply … he was just about to dismantle his light to check the contacts, when he realised that they were both still wearing their sunglasses.

My first dive in Mexico was at Cenote Pon DeRosa, a site which had been discovered by our hosts. As I had not worn back-mounted diving cylinders since my early sea diving days with BSAC, and since this was the established configuration in the Yucatán, I needed to be initiated into the use of a twinset and wing. At first I was too buoyant, and then since I insisted on wearing a helmet I couldn't see where I was going, and finally my primary light flooded. Our guide, Gary Walten, was very patient with me while Rick and Paul went off on their own. By the time the others returned I'd been on a traverse to Coral Cenote and had got the hang of it.

Since the trip was also supposed to be a holiday for Kate and me, we spent the next day together doing some sightseeing. The dive centre had some rickety old bicycles which we borrowed to wobble our way to Xel-Há Aquatic Park, south of Akumal. This is built around a natural inlet (or *caleta*) and featured a lagoon full of colourful native fish. It was like swimming in a big aquarium; the fish were small and generally shy of swimmers. On another day off, though, we encountered a solitary barracuda while snorkelling in an undeveloped bay; although it was alone, the creature would not move out of our way and fixed us with a beady eye as we swam around it.

For my next dive, I joined Gary at Cenote Mayan Blue to attempt a circular dive around the A and B tunnels. Rick and Paul, carrying stage tanks, accompanied us for part of the trip before heading off along the D tunnel for a longer swim. Taking another day off from the tough cave diving, I went with Kate by bus to the Mayan ruins at Chichén Itzá. The journey gave us an insight into the local economy; I swear that one passenger paid the driver with a box of household light bulbs!

For the final dive of the trip we all went to dive in Cenote Sac Actun. I carried a stage tank as well, although I lost the benefit of this as I started the dive breathing from my twinset rather than the stage. We dropped our extra cylinders at a convenient point, then the route became more constricted as we passed through a number of squeezes amid underwater stalagmites. Unlike the other flooded caves that I had dived in elsewhere, the cenotes of the Yucatán had been above sea level during the last ice age and this had allowed the development of cave formations – stalactites and stalagmites – before the sea had risen and inundated them once more. The caves were also full of a mixture of salt and fresh water. The salt water formed a distinct layer below the less dense fresh water, with a perceptible boundary layer (or halocline) between them. Because of the difference in optical properties, turbulence in the boundary between the two layers can make this look like the water surface when viewed from below, and when swimming in the mixing zone itself, the visibility is very hazy, as though your mask is coated with treacle.

One hour into the dive, Gary indicated daylight coming from Cenote Baham Chi. Since I had prematurely reached thirds on my back gas, we ran a jump reel up to the surface in the small cave. The party turned around and swam back to Sac Actun in a widely-spaced procession. Gary kept indicating that we should close ranks in case one of us had trouble, but since we were used to solo diving, we had trouble complying. Once in sight of daylight, we made a short decompression stop, made more interesting by a group of young women who turned up to bathe in the open cavern. In fact, Rick was so engrossed by the scene that he forgot to dump the air from his wing, and bobbed up to the surface amongst them.

## Coming to America

After a week in the Yucatán it was time for us all to go home. Paul and Rick took internal flights to Mexico City for their transfers across the Atlantic, and Kate and I returned to the US. Our flight took us back to Charlotte via Atlanta, where we had to clear US customs and immigration before continuing to our final destination. This process was straightforward for the US nationals on our flight, even though many of them did not have passports, since the immigration officials seemed to accept almost any form of identification, such as drivers' licences, utility bills, etc. But Kate and I were 'resident aliens' and so although we both had visas we were delayed in a long queue of holidaymakers. Although being amongst passengers who had disembarked from a flight from Newcastle-on-Tyne reminded us of home, we were in danger of missing our transfer. Eventually we cleared immigration, but when we reached the baggage claim our luggage (which had been checked in for the return flight) was missing. After a heart-stopping moment, we were met by the ground crew, who had collected our bags and put them on a trolley. Apparently they were holding our flight for us, and all we had to do was to push the cart through customs before our bags were loaded onto the aircraft. Avoiding the hard stares of the other passengers, we boarded the plane and arrived in Martinsville in the early hours of the following morning.

As I had now shown that I was at least a half-decent caver, Ron Simmons arranged for us to cave dive together in Virginia in May 1995. We met up at a convenient place in the middle of nowhere and drove over to the hamlet of Liberty in Tazwell County. We planned to dive at Lost Mill Springs – a series of three windows into the main drainage of Knob Mountain in the Appalachians. Ron showed me the resurgence, close to the road, but this was apparently not penetrable. A little way east, the river flowed across two karst windows, the larger of which had once contained a sawmill. Two smaller openings nearby also intercepted the underground flow, and the one further upstream had been explored underwater by Ron to a restriction at 15 metres depth and 80 metres in.

The dive base was reached by a steep descent down a muddy slope into a short section of cave which ended in a sump. As I was carrying my cylinders (the ones I had bought in Florida) down to the cave entrance, I slipped and broke the pillar valve on one of them, but Ron graciously let me borrow of one of his cylinders, so I set off breathing from my remaining good tank, reserving Ron's for emergencies. I reached the previous limit in 1-metre visibility, and tied a fresh reel onto the end of the line. A short amount of digging at

*Ron Simmonds, Lost Mill Spring*
*(Duncan Price)*

the gravel slope established that the passage opened out immediately, so I ploughed through the highest part. It was just like Wales! Beyond this, I followed the left-hand wall upstream until I reached a convenient chert knob. Consulting my watch (the one Ian Rolland had used in Agen Allwedd), I found it had stopped – presumably the five-year-old battery was getting weak and the cold water had caused it to fail. I had breathed a third of the air from my own cylinder, so I tied off the line and had to dig my way back out through the gravel squeeze before slowly swimming back to the surface in lieu of any decompression. Ron told me that I'd been gone 30 minutes, so my caution had been unnecessary. I gave Ron his cylinder back and he repeated my dive, but due to the poor visibility he didn't get any further either.

A few months later, my time was up in the US. I was glad to return to the UK. My assignment had been slow getting going and I'd spent several months at the start with little to do. Boredom had sapped my morale and allowed me to become homesick. Kate had felt the same way: she'd given up her teaching post in the UK and was not allowed to work in the US. Despite this, we'd made many friends amongst the locals and even joined a square dancing club. Once we got home, I resolved to put my energies into finding a more challenging job and get back into the UK caving scene.

I paid another visit to Martinsville at the end of August 1996, during a business trip to the US. But I didn't get chance to go caving with Ron Simmons and his friends, despite driving over to the Bat Ranch to meet up with them. Sadly, Ron was killed on 14 February 2007 while cave diving in Florida. He had been exploring and surveying Allen Mill Pond in Lafayette County on his own, when he failed to return from a dive. His body was found and recovered the next day from its maze-like network of constricted silt-filled passages. His tanks were empty, and it is surmised that he had used up too much air while preoccupied with exploring and mapping the cave. His problems would have been compounded by a line entanglement on the way out. His body was found 100 metres from the entrance, and he was wearing the same tanks that we had used on our dive together at Lost Mill Springs.

# 8

# Pilgrim's Progress

At the end of April 1995, I was still in the US. Three thousand miles away in Wales, Rick Stanton was diving into Sump 5, beyond the end of the San Agustin Way extension that we had found the previous year; we had hoped that the route he was following might lead directly into the underwater rifts beneath Against All Odds in Agen Allwedd, explored in 1990 by Ian Rolland. Supported to Sump 4 by Joel Corrigan, a rope access technician and keen vertical caver, Rick, wearing two of my 7-litre tanks, managed to push 55 metres beyond his previous limit into the sump.

After 10 metres, Rick broke surface – not in Agen Allwedd but in a short section of active stream passage – and 20 metres ahead he encountered a large boulder choke. Alone, and moving carefully through an area of unknown stability, he worked his way along the right-hand wall which dropped into a rift carrying the stream. But the route was blocked by a large boulder, even though he could see negotiable passage beyond it, and hear the sound of falling water. So Rick returned to Joel, and the pair made their way back to the surface. They made plans to go back and remove the boulder. They recognised that someone with access to the appropriate chemicals would be useful, so as an added incentive they left my diving cylinders behind at the Gloom Room.

At the end of my sentence in the US, I was keen to get back into the fray, and my diving gear accompanied me across the Atlantic in a suitcase rather than separately as air freight. This meant that as soon as I had retrieved my cylinders from storage I was able to get underwater rather than waiting several weeks for the shipment to arrive as had happened when I left the UK for the US. My return to action coincided with the Chelsea Speleological Society summer barbecue at Whitewalls, and I paid for a barrel of beer to lubricate the proceedings. My first cave dive back in the UK was a trip into Daren Cilau from Pwll-y-Cwm to exchange the wellington boots I had left in the cave for a better pair.

At the end of August a circus of divers converged on Pwll-y-Cwm. Lack of rain had reduced the resurgence to a static pool with the water level several inches below the lip of the pot; only a trickle of water leaking from the retaining wall, built upstream to divert debris away from the pothole dam, entered the pool, and even this was being reduced by the building activities of Arthur Millet and JC. A team of helpers (who were themselves planning to dive later) helped shift our equipment down to the water. Joel had already stashed some gear in the cave, leaving Rick and me to dive in, with our wetsuits and spare tanks strapped to our chests.

At the bottom of the Kings Road, we swapped our drysuits for the wetsuits, and made our way through St David's Sump and up to the Gloom Room. Collecting further equipment, we dived through to the San Agustin Way and each took a single cylinder up to Sump 4. After a briefing from Rick on the nature of the dive, we set off by pulling ourselves along on the walls of the sump rather than finning, thus saving energy and air. Despite the vulnerability that we felt on diving with no redundant cylinder, the underwater passage was roomy and inviting. After we surfaced in a long section of canal, we found the water got shallower, until we reached Sump 5 on a corner where a side passage led off. Part of this was an oxbow back into the sump pool, but there was also an inlet heading north which apparently closed down.

Sump 5 turned out to be a similarly pleasant experience. If anything, the visibility underwater had improved over the murk that we'd groped through during the long dive into the bottom of Daren Cilau. De-kitting, I felt that the trip was almost over: after all, this was the turnaround point. Rick led the way to the choke and the boulder which blocked the way on. Beyond this, we could see several metres along the rift to what appeared to be an arch or corner. We could hear the sound of a waterfall ahead, although this might just have been the stream running over rocks.

The plan had just been to blow up the obstacle and go away. But Joel had other ideas; he stripped off his wetsuit jacket and started to squeeze up into a small gap between the boulder and the cave walls. While Joel got stuck into this (literally), Rick and I clambered up the rock fall to look for alternative routes though the collapse. Finding nothing of promise, we had something to eat while Joel tried to free himself. Eventually Rick and I got fed up of waiting, and threatened to leave him there with the explosives for company (as an alternative to a lingering death). This gave Joel the encouragement he needed.

Having spent an hour longer at the sharp end than we'd planned, it was now time to Go Chemical. I set up the charge while Rick and Joel looked on like excitable children. After assuring them that I really did know what I was doing, I fired the slab of gelignite electrically from a safe distance. There was nothing more that we could do until the fumes from the explosion rolling down the passage in our direction had dissipated, so we donned our diving gear and set off out at 7 pm.

Five hours later, we were back on the surface. All the diving gear had been carried back to the King's Road where Joel left his kit for future retrieval. Rick and I both swam out, very heavily laden with two extra cylinders and a wetsuit each. Regulator problems halfway through the sump meant that I was forced to remain on one set for the whole sump, since the other regulator was free-flowing and I had to turn the cylinder off to stem the leak. When I reached the choke, I squeezed through – only to find my air supply cut off. Shocked, I let my mouth fall open, and dropped the mouthpiece. Fumbling around, I found the other regulator and shoved it in my mouth. But … no air! After a ghastly moment, I remembered to reach down to turn the cylinder on. Fortunately the misbehaving regulator was now functioning correctly and I had plenty of air to cover the last 20 metres to the surface. On investigation, I found the other cylinder had turned itself off when the rubber knob of the control valve had rubbed against the rock as I had squeezed through the arch.

In the early part of 1996, I made several solo trips into Daren Cilau to set up equipment for future use. It took the cylinders that I had bought in the US into the cave and left them just beyond the lake downstream of St David's Sump. I had tried to get the cylinders hydraulically tested when I returned to the UK, but the threads in the cylinder valves were an American specification, so I just filled them up on Rick's compressor and cached them in the cave. The water levels were quite high at the time and the approach to the sump was underwater. When the weather improved, I took the cylinders on to the Gloom Room with a full line reel for future use.

*Duncan at the Gloom Room (Tim Morgan)*

In June, I decided to dive in the Gloom Room to look for the downstream continuation of the sump. I had done several solo trips into Daren Cilau to move equipment, and I had no company for this visit either. The surface pool in the Gloom Room was static, yet as water was flowing into the upstream end of the sump there must have been an outlet. Reaching the first corner, I crossed the passage to the opposite wall and followed this downstream until the visibility deteriorated and I lost my way. Retracing my route in, I spotted the line reel across the passage from the main line and managed to loop the two lines together. Getting out of the muddy pool at the end of the dive involved an epic struggle; I dropped both my fins into the muddy water, and as I didn't relish the thought of trying to swim out without them, it took me some time to find them again. After this incident, I invested in a pair of brightly coloured buoyant fins that would be harder for me to lose.

In July 1996, Rick, Joel and I were reunited for another trip to the terminal blockage at the end of the San Agustin Way. Thirty minutes' work with a crowbar made no progress, so we set off another explosive charge. On the way out we had a look up the side passage before the start of Sump 5. We entered another 30 metres of rift, but this also ended in a mass of boulders which would need explosives to shift. Given that we had spent six hours getting there and would have spend the same time getting back, the prospect of tackling this site didn't appeal to us.

Rick and I went back to the end again in March 1997. We cleared the debris from the previous trip, and Rick managed to pass Joel's Squeeze to regain the route at stream level. This closed down after 5 metres in a more complete blockage, with the main stream flowing out over boulders to the left.

After this, Rick was less keen to carry on exploration in Daren Cilau. On my return to the UK, I'd been contacted by one Gary Jones who was training to be a helicopter pilot in the Royal Navy. He was keen to learn to cave dive, and I was happy to exploit his enthusiasm by dragging him along as my accomplice to various horrible places that I was interested in exploring. We spent some time following up my early trips with Ian Rolland, and more latterly Spanners, to dig out a bypass to Turkey Sump 2 in Agen Allwedd. We achieved success in the spring of 1996, and made many more visits in an effort to bypass Sump 3. By early July 1997 Gary had acquired sufficient experience and equipment to attempt the first exchange trip beneath Mynydd Llangatwg between Daren Cilau and Pwll-y-Cwm.

On the evening of Friday 4 July 1997, I put on Gary's drysuit and dived into Pwll-y-Cwm to check the condition of the choke and get accustomed to his gear. Gary is several inches taller than me, so I folded the excess material of his suit and secured it

*Gary Jones at Pwll-y-Cwm*
*(Duncan Price)*

with snoopy loops. The next day I dived from Pwll-y-Cwm to the bottom of Daren Cilau, where I rendezvoused (exactly on time) with Gary and his friend Andy Savage, who had caved in from the dry entrance in the quarries behind Whitewalls. I took off Gary's drysuit, put on my caving gear and, accompanied by Andy, made rapid progress out of Daren Cilau, while Gary dived out to the Clydach Gorge.

Since then, the through trip has been repeated a few times in one direction or the other but, due to equipment failure stranding him at the bottom of Daren Cilau, Gary Jones holds the dubious record of having done it once each way; he had no option but to come out the dry way and then walk back around the hillside to collect his car which was parked at the Drum and Monkey. I first heard of Gary's adventure when he rang me up to ask if could borrow my cylinders and regulators to retrieve his own equipment that he had abandoned in the cave. Fortunately he had had the presence of mind to wrap up his drysuit and bring it out of the cave.

In February 1998, Gary and I undertook a trip to re-examine the end of the San Agustin Way. We confirmed that all of the possible ways on at high-level were not promising, and remarked at the time that the area was of doubtful stability 'with the attendant danger of cutting off one's escape/head'. We found a sump beyond Joel's Squeeze where water entered through the boulders; I collected a cylinder and managed to pass this obstacle. The underwater section was only 2 metres long, but very tight. This gained a blind 3-metre-long fault-associated rift with a vocal connection through the boulders back to Gary. But we realised that further progress would need another diver in the final airspace of Against All Odds at the downstream end of Sump 4 in Agen Allwedd; we thought that this was close to the boulder choke that we were probing and that the separation between the two caves might be so little that we would be able to hear one another through the gaps between the rocks.

This trip marked the end of serious exploration directed at forging a direct link between Daren Cilau and Agen Allwedd, and our attention turned to other undived sumps in Daren Cilau that might offer easier pickings in terms of yielding new cave passage. One of these was 7th Hour Sump, which lay at the upstream end of Borrowed Boots Streamway. This had been discovered by Ian Rolland and Rob Parker in November 1985 after seven hours of caving from the Daren Cilau quarry entrance. Six months later, Ian had passed this sump after 5 metres, to reach 20 metres of canal ending in three more sumps. These were all deemed too tight, but the area was probably worth another look; dye tracing had showed that the water emerging from the sump came from Llangattock Swallet, a sinkhole between Daren Cilau and Agen Allwedd, and there was every possibility of finding a route between the two caves.

So in March 1999, Gary and I dived from Pwll-y-Cwm into Daren Cilau and carried some diving gear up 7th Hour Sump. The water emerging from the sump was really murky, so I chose not to dive there, and we left the cylinders out of harm's way for another attempt when conditions had improved. On the way out, Gary slipped and damaged his right shoulder by the pool near Duke's Sump. Although he was able to get out without too much difficulty, the resultant injury was sufficient to warrant a trip to the hospital when he got home. No bones were broken, but his arm needed to be immobilised, and Gary was signed off of work for three weeks.

We didn't get the opportunity to go back until the end of January 2000. Gary had dived in Pwll-y-Cwm the evening before our trip, and reported that the visibility underwater was good. We were joined on the inward journey by another one of my apprentices, John Volanthen, a mild-mannered IT consultant from Bristol. Gary set off first, but I overtook him underwater. Everything was going well until I realised that I hadn't seen the guideline for some time; I didn't have a search reel, having left it behind on a recent cave diving trip abroad, so I had to improvise a means of finding the guideline again. Reasoning that I had plenty of air, as I was carrying extra cylinders to get further into the cave, I simply sat on a rock to wait for someone to turn up and show me. A couple of minutes later, Gary's lights appeared across the passage, so I swam over to him as he was following the line, nonchalantly signalled OK, and continued into Daren Cilau. Gary remarked later that he had been wondering what I'd been up to.

In Daren Cilau, Gary and I changed into wetsuits and helped John into the cave as far as Duke's Sump. This is a site halfway between the upstream end of St David's Sump and the Gloom Room. John dived the sump but found that the water welled up through tight rifts at the end. Gary and I continued up to 7th Hour Sump, where the pool was crystal clear and very inviting, so I put a new line through Sump 1, and followed Sump 2 for 30 metres in a shallow 1-metre-diameter tube until the line ran out. I could see that the passage continued in a similar fashion; there was an awkward squeeze at the start of the sump, but the way on was wide open. We left the tanks in place for another push, and we had a look around the Restaurant at the End of the Universe (another underground campsite above the sump) before heading out.

A month later, we were helped into the water by Tim Morgan, our latest recruit to the CDG and a friend of Gary's from their student days at Nottingham University. Gary had a few problems kitting up, and arrived an hour behind me in Daren Cilau. On reaching 7th Hour Sump, he wound 70 metres of line onto the empty reel and free-dived through Sump 1, as it was only short and quite spacious. I reached the end of the line in Sump 2 and found a convenient head-and-shoulders airbell above the final tie-off, where I could attach the reel, then I laid a further 15 metres of line, to surface in a low canal; 5 metres further on I was able to stand up, belay the line and remove my gear, then 20 metres of walking-sized streamway got me to the base of a cascade. Climbing up this, I entered the side of a large chamber aligned east–west along a fault. The stream hugged the northern wall of the chamber then flowed amongst rocks littering the floor, but I could not follow it very far as at the eastern end of the chamber the way on was blocked by mud.

I returned to Gary after an hour's absence: in the meantime he had free-dived the static sump to the west of the one I had entered, to find a body-sized passage going off that might connect with the main sump. Gary also reported that as I'd set off he'd seen the glow from my lights in another pool further along the passage. As this might bypass the awkward squeeze at the start of the main sump, we took the diving gear up the squalid tube that led to it. But when we had got a couple of body-lengths into the sump, we found it uncomfortably tight, so we beat a retreat and exited – just in time to make the Drum and Monkey, where Tim had done sterling work propping the bar up to prevent it from closing early.

In May, Gary and I dived into Daren Cilau with John Volanthen, and met up with Tim, who had come in the dry way and stayed overnight at Hard Rock Café. In addition to our own gear, we had brought in Tim's wetsuit and extra diving gear. The four of us then took two full 5-litre cylinders to 7th Hour Sump, whereupon John went out while Tim waited at the bivouac site nearby. Gary and I dived through into the new chamber, which I had decided to call Pilgrim's Progress to continue a John Bunyan theme – explained later – and in tribute to Ian Rolland who had laid the groundwork for its discovery; I considered this expedition a pilgrimage to his 'shrine'.

We carried out a crude compass-and-tape-measure survey of the extension and checked out various possible ways out of the impressive rubble-floored void 7 metres across with a boulder-filled chimney to one side in the roof some 5 or 6 metres above us. Gary tried to climb up one side of the chamber to get into this, but decided that it looked very unstable. Our best lead was a side passage heading north out of the chamber: we explored this for 20 metres until it became too low. All the digging sites looked long-term, so after spending three hours beyond the sump we re-joined Tim for the gruelling slog out. Tim then camped underground for another night, while Gary and I struggled to stay awake for the dive though to Pwll-y-Cwm; we surfaced at 3 am after 17 hours underground, and the sun was rising as we drove back to Whitewalls with our gear, to turn in just as everyone else was getting up.

# 9

# Lesser Welsh Caves

Although my interest in cave exploration in Wales has been largely focused on the major cave system beneath Mynydd Llangatwg, my attention has occasionally wandered elsewhere. To the west of Mynydd Llangatwg lies Mynydd Llangynidr, an equally large expanse of barren moorland overlying the limestone below. But apart from a scattering of shake holes pockmarking its terrain, there are few indicators of potential ways into the extensive cave system which must lie beneath. Dye traces have demonstrated that water sinking in the area traverses long distances underground before emerging at springs at the head of the Clydach Gorge, upstream of Pwll-y-Cwm – but unlike at Agen Allwedd and Daren Cilau, there has been little quarrying activity on the flanks of the mountain to expose the cave passages which lie beneath.

In 1905 a pressing need had arisen to supply large quantities of water to the nearby steelworks which was undergoing expansion, so the local council started digging a tunnel to try to intercept the underground water flow to Ffynnon Cae Rhos, a large spring in Cwm Claisfer on the north side of the mountain about five kilometres away from Ebbw Vale. The tunnel was dug to a length of over 3 kilometres; it was lined with brick in the parts where the geology demanded it, and a concrete drainage channel was laid in the floor. In 1911 the diggers encountered an extensive shale band which continually collapsed, making the workings difficult and dangerous. Excavations stopped, and part of the adit was subsequently used as an overflow for the lower Cwm Carno reservoir (directly above), water from the surface stream linking the two reservoirs being directed through the tunnel to exit below the lower reservoir, to form the headwaters of the Ebbw Fawr.

Just over a kilometre from the entrance, the adit entered limestone and intercepted a number of caves. These voids were used as convenient places to dump spoil. In 1982, Bill Gascoine had negotiated access to the site for the purpose of clearing these cavities and prospecting for the hidden cave system that must be associated with them. After many years of hard graft, the Brynmawr Caving Club eventually broke into a major network of passages collectively known as Ogof Carno. The entrance to the natural cave is reached after 15 minutes walking up the tunnel – the adit follows a straight line for most of its length – and from here a spot of daylight can just about be made out from the entrance grille 1,750 metres away.

Over the course of exploration, over 9 kilometres of cave passages were discovered. However, Ogof Carno developed a reputation for being somewhat unpleasant as it is very flood-prone, which means that the lower reaches are frequently coated in thick mud; passage names like Southern Discomfort and Hotel Carnophobia reflect the nature of the place.

My first visit took place at the end of March 1992 in the company of Charles Bailey (one of the main activists in the exploration), Alan Brady (a young lad from Bynmawr Caving Club) and fellow cave diver Paul Whybro; Paul and I had done quite a hard trip down Agen Allwedd the day before. Paul had once described me as 'fit, but stupid!' – but the previous day's exertions must have taken their toll on his own faculties as he had forgotten to bring his oversuit and had to return to Whitewalls to collect it. After that late start, we undertook an 11-hour trip to the furthest extremity of the cave, a tiny upstream sump with a small stream emerging from it. The original explorers, not equipped for diving, had obviously been very disappointed to find their way barred by such an obstacle, as they'd christened it C*** Sump.

Having made a reconnaissance of the site and noted the considerable potential for further exploration, I arranged to make a return visit a month later. Access to the cave was controlled by Brynmawr Caving Club on behalf of Welsh Water, the landowner, and I managed to secure the help of Chris Brady (Alan's dad) to act as guide. I got up early one Saturday morning and drove from Coventry to Whitewalls. I found no one willing to come along to help, so I went to the cave entrance to meet Chris on my own. Neither of us was on top form for the trip – Chris had a bad back and I'd been suffering from a cold all week – but we decided to press on anyway.

It took us four hours to reach the brew stop at Pinnacle Corner, having collected a few items of use on the way. I was carrying a small bag containing my regulator, hood, mask and a modest amount of diving line, while Chris carried my 3-litre cylinder. After a cup of tea and a cigar (!) we reached the sump, where a brief inspection with a mask and torch revealed an open slot between the roof and a shingle bank big enough for a person. Chris fastened one end of the line around a suitable flake of rock while I put on my diving gear. Rather than bring a full-sized line reel, I had simply stuffed 25 metres of line tied to a block of lead into a mesh bag; considering the modest amount of air I had, this would be enough for an initial foray. I told Chris to give me half an hour and then, if I did not return, to go out; if I met with some mishap, there would be nothing he could do for me.

I ducked under the water and immediately my head popped up into a small airspace, just big enough to get my mask out of the water. Ahead, the passage continued underwater as a body-sized tube with a slot in the floor. I pushed my way along this (without fins) until I was forced to drop into the slot where the T-section shape of the passage became inverted; 18 metres from the start, I slid up through a narrow crack, to surface in a larger passage carrying a stream. I tied the line to a suitable belay and deposited my cylinder on a ledge, then set off up the open passage. But I kept my reconnaissance was brief, as I was very mindful of being out on a limb.

Returning to my gear, I had difficulty getting back into the sump and had to find an enlargement of the rift further upstream wide enough to admit me. Chris was waiting, and had realised from the movements on the line that I had passed the sump. I had more than enough air to go back through, but I decided to leave it for another time and continue the exploration with a partner. We left the lead and the partially depleted cylinder *in situ* and packed up the rest of my gear for the journey out.

I was very pleased at my discovery; it was the first time I had dived a virgin sump, and the way on beyond it was wide open. But I had no immediate plans to return, as I thought it might take a while to muster another diver to accompany me. Besides, I had other commitments; in the middle of the week following my trip I got a telephone call from Martyn Farr, who told me that he was going to dive the sump at the weekend. Martyn had heard that I'd just passed the sump and had left the continuation unexplored, but he had been planning an assault on the site for some time and had rallied a large support team to help him. I had been unaware of this until Martyn's call, and Martyn was adamant that he would be going ahead whether I joined him or not.

This news caused me a major headache; it was my wife's birthday that weekend, and my parents were coming up to see us both. Graciously, Kate told me to go ahead and join Martyn. So once again I found myself making an early start to drive down to Wales, where I found four of my club members waiting for me; they were not in fact there to help me, but were doing a high-grade survey of the cave. At Cwm Carno we met up with Martyn's team; there were eight of them (including Martyn), which was just as well since he had a lot of gear. My equipment was minimal in comparison – a container for my regulator, hood and mask, and another small bag with some food and surveying equipment. I gave the latter to someone else to carry as they were empty-handed.

*En masse* we headed into the cave, but since not everyone had been there before the team soon fragmented, those that knew the way in front and those that didn't at the back. We stopped for a chocolate break at one point; I had to wait for my food to arrive, as it was at the rear of the party. The diffuse nature of the group meant that I had finished my hot drink by the time everyone arrived at the brew spot, and I was almost ready to dive the sump long before Martyn was dressed. I was just finishing my preparations when I heard the sound of a wetsuit being removed and turned around to witness Martyn squatting in the stream – downstream of the sump, fortunately. As I was set to go, I suggested that I should go first to allow time for the water to clear behind me before Martyn joined me. He duly followed me through, cursing loudly at the zero visibility that he'd encountered underwater all the same.

Once free of our diving gear, we progressed upstream in a stooping-height passage with the water flowing towards us in a trench in the floor. The route onward developed into a tall rift containing jammed boulders at various heights, suggesting that there might be a choice of ways on at low and high levels. We stuck near the floor and popped out of the rift below a 7-metre-high aven. The walls were heavily eroded, with razor-sharp protrusions. Ahead, the rift continued, but soon narrowed to a point where forward progress was impossible, even though we could hear the sound of falling water ahead. Disappointed, I surveyed the passage back to the aven, where Martyn had found a passage going off to one side. With Martyn taking the lead, we made our way along this, the noise of flowing water growing ever louder. Martyn reported that the route ahead was too tight, so I squeezed down to a lower level where progress was easier. After a short distance, the stream emerged from a crack in the roof; backing up the passage a little, we squeezed along the top of the rift, to emerge in a 1-metre-high oval passage just above the point where the water disappeared below. Ahead of us the passage continued, but we decided to follow the source of the water along a low crawl which led around several bends to a restriction. This was too tight to pass, and the water appeared to emerge from a small pool. Another sump perhaps?

We surveyed back to the previous junction, and then went up the muddy side passage. This brought us to a balcony overlooking a 4-metre drop into a modest chamber. A small stream trickled from a continuation of the passage in the opposite wall, just out of reach; I contemplated launching myself into this, but thought better of it. Likewise, the overhanging climb down into the chamber below looked like it would need a rope and/or a ladder to traverse. We left a crowbar wedged in a crack in the floor to act as a belay point for future use and returned to the sump, taking notes for the survey as we went.

Martyn was first through the sump, and he packed up most of his gear to take out, leaving only a line reel and some lead behind. His sherpas had been busy digging a trench to try to lower the water level in the sump. My cylinder still had plenty of air left in it, so I cached it safely for another visit and packed the rest of my kit away in a couple of containers to take with me. The CSS survey team were just reaching the sump as we started our long journey out. I joined the advance party and made it to the adit entrance where we had stashed cans of beer for the stroll to the surface. We'd explored about 300 metres of passage in a 13-hour trip and there were a few leads still to investigate.

One of the honours of discovering a new section of cave passage is the opportunity to name it. Many parts of caves are simply called Big Chamber or Main Passage, and it's considered bad form to name something after oneself. As a schoolboy, I'd been forced to read the works of John Bunyan, and now I drew on this to dub the new section of passage The Slough of Despond, as it seemed to fit the rather depressing nature of the find.

After a short break, I returned to the fray accompanied by Arthur Millet. With my cylinder already in place, I only needed to carry a small bag containing my regulator and a bolting kit to fix anchors for the climbs beyond the sump; Arthur carried a length of rope, and we were to collect a wire ladder *en route*. Just as we were making our way down Southern Discomfort, a large rock I was standing on started to slip beneath me. I shouted a warning to Arthur and leaped to safety as it crashed to the floor below. Shaken but not discouraged, we continued. After a couple of detours to pick up kit, we arrived at the sump where I stuffed everything into the bag to take with me. I told Arthur I'd be a couple of hours, and dived through. The journey to the top of the climb was hard work, but soon I was preparing to descend into the chamber below; I tied the rope around a convenient flake of rock and fastened the ladder to the crowbar we'd left jammed in the floor, with the rope acting as a back-up. At the bottom of the drop I could see that the only way out of the chamber at this level was to follow the stream along a tight rift – this was obviously the continuation of the passage I'd explored from the other side on my previous visit. The only other lead out of the chamber was the point where the stream entered from a passage opposite the balcony I'd climbed down from.

Back at the top of the pitch, I decided to put an expansion bolt in the wall in order to better position the rope attachment point, so that I could attempt the traverse into the stream inlet. Fortunately I'd had the foresight to leave myself tied to the rope (still fastened to the rock flake), because as I leaned out to set an anchor into the wall, the floor beneath me collapsed into the chamber below, taking me with it in a heart-stopping drop. But my lifeline saved me, and I was able to get back up onto the ledge by climbing the ladder which was luckily still in place. I completed drilling the hole for the rock anchor and fitted an expansion bolt from which I re-hung the ladder. Then I extracted the crowbar from the crack in the floor and tied it to the end of the rope to act as a grappling hook. After several attempts. I managed to fasten a taut line across the gap – at full stretch I found that I could just about reach from toe to toe over the drop. Pulling on the line, I jumped across it, into the stream inlet.

Although I was now on a safe footing, I was disappointed to find that the passage closed down almost immediately. I freed the crowbar and pondered how to reverse my manoeuvre … I reasoned that if all else failed I could lower myself down into the chamber below and re-ascend the ladder hanging down the other side, but this seemed a little awkward. Fortunately, I was able to repeat the acrobatics that I had used to get across, and I was soon packing up my gear to return through the sump.

On the way back I decided to investigate another side passage that we'd seen on the previous visit. This turned out to be very muddy and rather squalid, but I was cleansed once more by my return dive through the sump with my arms full of equipment. Arthur was waiting for me, and as he wasn't wearing a watch he hadn't realised that I was half an hour later than planned.

On the way out we decided to visit the southern extremity of the cave. This terminated at a lake, which I swam across. A sandy beach at the far side ended at a blank wall, but I could see a climb above me which might go somewhere (the top of this was later reached by a route on the other side of the lake, and gained an active stream passage ending at more sumps). I thought that the lake might have some routes leading off underwater – and I was proved right when I returned in March 1993 with a local caver, Huw Durban; I dived down to about 12 metres to find that the cave continued underwater, but I could not clear my ears to go any deeper.

The final section of streamway was explored by Tony Seddon in 1993 and then by Martyn Farr in 1996. Nearly half a kilometre of passage was found, terminating in Sump 5. Martyn dived this for 50 metres before turning around just beyond a committing restriction, the way on still open. This is probably one of the one of the best cave diving leads to be found in Wales, and a prime candidate for someone young, fit and keen to tackle. But at the time of writing, access to Ogof Carno is denied by Welsh Water over health and safety issues, since a release of water into the entrance adit from the overflow for the Carno reservoir could trap cavers. The cave system itself floods to the roof in many places and can only be explored safely in periods of dry weather.

To the south-east of the Llangatwg escarpment lies another extensive band of limestone, beneath the former industrial settlement of Pwll Ddu. Although a few caves were known in the area, nothing of any note had been entered until October 1994, when the Morgannwg Caving Club achieved success at an insignificant hole in the hillside. The explored sections of Ogof Draenen (as it was called), grew rapidly; the cave passages known today amount to around 80 kilometres in length, making it the second longest cave system known in Britain. Most of the initial discoveries had occurred while I was in exile in the United States, and one of my first caving trips on my return to civilisation was to accompany Arthur Millet and John Cooper on a surveying trip to the downstream end of the cave, at Rifleman's Chamber.

Although the water from Ogof Draenen has been dye-traced to springs at Pontnewynydd (over 8 kilometres away), there is still a big gap between the explored part of the cave and its resurgence. Much of the system comprises a network of abandoned dry passages, a result of the complex hydrology of the area, which has seen several changes in water flow direction during the evolution of the caves over the aeons.

Ogof Draenen has very few sumps, and one of these lay at in an obscure side passage entered from a climb up from the main streamway. At the end of that passage, dubbed A Bit of a Dive, was a static pool known as Parrot Sump. The place had been investigated by Peter Bolt in February 1995, not long after the cave had been discovered. He had squeezed along a narrow slot at 3 metres depth for 20 metres, to reach a very small airbell. But his over-enthusiastic sherpas had destroyed his line reel *en route* to the sump, and he had to dive on a base-fed line. After checking with him that I wasn't going to tread on his toes, I decided to pay the site a visit in early November 1997.

Gary Jones, Andrew Savage and I had never actually been to Parrot Sump before, and we found the approach passage rather strenuous. My sherpas were gentle with my equipment, and I enjoyed the luxury of entering the sump with a 4-litre and a 3-litre cylinder plus a fully functional line reel. When I reached the previous limit, I passed a restriction beneath the airbell to gain a larger airspace after a further 5 metres, and a little further on I was able to stand upright, at the base of an awkward ascending rift. I removed my diving gear and climbed up the narrow chimney to find a tie-off for the line. A tight horizontal squeeze along the rift appeared to open out into larger passage beyond, but as we wanted to get out in time for a firework display I decided to leave this for another day, safe in the knowledge that the place was so unpleasant that no one would poach it from me. Exiting through the sump in zero visibility, I left my cylinders in place for a return trip.

Gary and I arranged to go back at the end of the month, each of us using one of the cylinders I'd left in place. But when I arrived at Whitewalls I discovered that the cottage still smelled of smoke due to an attempt to burn it to the ground. My club had recently applied for planning permission to extend the rear of the property, and even though the works would not increase the sleeping accommodation, or impact on the number of visitors, the plans must have escalated someone's ill-feeling towards cavers. The culprits were never identified, but we now have some new, more friendly, neighbours, and the caving club is very much integrated with the hillside community once more.

After a smelly night at Whitewalls, Gary and I entered Ogof Draenen and dived through Parrot Sump with some surveying gear and a crowbar, which we needed early on when a localised collapse required an hour's digging to pass. An uninviting static sump eventually barred our way. We had already found a bypass to Sump 2 *en route* and it looked like an aven near the final sump might offer a lead, ie a way over it; we called it 'Arse On Aven', as we couldn't be arsed to climb it at the time.

*Whitewalls in the snow (Duncan Price)*

Gary and I returned in April the following year. In the interim we had swapped some of the gear around, and now we both dived with a pair of cylinders each for security. On the far side of Parrot Sump, we extended the line and fastened it to a better belay point. We took a couple of cylinders to Sump 3, and I dived this on a base-fed line paid out by Gary. The sump was very short – only 4 metres – so I returned for Gary, and we both explored the 50 metres of passage beyond. A short dig through boulders led to Sump 4, a deep pool with a little stream of water flowing into it, followed by a ramp of boulders blocking the passage beyond. We didn't have enough line to enable us to probe Sump 4, so left it for another day. While I was diving, Gary scaled Arse On Aven, to find that it rejoined the main route just before the start of Sump 3.

Our final trip took place in November 1998, just over a year after my first dive there. Gary and I carried two very full 3-litre bottles to Sump 4 in a little over five hours. Then I dived into the pool and located a body-sized tube leading off at an estimated depth of 3 metres. I cautiously followed this feet first around a bend, thinking that going backwards would make it easier for me to get out again. At a second bend, I was able to turn around and finally see where I was going. The passage beyond continued, through a tight squeeze – but then I came up to a restriction so narrow that although I could see the passage continuing in crystal-clear visibility I feared I'd not be able to get back through it again. So I decided to stop there. The line reel was buried in the mud 30 metres from base at about 6 metres depth, meaning that my retreat was an interesting one, semi-blind. I attempted to survey the sump; but even when I was able to read my compass, it only pointed in the direction of my diving cylinders as I was unable to extend my arm far enough in the constricted passage to get a proper bearing. Gary and I struggled out of the cave with all of our gear, and surfaced after spending nearly 13 hours underground. We were exhausted and broken. The cave was still going but it didn't inspire us to return – we had more promising leads to explore elsewhere.

# 10

# The C-word

In February 1998 I resigned from my job in Coventry and took up a research post at Loughborough University. One of the attractions of the role was that my collaborators were based at Lancaster University, and I thought this might allow me to combine project meetings with caving trips to the Yorkshire Dales.

There was also an element of international travel to scientific gatherings, which occasionally took me to places where I could indulge in my hobby. An ideal opportunity arose in September 2000, when I was due to speak at a conference in Orlando, Florida. I flew into the USA a few days early, to go cave diving with a guy called Jon Bojar. I had been put in contact with Jon via the CDG webmaster, my old friend Rob Murgatroyd. Until I landed in the US, my only dealings with Jon had been via email, and as I phoned him from the airport it dawned on me that I had no idea what he was really like. Collecting a hire car, I drove to his apartment in Tampa, to be met by him and his girlfriend Karen, to find that he'd already got the measure of me, as he had bought some imported beer for me to drink as we swapped 'war stories' to seal our friendship. At the time I smoked roll-ups, and Jon remarked later that he'd been surprised when I pulled out some Golden Virginia and started making a cigarette. I did assure him that it was tobacco!

The next day we loaded Jon's truck with gear, and drove to the coast to join his friends for a dive in a spring located in the sea 200 metres offshore. We transferred the equipment to a kayak which we pushed through chest-deep water towards the entrance to Crystal Beach Spring. But by the time we neared the cave entrance the sea was choppy and our craft capsized in the swell, depositing its cargo on the sandy bottom around my feet. I was wearing a drysuit, but my weight belt was now on the seabed and I was too buoyant to dive down to retrieve it: all I could do was hold onto the boat while Jon (in a wetsuit) duck-dived to salvage everything.

We had originally intended to use scooters for the dive, but changed our minds and left them moored at the entrance. This was marked by an obvious boil on the surface leading down to a tight squeeze between boulders into the cave. Whereas everyone else had to remove their twinsets to pass the 'no-mount' zone through several restrictions into the Fitting Room where they put their gear back on, my side-mounted cylinders meant that I was able to get into the cave without removing them. Once we were in the cave proper, Jon decided to turn around while I continued to around 400 metres in, swimming against a strong current, before returning. Back on the surface, we discovered that the scooters had broken free and were now somewhere in the Gulf of Mexico … the trip was rapidly turning into what the Americans term a clusterfuck.

While Jon's mates went off to look for the errant items, he and I pushed the loaded kayak into the shallows in order to beach it and join the search. We were standing in the water up to our waists when I spotted a fin snaking through the water around us:

> Duncan: Is that a shark?
> Jon: No, it's a ray.
> Duncan: I think it's a shark.
> Jon: You're right!
> Duncan: What shall we do?
> Jon: I'll stand behind you.

The fish swam off, although Jon informed me later that an old man had recently been killed by a similar sand shark when he had jumped off a pier to go for a swim; the unlucky victim had landed directly on the creature.

We found our scooters, trapped in a circular current by the submarine spring. But in the meantime, the tide had gone out leaving our kayak high and dry, so we had to unload it to refloat it and push it back into deeper water before putting our gear back in.

The next day Jon took me for a couple of dives at an inland site known as Wayne's World (or, more formally, School Sink). This was an uninspiring waterlogged hole in the woods behind a public school, with wooden decking and steps to aid entry. Underwater, a jagged shaft gave way to a small tube into a large cavern. The conditions were similar to those at Crystal Beach Spring in that the floor was covered in dark-coloured organic sediment, although there was little flow here. The caves in the area communicate with the sea, which means that there is a halocline with a tannic saline layer beneath a lens of clearer percolation water.

We went for a familiarisation dive via the Bypass Tunnel to Main Street, and approximately 20 metres from the Asses & Elbows restriction we turned back again. After filling tanks at a dive shop nearby, we went back for another dive; the plan was for Jon to help me explore a side passage off the Deep Salt Tunnel, which required sidemounts to reach. Unfortunately, a regulator failure near the entrance resulted in our doing a shorter dive instead, via the Tourist Trap along the original Main Street line almost to the point where we'd been earlier. The promising lead would have to wait for another time, but I felt honoured to have been given the chance to do some original exploration.

Having received such a warm welcome in Tampa, I arranged to go out for a longer visit there the following spring. Even though Jon worked in computer networking and was largely home-based, I couldn't expect him to entertain me all the time, so I was accompanied by Tim Morgan.

## The C-word

Tim had only just qualified in the CDG, and had never been cave diving in the US. Our first dive was a short excursion in Wayne's World, as I knew where it was and was vaguely familiar with the line layout. The next day we drove up to Little River Spring in the cave country around High Springs. Jon Bojar and Brett Hemphill took time out to come with us, and we stopped off *en route* so that Tim and I could buy some umbilical dive lights.

Jon then took Tim and me for a dive in Round Sink back in the Tampa area. A large entrance pool housed a decompression trapeze of rope and PVC pipes suspended over to the entrance to the cave at around 25 metres depth. Beyond that, a large tunnel descended rapidly to a maximum depth of 45 metres, penetrating a white sulphide layer. Tim turned back early, feeling uncomfortable with the depth, while Jon and I continued to the connection with Nexxus Sink and then a little further beyond this, close to Stratamax Sink. On the way, the route 'surfaced' into clear fresh percolation water through two chambers, one being the entrance from Nexxus Sink. (This part of the Beacon Woods system headed towards Wayne's World, and in 2002 a connection was made with over 18 km of explored passage.) On the return journey, Jon pointed out some manatee bones lying on a ledge beside the line; the rib cage could be clearly made out.

Tim and I decided to drive back up to High Springs for a couple of nights so that we could visit some more of the popular tourist cave diving sites there. We dived in Devils Eye and Peacock Springs before heading back to Tampa via Manatee Spring, where we met Brett Hemphill who had brought some scooters for us to play with. But Brett had forgotten his qualification cards, and since the spring is in a state park, the rangers wouldn't let him dive. Tim and I had a good time, though, scootering all the way from Catfish Hotel to Friedman Sink in about 5 minutes against a ripping current.

Arriving back at Jon's, we were immediately talked into going for a sneak dive in Nexxus Sink. As the cave is located behind some shops, we waited until it was dark before changing into our gear in the parking lot. A steep slope led down to a pool full of branches. Underwater, we descended a rift and broke out into a flat-roofed chamber of crystal clear water at a depth of 22 metres. Jon took photos of us while we explored the place, and we made a quick foray down through the halocline to the line from Round Sink, where we'd dived a few days before.

Back in the UK, the caving scene was dramatically affected by an outbreak of foot-and-mouth disease that started in February 2001. Access to the countryside was severely restricted that year, and the caving community voluntarily suspended its activities; in the Brecon Beacons, my caving club bunkhouse was deserted except for a family of squirrels which moved in while it was unoccupied. One side-effect of this curfew was that I found that the money that I saved by not caving in the UK could be used to finance occasional cave diving trips overseas; I became such a regular visitor to Tampa that Jon Bojar reckoned I virtually had my own room in his apartment.

One of my cave diving ambitions was to visit Eagle's Nest. This site is famous for its depth (approaching 100 metres) and notorious for the number of fatalities that have occurred there as a consequence. Despite that fact that I had no formal qualifications in air diving, let alone using the mixed gases needed at depth, I wanted to go there. Jon lived close by, and could arrange to get the necessary gas mixtures (no questions asked) to dive there, so it was with that in mind that I arranged to pay him a visit over the May Bank Holiday weekend in 2001.

The morning after my arrival in Tampa found me driving Jon's jeep around the neighbourhood to return a cylinder of helium we had used to blend the gas mixtures we were to dive with. While living in Virginia I had gained a US driving licence and was familiar with driving in the country. I had, however, never handled a left-hand-drive car with a manual ('stick shift', to use the colloquial expression) gearbox – particularly one with the controls on the steering column. It's probably just as well that Jon wasn't in the vehicle as I ground through every intersection.

A couple of Jon's friends came with me, and we drove through the woods, following a maze of hunting trails to the cave entrance, blissfully ignoring the signs informing us we were on private property. At the time, the site was off limits to cave divers, but access has since been formalised by the Chassahowitzka Wildlife Management Area, with decking and steps constructed to aid entry to the water. But we of course had no such luxury, and assembled our gear on a muddy beach beside a large pool with a fallen tree at the bottom.

I was using my familiar configuration of side-mounted primary cylinders with additional tanks of travel and decompression gases clipped by their bases into the belt loops of my harness and with the tops of the cylinders tucked under a chest-loop of elasticated cord. The size of the cave hardly warranted such a rig, but it was what I was used to, whereas the others employed more typical Floridian gear – back-mounted bottom gas, and side-slung stages. Out of deference to the depth I was aiming for, I wore an ABLJ as a back-up for my usual means of staying afloat – i.e. letting some gas directly into my drysuit. None of us wore gloves for the dive, although I attached a thin neoprene pair to my oxygen cylinder to help stop me getting chilled in the final part of the decompression.

The base of the pool funnelled down to a small chimney, and we dropped through this in single file. This opened out in the roof of a large underwater chamber where I staged one of my decompression mixes on the line at around 20 metres depth. We descended the shotline to a cone of rocks at 40 metres depth and switched over from our travel mix (nitrox-35) to the bottom gas of trimix 14.5/45 (a gas mixture of 14.5% oxygen and 45% helium, the balance being nitrogen). Up to that point I'd only ever done any diving breathing air, and had never dived below 55 metres.

The problems with breathing air in deep diving are twofold: nitrogen narcosis and oxygen toxicity. The 'narcs' strike first, as nitrogen acts on the nerves in a similar way to alcohol, but with its influence increasing as you go deeper. As with alcohol, the effect is subtle at first, but then you realise you can hardly function; the level of impairment depends on the individual, and on other factors which can vary from day to day. But whereas nitrogen gives you the 'narcs', helium is inert and has no discernable narcotic effect at depth, hence its use. At the time I learned to dive, 55 metres was the recommended maximum depth on pure air, though nowadays the limit is much more conservative, depending on the training agency – some divers won't use air for anything more than inflating their car tyres!

Another physiological limit to breathing air under pressure is oxygen toxicity. There are a number of different considerations, including long-term exposure at moderate pressures which can cause lung damage, and the more immediate high-pressure effects that affect the nervous system. The current view is that pure oxygen should not be breathed at a partial pressure higher than 1.6 bar. Since the absolute pressure experienced by a diver increases by one atmosphere (1 bar) for every 10 metres down, this means that oxygen cannot be breathed below 6 metres. Again, individuals' tolerance varies, and this chapter is definitely not a 'how to' on mixed-gas diving – in fact, this whole book is, if anything, a 'how *not* to' on cave diving in particular and lifestyle in general.

Since air contains about one fifth oxygen (20.9% to be exact) the 1.6 bar limit is reached at a depth of around 70 metres. Eagle's Nest goes to 100 metres – and at that depth not only would you be off your trolley with nitrogen narcosis, but there is a real risk that your body would be racked with convulsions from toxing. Jon told me he'd actually been to the bottom of Eagles' Nest on air, and had experienced the full panorama of tunnel vision (narcosis), pins and needles (oxygen toxicity) etc. People have dived deep on air, and some still continue to do so, even though for some divers it was a one-way trip – and it is now generally considered a BAD THING.

So there I was at 40 metres, breathing a gas mixture that had the same narcotic load as air at 15 metres. If I'd been breathing from that cylinder on the surface, the reduced oxygen content might have been a problem – but at this depth the pressure was five times greater (that's one atmosphere for every ten metres, plus the one atmosphere you started from). Technically, any breathing mixture with an oxygen content lower than 20.9% is termed 'hypoxic', and although the human body can tolerate reduced oxygen levels to some extent (e.g. at altitude), there are limits beyond which too little oxygen gets into the bloodstream and you pass out. So while at normal atmospheric pressure an oxygen content of 14.5% might cause me to pass out eventually, at 5 bar pressure there was plenty of oxygen for me to metabolise. (Once, on the surface, I'd had a go at breathing a mixture with only 10% oxygen; I felt very unhappy, but came to my senses before I lost them completely.) Doing the mathematics meant that the trimix we were breathing wouldn't have a partial pressure of 1.6 bar until just over 100 metres depth, at which point the equivalent narcotic depth would be about 46 metres. We were not planning on going that deep, but if we did we'd still be OK.

Of course, going down is the easy part. Not only does nitrogen make you feel like you've had one too many beers (or put another way 'like drinking a martini for every 10 metres you descend'), but under pressure it dissolves in the body's tissues, which is unnoticeable at the time. Although nitrogen narcosis clears up immediately as you come up, the gas in your tissues takes time to diffuse out again. Come up too fast and, rather than harmlessly going back into the bloodstream and out of the lungs, nitrogen can form bubbles in the joints ('the bends') or worse (the brain). And even though helium doesn't give a diver narcosis, it too percolates into the body tissues and needs time to escape safely. Diving physiologists have studied this process for over a century, and computer programs are now available to calculate the necessary tables to minimise the chances of a problem. The nitrox mixes and the pure oxygen were there to accelerate the gas exchange on ascent and help us get back up to the surface safely. Jon and I had transcribed our tables for the dive onto waterproof paper; in deference to my nationality, he'd written my decompression stops in metres whereas the American divers had their stop depths in feet.

One of the divers had brought a scooter, but the rest of us had to swim upstream along the massive underwater tunnel. The depth increased as we cleared the breakdown in the entrance chamber, and we travelled for over 300 metres through the next big chamber (the Super Room). At this point, we were about 15 minutes into our bottom time, and I'd seen enough of the cave. I indicated this to Jon by making a crude gesture with one hand encircling an imaginary phallus. Jon understood, and signalled to the others to turn around. On the way back I spotted a depression in the floor of the Super Room, and headed for it with my right arm outstretched; finding the deepest point, I shoved my depth gauge into a hole until it read no less than 85 metres.

Nearing the shotline, we made the first of our mandatory decompression stops – at 48 metres. This, like the other deep stops, was brief, maybe only a minute or two, but enough to allow me to reflect that I was decompressing deeper than many divers had ever been down to. Nearing the cylinder of nitrox-35 which had been left at the base of the shotline, I switched to it immediately. I realised that it was a little high in oxygen for this depth and thus I risked toxing. The normal

*Duncan at 40 m in Eagles Nest (Jon Bojar)*

protocol is not to take gas mixtures below their maximum operating depth (usually defined by oxygen content) but this is not always practical, and in this case rather than tie our tanks to the shotline (as we had done with the next and richer nitrox mix) we had found it expedient to drop them slightly deeper, onto the floor of the cave. Fortunately, the effects of too much oxygen depend not just on the level but also on the duration of exposure, and a short 'spike' wasn't going to hurt me.

As we got shallower, the stops got longer. At a depth of 20 metres I was breathing from my second nitrox mix, and Jon took my photograph. Slowly we made our way up the entrance tube into the surface lake; here, I found myself usually decompressing deeper or shallower than the others, as their stops were 10 feet apart whereas mine were at 3-metre increments. The final hang was the longest, done on pure oxygen from cylinders that we'd left by the fallen tree. I put on my gloves to keep my hands warm, sat astride the tree-trunk and put my thumbs into a convenient hole for balance. I was quite comfortable and

# The C-word

thought that I might have a snooze to pass the time – but just then I felt something grip my right hand. I pulled out my thumb to find a catfish on it, so I bashed my hand against the tree until the creature let go and swam off in disgust. This commotion had caught the attention of the others and I could tell by their exhaust bubbles that they were laughing at my predicament.

After our deep dive, Jon and I took it easy for a couple of days, visiting a few small shallow caves in the area. Then the day before flying home, I went to Wayne's World on my own. My aim was to extend the line in a sidemount passage off Deep Salt Tunnel, which was thought to loop back around to connect with the downstream sector of the cave; this was the same passage that Jon had wanted me to look at on my first dive there with him in September 2000. But as in my previous attempt I was beset with equipment problems; five minutes into the dive one of my regulators suffered a first stage leak, so I had to return to the surface. I fixed it and started again.

The Deep Salt Tunnel line started with a left-hand bend off the main line, with a short gap between them. I laid a jump line to join the lines temporarily, but this was probably not necessary. A T-junction marked by a float on the line beyond this indicated the start of the new lead to the right. The passage was low with no flow, and I pushed several silt screws into the mud to act as anchors for the line. The time taken for this activity prevented me from reaching the end of the line before I had to turn around, but at least I'd done something useful.

I'd had a great time diving with Jon, and we made plans for him to cross the Atlantic so that he could join us for a two-week cave diving holiday in France. Caving in the UK was still on hold, but there was nothing to stop us popping across the Channel to enjoy the delights of cave diving on the continent. Or so I thought …

During my visit to the US in May, Jon had noticed that I didn't seem to be smoking as much as usual. I passed it off with a remark that I had a slight sore throat, and didn't mention that I could feel a lump in the right-hand side of my neck. I had dislocated my right shoulder a couple of times when skiing (my physiotherapist casually remarking that if I did it again maybe I should take skiing lessons) and I would occasionally massage the area when it ached, so I had found the lump quite early on. But now it seemed to be spreading, and I suspected the worst. When I returned to the UK, I went to see my general practitioner; the initial diagnosis was that I probably had a virus and I was told that if there was no improvement I should go back in a month.

The next time I saw my doctor, he referred me to an ENT specialist. While I was being examined by the surgeon at the hospital, I noticed a sheet of paper on his desk with the terse heading 'FAX REFERRAL FORM FOR CANCER' and my name on it Not good!

Ten days before Jon was due to arrive for our trip to France, I went into hospital for a biopsy on the lymph nodes in my neck. I had a line of stitches in my neck from the operation. I told the surgeon that he should have made the incision a bit longer to look more impressive – 'like I'd been in a fight!' – but he took a dim view of this, especially when I asked for the sutures to be removed early so I could go on holiday. I signed a form to confirm that I'd asked to have my stitches out prematurely.

We went to France, anyhow ... more about that later. Then, by the time I returned home, I expected to have heard from the hospital. However there was no letter. Thinking that no news must be good news, I relaxed. But a week before my 37th birthday, I was summoned by the specialist. I had cancer, lymphoma – just like my friend at Exeter University, Piers Leonard, who had had died from the same disease, aged 20, a year after I'd graduated. To be honest, I took the news in my stride – I was surprised to have lived so long already, considering all the daft things I'd done. The prognosis was good, though, as the cancer had been detected at an early stage and there was a 95% chance that I could be fixed. Since the chances of anyone dying on a cave dive in Britain during the 1970s had been as high as 5% per dive, the odds didn't seem so bad to me.

The next few weeks were a whirlwind of tests and treatments. I had told my oncologist that I'd been invited to give the plenary lecture at the annual conference that I attended in the US. He said that if I started chemotherapy straight away then I might be able to travel at the end of September, in the recuperation period before I had radiotherapy.

Before treatment could start, I had to have a MRI scan. This was due to be done on the day after my birthday and I was not to have anything to eat or drink after midnight the day beforehand. Needless to say, I had quite a party (cum wake) on the evening of my birthday, and arrived at the hospital with the biggest hangover of my entire life. I was given a cocktail of chemicals to sip before the procedure, but necked them back in one go owing to alcohol-induced dehydration ... I received four weeks of chemotherapy. Then I flew to the US.

At the end of September 2001 I caught the Continental Airlines flight from Birmingham to Newark; the smouldering ruins of the World Trade Center buildings were visible out of the aircraft window as we came into land. I was asked if I was nervous about flying after the attacks of 9/11, but under the circumstances that was the least of my worries. I was still on medication, and the full side-effects of my treatment had not yet kicked in. My goatee beard fell out onto my T-shirt during the transfer flight to St Louis and when I reached my hotel room I shaved the rest of my hair off to save the embarrassment of losing it in handfuls during the conference.

I flew down to Tampa to see Jon at the end of the week. I had given my keynote lecture on the last day of the meeting and was still wearing a business suit for the flight. This, combined with my bald head, meant that Jon didn't recognise me at the gate. Despite my medication, I felt fit and well, and much to my oncologist's dismay I had even been cave diving in the UK during my treatment – in fact, when I heard about the terrorist attacks in New York I was actually on my way back home from a cave dive.

My first dive with Jon in Florida was in Wayne's World; this time I was to explore a sidemount passage off the entrance room while Jon surveyed along Mainstreet and around the shortcut loop back to the entrance. On arriving at the sink, we met another diver forlornly waiting for his dive buddy to show up; he was easily persuaded to assist Jon after I'd been shown the jump to the sidemount line. On reaching the end of the fixed line, I tied on a reel and pushed through 10 metres of low passage to a point where it became apparent that further progress was inadvisable – I could see that the route continued, but silt screws would be needed to secure the line in the rather mobile mud floor to make it safe, and I hadn't got any. So I wound the line in, and took a tour down the short cut to meet the survey team. But although I had ample gas reserves, the visibility beyond the meeting point had been ruined, so I returned to the surface a few minutes ahead of them.

The next day, Jon and I visited a cave known as Lost Forty; *en route* to the entrance, Jon's jeep got stuck in the sand and I had to dig him out. The underwater entrance to the cave was full of rubbish, and the fixed line into the cavern passed between a newspaper vending machine and other junk. At this point the lines split: Jon followed the right-hand line which was buried and had to be pulled out of the mung. I took the left-hand line, having to extract it from the silt as well. After a tie-off at the deepest part of the cave, the line turned right along the wall of the chamber at a depth of 48 metres. I followed this until I met the second 'up' line and took this out. This too had to be pulled free, until I reached a point where the line was utterly buried beyond recovery (Jon encountered similar problems and had followed me to the base of the chamber). I turned back and returned the way I'd come, meeting Jon *en route*. Our exit was made more interesting by the collapse of some of the debris at the entrance, which meant that we had to dig our way out through a refrigerator.

The final dive of my visit was to Rock Bluff Spring in Gilchrist County with Brett Hemphill and Jon. The spring was marked on the DeLorme Road Atlas just north of the point where the 340W from High Springs crossed the Suwannee. I was map reading for Brett, and we overshot the boat ramp where we had to launch our kayak to get to the site. 'We've done driven too farr south!' I said when I realised my mistake. 'You've been here too long!' chorused Brett and Jon.

The spring was situated up a creek on the east bank, and although the land around it was on private property, the cave was in navigable water so it was legal to visit so long as we didn't go onto the shore. The owners were away and there was a family sunbathing on the sand. The entrance was quite snug and Jon had to drag me through it against the current; Brett got in unaided, by flipping on his back and pulling himself along the roof. After that, we had a very pleasant dive, finally turning around at a surface entrance inside the cave, further upstream.

A few weeks after returning to the UK I started a course of daily radiotherapy treatments. This was far more gruelling than the four sessions of chemotherapy I'd already undergone. I would turn up at hospital each day to be zapped and then told when to come back for my next dose. The appointments did not follow a regular pattern, and by the end of it all I was exhausted. Nevertheless, when Jon and Karen came to visit the UK in November, Tim Morgan and I took Jon for dives at Wookey Hole and Pwll-y-Cwm before they returned home.

*Brett Hemphill and Duncan (Jon Bojar)*

# 11

# Saturday Night at the Movies

With the exploration of the upstream limits of Daren Cilau at an apparent impasse, Gary Jones, Tim Morgan and I decided to turn our attention to an obscure series of passages at the bottom of the Borrowed Boots Streamway. Ian Rolland, Steve Jones and Phil Rust, having first entered a half kilometre of passages in February 1986, had named the network Saturday Night at the Movies. It contained five sumps, and Ian free-dived one of these using a collection of caving belts tied together to form a safety line; they called these the Troll Belt Sumps after the brand of caving gear they had used. Despite the discovery of more dry passages on a follow-up trip a month later, and even though Ian had left a stash of gear there before his death in 1994, no actual diving had taken place there. So in February 2001, Gary, Tim and I were ready to mount our first expedition there.

I kitted up quickly and was first in the water. This was because I'd learned a few secrets from Rick Stanton; being in front would afford me the best visibility, undisturbed by silt knocked from the roof of the passage by other divers' exhaust bubbles or sediment kicked up from the floor by a careless fin stroke. This allowed me to swim efficiently and use less air. Then, once I had surfaced in Daren Cilau, I would be able to select the choicest spot to remove my gear, thus giving me the same advantage on the way out.

Tim dived second, but had problems with his trim halfway through the sump; he ended up pinned to the roof by air that had migrated into the feet of his drysuit. But unlike the same problem I'd had during my first traverse of the sump ten years before, Tim was in a larger part of the passage and so was unable to retain contact with the guideline. Worse, a bag of gear he was carrying on his chest prevented him from tucking into a ball to recover from this situation. So he ditched the bag and cut several holes in the feet

*Tim Morgan at Pwll-y-Cwm (Duncan Price)*

## Saturday Night at the Movies

of his suit to vent the air. Fortunately he then dropped straight back onto the line, tied his bag onto it, and made a prompt exit in his now-flooded drysuit, passing Gary *en route*. On reaching Tim's abandoned bag, Gary decided to turn around to investigate what had been happening, bringing the bag out with him.

Meanwhile, I'd arrived in Daren Cilau and changed into my wetsuit. After waiting for over an hour, I wandered up to Hard Rock Café and had a cup of tea with the campers there. But with still no sign of the others, I went to Duke's Sump and followed an assortment of lines through to the airspace beyond. I tried to dive down the rift at the far end, which was disgorging a fair amount of water, but despite levering aside several blocks at the top, I could only penetrate this to a body-length before it became too tight. I did a number of other useful chores in the area, such as making use of a hammer and bolt driver to set expansion bolts into the walls at strategic points to fix or reposition various handlines that we'd left to aid our progress. Somehow I managed to while away 10 hours underground before I dived out – to find out eventually that Tim and Gary had spent most of the day in the Drum and Monkey watching rugby on TV.

Our next outing took place in June, by which time the countryside was being devastated by the foot-and-mouth epidemic. The hillside around Whitewalls was out of bounds to visitors so the house was shut. But fortunately the Clydach Gorge was still accessible on foot, so Tim and I decided to go ahead anyhow; we spent Friday night at Arthur Millet's house in Crickhowell before diving into Daren Cilau the next morning. On reaching what we believed to be the downstream sump at the south-eastern arm of the complex network of passages, I geared up and plunged in. This proved to be an easy 10-metre-long dive into a section of canal ending at another sump. I met Tim back at dive base; we each used a single cylinder to go back through, and I explored the next sump for 20 metres until it closed down. Halfway along the canal, I could see an underwater rift heading off to the west. I dived along this to a T-junction, and then northwards again, to surface back where we had started. The area was obviously more complicated than we'd been led to believe, and we cursed ourselves for forgetting to bring a copy of the survey.

Now it was Tim's turn to explore. He went through the Right-Hand Sump (as it became known), reaching an underwater chamber where there was a choice of routes. He followed the passage ahead around to the west, to surface in an airbell where he tied off the line. Next, he headed south from the junction through a low arch, to surface in another airbell; then he dived through the underwater continuation to another short section of dry passage. Then, feeling very cold, he returned. I went back in to push this lead – to my astonishment finding a live frog in the section between the sumps – and laying out another 30 metres of line in a roomy tunnel before my air margins forced me to retreat. I'd seen that the end of Frog Passage was wide open and heading into the blank area between Duke's Sump and the Gloom Room; Tim and I were pleased that between us we had discovered nearly 200 metres of cave, much of it underwater.

We spent the night underground at Hard Rock Café, and when we eventually consulted the survey the next day, we discovered that we had not actually dived any of the sumps marked on the survey. The site we had originally investigated was marked on the maps as

'Pool +2 m deep', which left us at least five more sites to investigate, in addition to the going leads that we had discovered on our first visit. But in mid-July access to the Clydach was suspended due to the spread of foot-and-mouth, so we had to wait until November 2001 for another chance to continue our explorations.

The next trip included Gary Jones as well as Tim and me. Gary was last to enter the water, but he was forced to turn back about two-thirds of the way though the sump, having used up a third of his air supply. It turned out that this was because he had been wearing a new low-volume mask which had a slight tint to it, and in the poor visibility he'd had to spend a lot of time trying to follow the line, thus using up a lot of air. Tim and I decided to go to Hard Rock Café for a hot drink and wait for Gary there. We left a note by our gear, but we suspected that he had encountered a problem and had turned around. In any case, we decided to give him a little longer to show up, as he was a notoriously slow swimmer and always last to arrive even if we let him dive ahead of us.

After an hour's wait there was still no sign of Gary, so Tim and I adopted a revised plan, which involved putting Tim into the Gloom Room Sump to continue exploring the downstream route. Earlier in the year John Volanthen had dived here under high-water conditions; with the benefit of an increased current, he had successfully located the outlet and laid out 25 metres of line to a restriction. He had turned around here, as the flow had increased to a point where he was in real danger of being unable to get out. But Tim's dive was less successful, as the visibility was so bad that he was unable to read his gauges, let alone find the line downstream. During this trip another event gave us pause for thought ... a major rock fall had occurred at the bottom of the King's Road; a section of the roof had peeled away and landed on the place where we usually left our gear when changing. We speculated that the collapse might have been caused by an earthquake and were very glad that we hadn't been there to witness it.

At the end of March 2002 Gary, Tim and I had a more successful trip when we finally managed to return to Saturday Night at the Movies. John Volanthen had gone in ahead of us to push downstream from the Gloom Room, but (like Tim before him) was thwarted by poor visibility. Evidence of major flooding over the winter was apparent everywhere: the debris at the bottom of the King's Road had been washed into the start of the sump to create a sandbank which we had to crawl over in order to get out of the water; further into the cave, the fins and reel that we'd left behind in November had been washed into various nooks and crannies. Tim set off into Frog Passage and added 65 metres of line in an active river passage until he reached a tight ascending rift. I started tagging the spare line that we had carried in, while Gary investigated the Main Downstream Sump for a short distance, using a single set of spare gear.

Tim came back after 40 minutes, allowing Gary to go back into the Main Downstream Sump with two cylinders. He continued straight on through it, to reach an underwater chamber; here his ascent of a rift took him into a strong current. He followed this upstream, to surface in 50 metres of open streamway, terminating at two sumps. Gary sentimentally named the new find Bunny Passage, as his pet rabbit had just died.

He had been gone for over an hour, and we were just about to give up on ever seeing him again when he reappeared. So I dived into the Main Downstream Sump to locate the exit for the water flow, but I couldn't find it so I surfaced in Bunny Passage and explored the northerly (static) sump. I passed this after a short dive to gain airspace at Steve's Real Sump, which had been discovered in 1986. Then I discarded my gear and travelled back overland to meet the others.

In the meantime Gary and Tim had come across Ian Rolland's cache of dive gear high on a ledge, and were raiding it for anything useful. I felt quite emotional as the others handed down bits of equipment that had once belonged to Ian; the haul included a mask, a pair of fins, a line reel and some dodgy-looking cylinders (one with a regulator still attached). I decided to take out Ian's 1980s-style low-volume mask for repair, but it turned out that the rubber was too perished to seal. Another memento of the era was Ian's diving knife (more like a dagger used to fend off sharks) which we passed on to his son, Connor, several years later. We left the rest of the haul underground, as we thought we might have some use for it later.

The diving conditions at the time were excellent, and since we had a number of going leads, we came back the following weekend to continue our exploration. I was inserted into the Right-Hand Sump and reached the end of Frog Passage without difficulty. The continuation was too tight to follow so, diligently surveying the route, I returned to the others. Meanwhile Gary and Tim had explored and surveyed 40 metres of the passage carrying the Borrowed Boots Streamway water into the area. This was upstream of the dive base and included yet another sump.

Once I'd returned, Gary donned my depleted cylinders and pushed on into the active stream sump entering Bunny Passage. He explored this for 50 metres along a roomy passage with a maximum depth of 7 metres. While Gary was gone, Tim and I occupied ourselves by exploring the inlet heading north below the alcove where we'd found Ian Rolland's gear. We followed this to a squeeze, beyond which we could hear water flowing. Although the passage showed no signs of having been entered before, we reckoned that it would link with the Borrowed Boots Streamway, so we called it Rolly's Secret Backdoor. On the way out, Tim climbed down into the end of Borrowed Boots Streamway and confirmed that the new passage did connect, but the squeeze would need enlarging to make it a viable shortcut into Saturday Night at the Movies.

Up to this point, our regular trips through the long sump between Pwll-y-Cwm and Daren Cilau had all been done following the original guideline laid by Martyn Farr in 1986. But even though this had been tidied up in several places, it was in poor shape. Furthermore, the layout of the underwater passage was based on a few compass bearings and a lot of guesswork. Although it could be argued that since we knew where both ends of the sump were a more accurate plan was not needed, I wanted to do a better survey of the route. Finally, we all agreed that a lot could be done to improve our journey through the sump by putting in a completely new line, away from obstacles and alcoves.

So I sourced a kilometre of tough 6-mm diameter hawser-laid polypropylene twine from an army surplus shop, and we began to replace the old guide line in 100-metre sections. We marked each length at 5-metre intervals with a pair of cable ties around the line: one green with a short tail, to face in the direction of Pwll-y-Cwm, and the other red with a long tail. In addition to the directional information provided by the markers, we attached a piece of insulation tape next to each one, labelled with the distance from the surface. Since the tape might fall off or become illegible, we also attached engraved plastic discs every 50 metres as a more robust means of measurement. We started replacing the line on Friday evenings during the usual check-out dive to make sure that the choke was open, but once we were further in it made sense to combine the line replacement with the longer working trips into Daren Cilau.

After a two-week break from our siege of Daren Cilau, Tim and I returned to the fray. Andy Stewart, a former marine commando from Devon and friend of Martyn Farr's, turned up to have a dive and help with our gear. *En route* into the cave, we replaced the line from 200 to 300 metres – but unfortunately I dropped one of my two 7-litre chest-mounted cylinders while doing this, and didn't notice until it was too late to go back to search for it. Luckily Tim and I were both carrying plenty of spare gear and the loss of one cylinder did not affect our plan to put me into the Gloom Room Sump.

Reaching the site, I set off looking for the downstream line laid by John Volanthen. The visibility in the start of the sump was atrocious, and I was relieved to break out into clearer water when I reached the main passage. Having been up and down a large part of the sump looking for the other line, I found it in near-zero visibility, close to the start of the sump. Under the circumstances, I decided not to continue, so Tim and I went out, collecting my lost cylinder and removing the old line that we'd replaced *en route*. Andy met us on the surface … and he carried our four 15-litre cylinders up the hill to the cars in one go – that's over 70 kilos!

Gary, Tim and I waited until August for our next foray to Daren Cilau. The visibility in the sump was very poor, so on arrival in Daren Cilau we decided not to take any diving gear to Saturday Night at the Movies, as the water there was unlikely to be any clearer. Instead, we used a rope, ladder and bolting gear to rig the climb down into the bottom end of the Borrowed Boots Streamway. We enlarged the squeeze into the upper end of Rolly's Secret Backdoor by using a lump hammer and chisel, but this passage still proved to be a harder way in than the original route. We toured around some of the dry passages in the area, and descended a climb we had come across on a previous visit. This ended at a static sump, so we left a handline there, ready for use another time. I free-dived a short distance into the first of the Troll Belt Sumps, far enough to determine that it was worth a return visit with breathing apparatus.

On our next dive into Daren Cilau, Gary and I were joined by John Volanthen, though he was just going in and out to test his chest-mounted rebreather. We carried in two extra reels of line, to replace the line between 350 and 500 metres. *En route*, I dropped the first reel (marked up for 350–400 metres) and left the second at the 350-metre mark, as it was now superfluous to the day's plans; fortunately John found the reel I'd lost, and put it with the other one before diving back out from Daren Cilau. Gary and I took a single cylinder to

Saturday Night at the Movies, whereupon Gary used it (in combination with another tank left in situ) to dive upstream in Bunny Passage. He explored 45 metres of roomy sump before the passage abruptly closed down into a narrow rift. The way on wasn't obvious, so he tied off the line at floor level at a depth of 10 metres just before the end. While Gary was diving, I checked out Ian Rolland's old cylinders; one of the tanks was completely unserviceable and the other only held 40 bar of something, so I decided to wait until Gary returned before diving Troll Belt Sump 1 (the sump I had previously free–dived); using Gary's left-over gas, with only 50 bar of air in the set, I passed the sump after an easy 10-metre dive. After a short climb and 40 metres of mostly dry passage I ended up at another static sump, Troll Belt Sump 0. On the way out to the surface, I had sufficient air to collect the abandoned line reels and complete the job of replacing the line from 350 to 500 metres. As a consequence, Gary surfaced before me, and he even managed to make last orders in the pub. I was not so lucky.

*Laura Trowbridge and Ivor Cashmore (landlord of the Drum & Monkey Inn) (Duncan Price)*

John Volanthen and I went back in December 2002 to continue renewing the guideline. We replaced the section from 500 to 600 metres on the inward dive, leaving less than 50 metres to go. Changing into wetsuits and diving through St David's Sump, we trekked up to Saturday Night at the Movies, where I went to Troll Belt Sump 0, but finding no tie-off for the line, I removed a block of lead from my weight belt and fastened the line to it. The first part of the sump turned out to be 20 metres of deep-water canal beyond a low arch, but eventually the route lay underwater and I laid out a further 30 metres of line; then I entered a larger passage with an orange line already running along it. At the time, we believed this to be the upstream line from Bunny Passage, but we weren't sure as the survey data was a little confusing. On the way back to John, I was able to find a rock to replace the weight I'd used as a belay for the line. We offered John a dive in Troll Belt Sump 2, but he declined as he was feeling cold, so we left the cylinders there for another time. We exited – to find that because snow on the hillsides had been melting while we'd been underground, the water level at St David's Sump had risen by a metre. Fortunately we had placed our gear well above this *(see colour section)*.

In March 2003, John dived the static Troll Belt Sump 2. He passed the short sump to gain a 2-metre-long airbell first reached by Ian Rolland in 1988. The next sump turned out to be 4 metres long, leading to a section of low water-filled canal ending in a vertical rift. John took his diving gear off and started to climb, then discovered a rope hanging down that Gary, Tim and I had placed the previous August. I had a look in the Right-Hand Sump following the line laid by Tim on our first trip there in 2001; a body-sized tube continued underwater beyond the final air space for 10 metres before surfacing at a larger dome and a junction of two lines. I followed the right-hand line back, to emerge between the Downstream Sump and Right-Hand Sump, then replaced the remaining section of Martyn Farr's original guideline and tied it off to a rock at the 650-metre marker in the sump pool at the bottom of Daren Cilau.

In August 2003, Gary Jones and I went back to mop up a few remaining leads in Saturday Night at the Movies, when I dived the Mainstream Sump towards Bunny Passage. Instead of surfacing in Bunny Passage, though, I fastened a line at the point where I expected the downstream continuation to go off, and then laid 35 metres of line along a roomy underwater tunnel, continuing until the route connected with Frog Passage, as I'd anticipated. With ample reserves of air, I surfaced in Bunny Passage and swam to the end of the line in the upstream sump laid by Gary a year earlier. In good visibility I found the way onward was on a ledge to the right, where a handsome passage continued upstream. But I didn't have time to explore this – and I hadn't found the line from the Troll Belt Sump, either.

Two weeks later, conditions were still exceptional, and Alec Wallace, a diver turned cave diver, helped me get to the Gloom Room Sump. This time everything went as planned, and I found John Volanthen's downstream line without difficulty. I followed it to his tie-off at a boulder restriction, and as the water level was low I was easily able to pass this obstacle. After 60 metres of progress I reached the upstream limit of exploration in Bunny Passage.

We had established that the river flowing through the San Agustin Way (which would have come from Agen Allwedd) continued through Saturday Night at the Movies (and the confluence with the water from Borrowed Boots Streamway, sourced from 7th Hour Sump and Llangattock Swallet), to emerge from Duke's Sump and then out to the daylight at Pwll-y-Cwm. The only question that remained was where Troll Belt Sump 0 fitted in, as we had not yet found the connection point.

The weather was kind to us and diving conditions remained superb; the visibility was so good that I was able to use my scooter to dive into Daren Cilau two weeks later. The original plan had been for Rick Stanton and Phil Short, who was a lot keener and tougher than me, to go to the downstream end of Sump 4 in Agen Allwedd, to try to make vocal contact between Against All Odds and the terminal point of the San Agustin Way in Daren Cilau. John Volanthen and I were due to go to the end of Daren Cilau, but it transpired that Phil couldn't make it, so a team was dispatched into Daren with no clear purpose. Irish cave diver, Natasha Mitchell and Ian Pinkstone, an up-and-coming cave diver, accompanied us into Daren Cilau, Natasha becoming the first woman to make the through dive. This was all the more remarkable because not only had she never dived at Pwll-y-Cwm before, but also because she was wearing a back-mounted twinset; when she reached the choke, she coolly removed her cylinders and pushed them ahead until she was through, then replaced them.

With a new guideline in the middle of the passage and with the visibility exceeding 10 metres, I was pulled through the sump in about 25 minutes. But on reorganising our gear in Daren Cilau, it was apparent that one of my regulators destined for the onward dives had a slight high-pressure leak, so we decided to support John up to the Gloom Room and allow him to do a reconnaissance dive upstream to the start of the San Agustin Way. This proved very useful: he was just 5 metres from the end of the sump when he encountered another guideline entering the main tunnel from a previously unnoticed side passage in the right-hand wall. This was my line from Troll Belt Sump 0 – and the final piece in the jigsaw fell into place. Over the course of our explorations in Saturday Night at the Movies we had successfully explored over a kilometre of new territory, half of which lay underwater.

At the end of July 2004 I made a final visit to the area on a solo trip. I dived into Saturday Night at the Movies via the route downstream from the Gloom Room into Bunny Passage and then through Steve's Real Sump to collect the gear we'd left behind. I'd intended to complete a circuit by following the route from the Troll Belt Sumps into the upstream end of the Gloom Room sump, but I thought better of it and returned the way I'd come. It's interesting to speculate that had Ian Rolland carried out his planned dives in Saturday Night at the Movies, then he (rather than Rick Stanton) might have discovered the San Agustin Way.

## 12

# An Unwelcome Guest

In March 2002, Tim Morgan and I decided to return to Florida to pay Jon Bojar another visit. I'd completed my cancer treatment and was in good health once more. Rick Stanton came with us – he had just bought a KISS rebreather and wanted to get some dives in with it; he'd taken part in the 1998 Wakulla Springs project and had gained a great deal of experience with the Cis-Lunar Mk-5 rebreather under the guidance of Bill Stone and Richard Pyle. Engraved on the scrubber canister of the KISS rebreather is a helpful reminder of its inherent dangers: *This device is capable of killing you without warning.* This caused a few raised eyebrows when our bags went through security, and for the flight home Rick hid the warning under some duct tape with his name written on it *(see colour section)..*

We flew into Orlando and drove west to Tampa for a stopover with Jon to collect some cylinders before heading north to our accommodation in Luraville. Rick had specifically requested a cylinder of trimix with a high helium content for use with his rebreather. This task had been subcontracted to one of Jon's associates, Brett Hemphill, but by the time we all turned in the item hadn't arrived. In the morning we awoke to find the cylinder of trimix waiting for us outside the door to Jon's apartment. Attached to it was a long and rambling note from Brett (who fancied himself as a man with his finger on the pulse of local cave diving), which started: 'I don't know where you are planning to use this cylinder, maybe [long list of deep caves] with [long list of cave divers] …' Brett had obviously thought that Rick was up to some subterfuge, so we dubbed the cylinder the 'tank of paranoia'.

Having caused enough trouble in the first 12 hours of our visit to this country, we decamped to the Dive Outpost near Peacock Springs, where we made our first cave dive of the trip. Tim, Rick and I set off upstream following the route that Rick and I had taken on our first dive here in 1994. This time we made it to Challenge Sink, where we stuck our heads out of the water. Rick wanted to continue to the other end of the traverse at Orange Grove Sink, but I was concerned that Tim and I did not have enough air to make the trip safely. We had also left a jump line in place between the Peanut Tunnel from Peacock Spring and the main line; Tim volunteered to go back and take this out before going on to exit via Olsen Sink. Rick assured me that we could share the (untouched) bailout tanks he was carrying for his rebreather, so the two of us could complete the through trip.

*Forrest Wilson and Duncan at Cow Spring (Cindy Butler)*

Surfacing at the upstream end of the cave system, we faced a long walk back to our vehicle, which was parked beside the head spring. We had just climbed the wooden steps out of the sinkhole when I came across a familiar face. Although we'd never met before, I instantly recognised the man with the Santa Claus white hair and beard – fabled inventor of the line-arrow: Forrest Wilson.

He stuck out his hand to greet me: You must be Duncan Price from England!

Me: Where am I?
Forrest: Orange Grove Sink.
Me: That *was* a long swim!

Forrest gave us a lift back to join Tim on the other side of the park. We must have looked a curious sight as, still in our dive gear, we hung onto the sides of his van as it sped along the dirt track.

Over the course of our stay, Rick introduced us to many of the friends he'd made during his visit in 1998. We visited several sites in the area before returning to Tampa to meet up with Jon. Tim had to drop out of diving for the last few days as he'd come down with an ear infection, although we all enjoyed the Gasparilla parade in Tampa. It turned out that Rick never did use the 'tank of paranoia' in anger.

Through my contacts with local cave divers, I was asked to give a seminar on sidemount diving techniques at the National Speleological Society Cave Diving Section meeting in Gainesville at the end of May 2002. This was quite an honour, and I persuaded John Volanthen to come along with me for the trip. I arranged to go out a few days ahead of him, and was to pick him up at the airport when we collected our hire car. John had also recently acquired a rebreather (an AP Classic Inspiration) and wanted to use the trip to build up experience with it.

Before John arrived, I made a few cave dives. Jon Bojar and I drove over to Blue Springs near Orange City. The spring is in a state park, and we didn't arrive at the entrance until 15:15, having been delayed by getting stuck in sand in an orange grove while looking for another cave. The warden told us that the latest time that divers are allowed in was 15:00, but he admitted us on the condition that we were out by 17:00. The entrance to the head spring dropped down a roomy vertical rift to 36 metres depth, whereupon a considerable current emerged from a narrow slot.

Then Brett Hemphill, Jon and I went to Wayne's World to shoot some video footage for the forthcoming National Speleological Society Cave Diving Section (NSS-CDS) workshop. Brett was on the camera and Jon was the model, while I held the lights. Things quickly went awry; first I got lost in the entrance when placing the deco bottles. Then Brett proceeded to film the first two sequences with the lens cap on … our saving grace was the post-dive debrief in The Cricketers, an English-themed pub nearby that served passable imported ale.

The next day I returned to visit Wayne's World, to follow up on a lead discovered by a visiting Canadian diver, which Jon and Brett had disclosed to me while under the influence of alcohol in The Cricketers. It was called Tornado Alley, and it lay off the Deep Salt Tunnel opposite a passage I'd investigated on a previous visit. I dropped a stage tank off at the start of a low section, and I soon reached the limit of previous exploration. The way on being wide open, I quickly laid out 120 metres of line heading south and then east, even though this was against a strong current, in a 2–3-metre diameter tunnel at 30 metres depth. My reel ran out at a low duck-under, and I belayed the end of the line to a silt screw which I'd found *en route*. I surveyed the route back, and presented Jon with the data for him to add to the map.

After the dive, I met John Volanthen at the airport and we headed north to stay at the Dive Outpost. I hadn't spent much time with John before the trip, but I knew that he didn't drink, smoke or chase women, so I wondered how we would get on. 'It's only a week,' I thought. 'I'm sure I can put up with him'. It turned out, in fact, that despite our different lifestyles we got on very well, particularly as John was not averse to driving me back from the bar in the evening.

John and I had arranged to borrow a couple of Tekna scooters from Harold and Cindy Geick, a couple who had helped out on the 1998 Wakulla Springs Project, where they had met Rick Stanton. We didn't get chance to use them for our first dive at Peacock Springs as they had been banned for conservation reasons, but the next day we took them to Devil's Eye and cruised as far as the Hinkel Restriction (about 1,000 metres from the entrance).

We were due to relocate to Gainesville for the start of the CDS meeting, so John and I dived the nearby Telford Spring, following it for about 800 metres, to where the line split at the end of the Expressway. Back on the surface, we hung around in the sunshine for a while; then I went back in for a try-dive on John's rebreather. I didn't go far because I was

## An Unwelcome Guest

*John Volanthen at Devils Eye (Duncan Price)*

only wearing my swimming shorts – but on the way out of the cave I became caught up in the line. I wasn't prepared for this as I didn't have a knife to cut myself free with. The rebreather had plenty of time left on it so running out of air wasn't an issue – I was more likely to succumb to the cold first. By feeling around the unfamiliar equipment, I was able to work out where the line was caught and untangle myself. After what seemed like an age, I returned to John with only mild hypothermia … *(see colour section)*.

The CDS meeting proved a lot of fun and my contribution was well received. The afternoons were free of commitments, so John and I were led off on a cave chase by Brett Hemphill before going for a dive at Suwanacoochee Spring. On the second day of the meeting, John and I split up, as he wanted to do a deep dive in Peacock 3 while I visited Luraville Spring with a couple of other divers.

Luraville Spring is part of an underwater cave system which is connected downstream to Telford Spring. We had to put our gear on while standing straddled across the waterlogged entrance chimney to the cave – but I lost my footing and sank to the floor of the cavern. Although I was wearing my cylinders, I was without my mask or lights. All I could make out was blurry sunlight coming from a little hole above me while I fumbled for a regulator to breathe from. But of course my cylinders were also turned off, so not only was I virtually blind, but also I had no air and was negatively buoyant. I needed to get back to the surface. Urgently! I managed to turn my air on and connect one of my cylinders to my drysuit inflator valve and float to the surface. Despite this eventful start, we explored the cave for nearly 400 metres whereupon the passage became very low; I continued downstream alone for another 100 metres to a five-way junction where route-finding became difficult, and I retreated.

On our final day of diving in Florida, John and I drove back to Tampa to return our borrowed cylinders. We stopped off at Wayne's World *en route*, with the Geicks in tow.

John went for a tourist dive while I returned to the end of the passage I'd explored at the beginning of my visit. I used two stages of nitrox-30 to reach the start of the new section, then conducted the rest of the dive on air. I reached the end of the line after about 40 minutes, and discovered that the route directly ahead was too low. I found a way around this that emerged through a ring of rock flakes shaped like some monstrous jaws into a large chamber with a fresh water layer in the roof. After blundering around looking for the way on, I eventually deposited the contents of my reel along a handsome 3-metre diameter tube heading south. I breathed the nitrox on the dive out, and then decompressed on oxygen in the entrance shaft.

The next day, I returned to the UK and, ever economical with my annual leave, drove directly from the airport to work. When I finally got home later in the afternoon, I unloaded my bags from my car and went to the bathroom to empty my bladder; I must have been quite dehydrated, as I don't recall needing the toilet all day until then. I noticed a bit of fluff on the end of my penis – trying to flick it off with a finger I was horrified when legs popped out of it. I had a tick on my dick! I knew enough about ticks to realise that they could be tricky to remove without leaving the head still attached to me, so given the location of the offending arachnid, I decided to seek medical attention in the local health centre rather than trying to do it myself. The clinic was still open and I had enough time to get an emergency appointment with a (male, luckily) GP. I left a note for my wife to say I was back home again, but had just nipped out to see a doctor.

I explained to the doctor that I'd brought back an unwelcome visitor from Florida. I guessed that the tick must have snuck into my clothes while I was changing at Wayne's World, and had looked for somewhere warm to feed itself during my journey home. I showed the doctor the problem, half-expecting him to say 'It looks like a willy – only smaller!' But the doctor merely explained that he'd never done this before and sought a second opinion. Another – fortunately – male doctor came in, and the pair of them debated what to do.

One of them consulted a medical textbook; apparently there were two methods of removing the tick. The preferred approach was to cut the skin away around the creature, thus ensuring that none of it remained embedded in my body. 'But I'm Church of England!' I stammered, as I didn't relish the thought of an emergency circumcision. Having discounted surgery, there was another way (known as the 'outback method') which involved dousing the tick in petrol until it suffocated, tying a loop of thread around its head where it was attached to me, and pulling it off. 'We suggest you try this at home,' was the doctors' advice.

I went home with a prescription for some antibiotics and a sample bottle to put the tick in so that it could be sent to a laboratory in Leicester for identification. There was a chance that I could catch Lyme disease. After decanting some fuel from my portable compressor, I went upstairs to the bathroom to perform the deed. I was just in the middle of splashing petrol over my wedding tackle when my wife burst in. She'd come home unannounced and had seen my note. Given that I had recently been treated for cancer, she feared the worst. Thinking quickly, I pulled a stray hair from her scalp and tied it around the tick. After putting up a struggle, the tick parted company with me, and I dropped the dead insect into the container, to be returned to the medical centre the next day.

Fortunately there was no lasting damage, although I would advise you not to try this for yourself. Tick removal tweezers are available, and if you're going out into the countryside where ticks are prevalent, one of these might be a useful addition to a first aid kit. Alternatively, if you have a tick on your privates, visiting a vet might be more rewarding; pets frequently collect them, so vets have a lot of expertise in their safe removal!

(I was telling this tale to some friends of mine in the local badminton club when one of them, Paul Schober, a consultant in genitourinary medicine at Leicester Teaching Hospital, asked me if I had a photograph of said tick. I admitted I'd taken a digital photo of it while it was still attached to me (and why not, indeed?). Paul said he'd like to have a copy to show to his students. So not only can I claim to have invented the glue that holds the wallpaper on in aircraft toilets, but my penis features in a lecture course on venereal diseases!)

I made my third 2002 trip to the US at the end of September; as I was going to a conference in Pittsburgh I went alone. Jon and Karen were getting married a week after the meeting finished. This gave me some time off to spend in Florida before the ceremony. Since Jon would be otherwise occupied with more important matters, I swung by his house to borrow some cylinders before driving to Gainesville to meet up with Forrest Wilson and a friend of his, Cindy Butler, for a few days of cave diving mayhem.

Our first dive was at Alachua Sink, which is situated just behind a restaurant. I'd heard about the site on my very first visit to the area in 1994 – access is strictly controlled on account of a number of fatalities that have occurred there. Fortunately Cindy was a guide. I had never dived with either of them before, but I knew Forrest to be a long-time caver and 'sump diver', to use American terminology. Cindy must also have been curious about my strategy of utilising my drysuit for buoyancy control rather than relying on a separate wing or compensator; she later admitted that she'd feared that this meant I would be a 'silt monster'.

The surface pool at Alachua Sink was tannic, with less than a metre of visibility; dropping down on the line, I could only just make out Cindy's lights ahead of me. At a depth of 35 metres, the cave opened into a chamber with a junction of lines heading upstream and downstream. Here the water cleared and I was able to impress the others with my perfect trim and buoyancy control. Forrest had requested that we didn't swim too fast at depth, so for the next 30 minutes we adopted a leisurely pace, as far as the drop-off to 60 metres (the average depth being about 45 metres). Here Cindy signalled to turn around, but not before I had done a bounce dive down the shaft to see how far it went. Forrest led out and being 'old school' set a cracking pace in order to minimise decompression; only 20 minutes later we were making our way back up through the murk and occasionally bumping into one another during our stops. At one point I believe that I was actually standing on Forrest – I could hardly see anything.

The next day, Cindy and I met up with her friend Alan Heck, and we drove to Luraville. We were running a little late and Forrest was already diving, so we decided to check out

Bonnet Spring as a possible dive site. We walked over to see if its large alligator was in residence. The spring pool was very small and the water level extremely low. Cindy cleared off some weeds and I went up to the edge to probe around with a log and check the visibility; I'd only just turned around and stepped back next to Alan when the rock and ledge I'd been standing on collapsed into the sink. No alligators had been harmed by our actions, but we decided that a different dive site might be in order.

As an alternative to Bonnet Spring, we did a stage dive in Peacock 3 before heading over to Telford Spring to meet up with some of the regulars from the Cave Divers' Forum online community. I demonstrated that the water temperature was 'balmy' in comparison to UK conditions by going for a dive dressed only in my swim shorts and wearing a couple of aluminium stage cylinders jury-rigged onto my sidemount harness. This time I didn't get caught up, although I had remembered to take a diving knife with me.

For our next dive we met Forrest at Cow Springs where I gamely tried out the rebreather he had made, before going for a longer dive on more conventional equipment. Forrest then had to drive back to Georgia, so I spent the next few days being taken to a variety of lesser-known caves, many of which required a kayak to reach, before making my final dive in the area at Peacock Springs.

At the end of the trip I returned to Jon and Karen's place in Tampa before flying up to their wedding in Rhode Island. *En route* I stopped off at Wayne's World for another exploration dive in the passage I'd discovered in May. Unfortunately the conditions were very poor with a lot of particulate matter in the water, so I only added 35 metres of line in what appeared to be a roomy tube before retreating in disgust. Although I prepared to dive again the next day, I never returned to the passage. The route was subsequently connected back into the main cave – not by me, but I was satisfied to have played a part in the exploration of Wayne's World, and felt rewarded by my name appearing on the survey.

Leaving Florida behind, I went to Jon and Karen's nuptials. Tim Morgan (also in the US on business) and I acted as ushers for the ceremony. The event was a fancy-dress affair and I'd hired a suitable medieval costume; Jon and Karen provided me with a large ceremonial sword to complete my outfit, and I played the part of 'Duncan the Destroyer' since I had acquired a reputation for being a bit clumsy around their house.

In 2003 and 2004, I made more visits to the Sunshine State, although I did most of my diving in northern Florida rather than the Tampa Bay area. My widening circle of contacts gave me the chance to explore several sites that were off the beaten track or required special permission to access.

Then I took a break from visiting the Florida springs until May 2014 when I returned in the company of Rick Stanton. Forrest Wilson was our host, and we put in an appearance at the NSS-CDS workshop in Lake City. After the meeting, a group of us went for dinner in a restaurant. Once we had eaten, we split the bill and paid with an assortment of credit cards and cash. When the waitress came back with the receipts for us to sign, she called out my name first:

## An Unwelcome Guest

Waitress: Dr Duncan Price?
Duncan: Yes, that's me!
Waitress (handing me the receipt): Have I seen you on TV?
Duncan (bluffing): Well … you might have done … I do a show for the BBC called 'Dr Duncan Does Science' – we make rockets and stuff …
Waitress (falling for my story while my co-diners are trying not to snigger): Oh wow!
Duncan: … last season we made a mini-sub and drove it around a lake.
Waitress: Can I have your autograph?

We found some paper and I asked her name in order to dedicate my message. While I was doing this, she glanced at Rick (who wore a CDG polo shirt like mine and was keeping a straight face) before turning to ask me if he had also been on TV.

Duncan (pokerfaced): Yeah, we did a special on diving with sharks – it was awesome!

# 13

# Dodgy Devices

There were concerned expressions on everyone's faces when I slipped into the Santa Fe River for the first dive on my homemade rebreathers – the device looked more like a cross between a set of bagpipes and a vacuum cleaner than any form of life-support apparatus. I silently disappeared without a trace. Then there was an eruption of bubbles, and the audience broke into laughter as I emerged holding the contraption in two pieces with water pouring out of it. Back to the drawing board!

I stress that using home-made life support apparatus is very hazardous. Messing around with rebreathers can leave you looking stupid, dead or both. Furthermore, such an enterprise might not actually save you any money. View it as a form of adult entertainment, though, and you won't be disappointed.

Rebreathers are old technology, pre-dating the development of the aqualung by well over 100 years. The principle of a rebreather is very simple: the diver's breath is continuously recirculated between the diver's lungs and a breathing bag (or counterlung). Some means of adding oxygen is used, to replenish that which is metabolised by the body during respiration; the expired carbon dioxide is removed by a bed of chemical absorbent based on a mixture of sodium and calcium hydroxides (sodalime). The advantage of this closed-circuit arrangement is that a diver's gas supply can last many times longer than in normal open circuit scuba, where the wearer's expired air bubbles out at the end of each breath.

For example, whereas a 3-litre cylinder of air filled to 200 bar would last about 25 minutes on the surface when breathed on open circuit, at a depth of 40 metres (five times atmospheric pressure) it would last only 5 minutes. But if the cylinder were filled with the same amount of oxygen and breathed on a closed circuit rebreather, the duration would be over 5 hours on the surface – and the same at 40 metres, so long as the scrubber canister held enough absorbent. Of course, oxygen toxicity would be a problem at this depth, so it is essential to dilute the oxygen with nitrogen (using air) or a helium/nitrogen mixture (trimix) to mitigate this. In order to maintain oxygen levels adequate to support life, some form of electronic monitoring is also advised, as the body's response to too little oxygen (unconsciousness) or too much (seizures) is not a particularly convenient indicator. This monitoring can be done with electrochemical sensors that produce a current proportional to the concentration of oxygen surrounding them; their output can be measured and converted to the partial pressure of oxygen in the breathing loop for control purposes.

Should the sodalime become ineffective – by being used up or just by getting wet – carbon dioxide will build up in the breathing loop. Although it's easy to measure $CO_2$ levels in the laboratory, devices that can do the same thing underwater in 100% humidity and consume little power are not widely available. Carbon dioxide poisoning manifests itself as headaches, apprehension and confusion, and can result in cardiac arrest (trust me on this – I've experienced all but the last one). Flooding the scrubber is also bad news, since the 'caustic cocktail' produced by wet sodalime can be inhaled with uncomfortable consequences (been there, done that, too).

The most basic form of rebreather is nothing more than a mouthpiece communicating with a suitable counterlung via a scrubber, in an in–out–in–out arrangement. So long as the circuit is purged of nitrogen and the diver goes no deeper than 6 metres, pure oxygen can be used without any form of electronic monitoring. An advantage of an oxygen rebreather is that no exhaust bubbles are produced. This feature led to the adoption of such devices by the Italian navy in the World War II; their users caused great consternation to Allied forces by sneaking up undetected on warships and placing limpet mines on them. But then the British copied them – and after hostilities ceased, the fledgling Cave Diving Group managed to buy some sets of war surplus diving apparatus and used them to explore underwater caves. But by the 1960s, open circuit scuba gear had proved to be more versatile and easier to use, so this technology fell out of favour with British cave divers.

But then in the 1990s, spurred on by the desire to dive further and deeper, the cave diving community started looking at closed circuit rebreathers again. The American cave explorer Dr Bill Stone had realised the limitations of off-the-shelf diving gear and had developed his own highly sophisticated family of computer-controlled rebreathers, culminating in the Cis-Lunar Mk-5. An earlier unit, the Mk-4, had been used by Bill and his team for the 1994 Huautla expedition; Ian Rolland had been wearing one of these when he died. Rick Stanton had been on that trip and had subsequently taken part in the 1998 Wakulla Springs Project, where he had acquired a lot of useful experience. I became infected by the rebreather bug after Rick had brought one of his homemade units to a swimming pool in Derby and let me have a go on it. *I wanted one for myself!*

The easiest way to start was to build a simple pendulum-style oxygen rebreathers, as described above. This would be limited to shallow water diving, but would also be useful for decompression. A problem particular to this type of rebreather is that the pipe between the mouthpiece and the scrubber is not cleansed of carbon dioxide. But by modifying a BC power inflator with a bayonet on/off switch, I could use this as a mouthpiece and also add oxygen ahead of the dead space, thus sweeping any carbon dioxide back into the scrubber. The design was hardly original, but it was surprisingly effective. Since I only ever dived in caves or mines, I did most of the testing underground. A steep learning curve awaited me …

Back at our HQ near Peacock Springs, I made some modifications; I pressed a spare ABLJ into service as a counterlung, and fastened the scrubber to it. This time, trials in the head pool of Peacock Springs under the watchful eye of the Park Ranger were more successful. A couple of days later, the P1SS (as it became known) was moored in the entrance to Manatee Springs while I scootered a mile into the cave and back. This was the first serious trial of the device as a decompression tool. On reaching the rebreather, I had to figure out a way of breathing from it without flooding it: I achieved this by opening the inverted mouthpiece while injecting oxygen and putting the bubbling end between my lips. This worked very well. But then I made the mistake of trying to put the ABLJ over my head, dislodging my mask and nearly drowning.

I carried out subsequent trials at Wayne's World, and then at Round Sink near Tampa. This time everything went to plan, and I learned that it was easier to stick my arm through the head opening of the ABLJ and carry the rebreather over my shoulder. Back in the UK, I used the P1SS for some short, shallow cave dives in the Yorkshire Dales and at Wookey Hole, keeping an eye on my depth to make sure that I strayed no deeper than 6 metres.

The rebreather could also be used as a flotation device, by having more oxygen in the counterlung than was required to breathe. This feature came in handy when Gary Jones, a recent recruit to cave diving, Laura Trowbridge and I did a through trip from Old Ing Cave to Birkwirth Cave in Ribblesdale, North Yorkshire. The sumps there are not long or deep, so I decided to use my toy while the others used conventional open circuit gear. Laura surfaced into the deep canal at the end of Birkwirth Cave, over-weighted and minus a fin and a wellington boot … and started to sink … Unlike our open-water counterparts, cave divers do not have quick-release diving weights as the consequences of losing weights and thus being trapped on the cave roof outweigh the advantages of being able to shed them quickly. So I rapidly injected oxygen into my rebreather, fully inflating the counterlung and thus creating extra buoyancy, then grabbed Laura and towed her to safety.

The P1SS's next outing was in early May 2002, a ten-day excursion to the Lot and Dordogne areas of France. A 3-litre cylinder of oxygen and a few changes of sodalime lasted me the entire trip! I used the rebreather mainly for decompression stops at 6 metres, although I did also make a 500-metre cave penetration solely on closed circuit; I also carried an adequate open-circuit bail-out, which included fitting a second stage to the oxygen cylinder driving the rebreather.

Back home, I needed somewhere to play with my toys; a place unaffected by the weather and with lots of underwater passages to explore. To the north of Birmingham around Walsall and Dudley is an area of limestone, devoid of caves, that was once mined to provide lime for steelmaking and agriculture. Linley Caverns Limestone

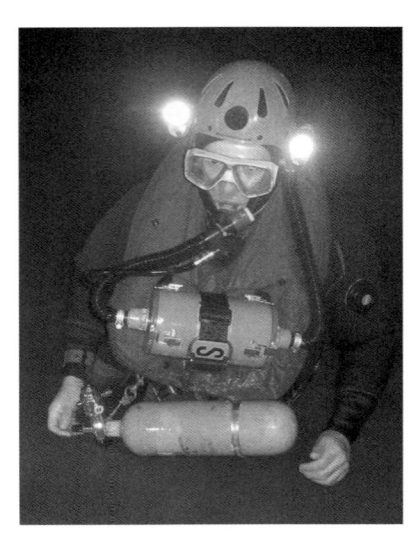

*Duncan and P1SS rebreather at Linley Caverns (Pete Mulholland)*

Mine is one such site, unworked since the 1930s and now flooded. During World War II, its upper levels had been drained and reinforced, with the intention of housing munitions away from the attentions of the Luftwaffe. However the mine could not be made safe as an underground bomb depot, so the weapons were kept on the surface. After the war, the site fell into disuse, and it eventually filled with water again.

*Rick Stanton watches Clive Westlake enlarge the entrance to Linley Caverns (Duncan Price)*

    The Linley Caverns had received no attention from cave divers until Jim Lister and Clive Westlake, both experienced cave divers from the Derbyshire Section of the CDG, took an interest in the site. Underwater, the visibility was exceptional and the mine workings were developed on a pillar and stall network with many large open spaces up to 15 metres across and 10 metres high. The entrance was a small hole opening out into the workings, which were situated in woodland alongside a container depot. In office hours, there was often a burger bar in attendance. It was an ideal training site, especially as I was living near Loughborough at the time and it was close enough to go for a dive after work (or, sometimes, instead of work).

    I became involved in exploration of this maze at the beginning of January 2002, when I was invited along for a tourist dive to the end of the Western Line. This was a route that headed deep into the mine. The team had also explored the upper level to the north, where the munitions were to be stored. Weird, calcified fungal growths from buried timber stuck up out of the floor like stalagmites, and there were signs on the walls dating from its wartime use. On my first visit I reached the end of the westerly route and even managed to lay out the rest of the line on the reel which had been left there. My explorations continued beyond this point to a blank wall, where a small opening (The Hole in the Wall), less than a metre square, with a wooden prop to support the roof, gave way to what was obviously a different mine.

A friend at the British Geological Survey gave me plans of the workings from the records of a contractor who had carried out a survey of the area; part of the road leading to the mine had recently collapsed. The documents presented me with an intriguing possibility: it should be possible to dive in a big loop from this new mine north into a third mine, west into another mine and then back to the entrance. With the approval of the original team of divers, I started working towards this goal.

After a couple of false starts, I found my bearings and started going northwards along a series of workings that I called the Deep Northern Line. I already had a map of the mine and was able to navigate by dead reckoning through the maze. I made zigzag progress in the right direction to a substantial collapse at a depth of 30 metres. In trying to go over this, I made a very frightening ascent though the boulder chaos to a depth of 20 metres, before deciding that a better option would be to go to the west, skirting around the unstable area. But I saw that this would have taken me deeper, so would have involved using mixed gases to minimise the effects of narcosis; it would also add to the decompression penalty that I would accrue. So I decided to put the project to one side.

My interest was rekindled when I learned that another pair of divers from the Derbyshire section of the CDG, Marcus Crabbe and Colin Hayward, had explored the shallow northerly trending tunnel into the original East Anglian Cement Company workings. They had followed the levels that had been modified during the war, which we called the Munitions Tunnels. At their furthest point they'd found the main adit entrance blocked with big steel bombproof doors, and had followed the line of a railway track westwards, to a depth of 20 metres. This was the limit of their equipment and experience.

In the meantime, I'd perfected a lightweight fully closed circuit rebreather, using components sourced from an East German tank escape rebreather and the contents of the plumbing department of my nearest DIY store. Again, I employed an ABLJ as the counterlung, but this time I'd fitted the scrubber with a couple of oxygen sensors whose output was displayed on a pair of butchered voltmeters enclosed in a waterproof box. The development of the R1P (as I dubbed it) was accompanied by an exciting episode; while testing it at Pwll-y-Cwm I'd inadvertently breathed pure oxygen at 15 metres depth and experienced the preliminary symptoms of oxygen poisoning.

At the end of June 2002, Rick Stanton and I swam up the Munitions Tunnels and headed west, following Marcus and Colin's line. We both wore our homemade rebreathers, allowing us to extend their line for 200 metres due west to a depth of 30 metres. The dive was not without incident: at one point my fins caught the line and I pulled an abandoned crane over. Rick was behind me and saw this happen in slow motion as the toppling frame narrowly missed me. We managed to find our way out of the heavily reinforced workings (a relic of the mine's proposed wartime role) into a more cave-like environment (i.e. devoid of concrete, brick and ironwork) *(see colour section)*.

Rick and I having made significant progress towards joining up the loop, I paid it another visit the following weekend, this time with Tim Morgan and John Volanthen. John and I set off to the end of the Deep Northern Line on scooters. Here, I laid out the rest of the line on the existing reel (on open circuit). Leaving a fresh reel tied on at the end, I turned around and let John continue, using his rebreather. He went only a little further, though, before heading out, owing to uncertainty over his decompression obligations; his main dive computer had not turned on and he was using his backup. The depth at the end was now approaching 45 metres. Meanwhile, Tim swam north up the Munitions Tunnel, then west to the end of the Cement Works Line, and added another 100 metres of line to a depth of 40 metres.

Ten days later, John and I went back for a midweek evening dive. John scootered to the end of the Deep Northern Line and continued north, laying line until the reel was empty. Adding a fresh reel, he continued to head in the same direction to a depth of 55 metres, where the floor of the mine was covered in a white mung of rotting timbers. With no tie-offs, John wound himself back to the previously dumped reel. Meanwhile, I scootered to Tim's limit on the Cement Works Line and tied on a fresh reel, but I'd put far too much line on the reel and it kept jamming as I swam along. The depth and level of narcosis (I was breathing air) didn't help matters. After several worrying moments, I eventually got the reel spinning again, and I set off in the right direction. Then, 100 metres from where I had parked the scooter, I was approaching thirds and about to turn around, when I reached a T-junction. Across the passage from me, a familiar orange line ran from left to right, I tied in to this, and headed back the way I'd come. Meanwhile John returned and discovered my line. After collecting his scooter from the previous limit less than 20 metres away, John continued around the circuit, meeting me when I was on my 6-metre decompression stop.

As it was me who'd completed the project of linking up the mines underwater, it was only right that I should do the circuit. My birthday was a week later and I decided to celebrate by taking the day off to go diving in Linley Caverns. We hadn't surveyed the connection point, and my intention was to rectify this during the trip. From experience, I knew that I'd have to do something to combat the narcosis levels at depth, so I brewed up some heliair-30 mix to keep a clearer head, as well as some nitrox to cut down the decompression time; heliair is a flavour of trimix brewed up by partially filling an empty diving cylinder with helium and topping it up with air. The advantage of this approach is that you can check the helium content by measuring the oxygen percentage in the mixture, and as in the added air there is roughly four times as much nitrogen as oxygen, it's quite simple to calculate the balance (that is, the helium). Also, blending heliair doesn't require handling high-pressure oxygen (which can be a hazardous procedure). The major downside of heliair is that it is by definition hypoxic to breathe on the surface, and only safe to breathe once the partial pressure of oxygen has risen to a suitable level.

At this point, I ought to reiterate that my highest diving qualification outside the Cave Diving Group was (and at the time of writing still is) BSAC Snorkel Diver. What I knew about rebreathers and mixed gases was purely based on what I'd learned from the internet and my friends, or had worked out for myself. Rick Stanton (who has no formal diving qualifications either) once gave me accelerated onsite tuition in the use of his homemade rebreather at Linley Caverns before letting me take it for a 400-metre penetration to a depth of 40 metres (on my own); his instructions amounted to: 'Breathe in. Breathe out. Add gas (oxygen or diluent) as required'. His approach to mixed-gas diving was equally simple: 'What's the maximum partial pressure of oxygen you're prepared to tolerate?' and 'How much helium can you afford?' Since I had access to free high-purity helium and oxygen at work, and had bought my own portable air compressor, I was well set up for mixed-gas diving.

For my birthday, I talked Alec Wallace into providing some company. It was his first visit to the mine and he was just planning to take a tour of the nearer parts for familiarisation. We took a mountain of kit underground and left a handline by the entrance to aid getting up and down the muddy slope to the water. Somewhat overladen – with two side-mounted 15-litre tanks of heliair-30, two chest-mounted 12-litre tanks (nitrox-30 and nitrox-40), a scooter and an oxygen rebreather – I set off. Dumping the rebreather at 6 metres depth and about 30 metres from base, I promptly upended and hit the roof feet first; one of my chest-mounted cylinders had pressed on my drysuit inflator and filled it with air. Sorting myself out, I dropped back to the floor, fortunately directly onto the line. Regaining my composure, I adjusted my trim and headed west to the Hole in the Wall, breathing from my tank of nitrox-40.

*Dive base in Linley Caverns (Will Smith)*

With all my gear on, it was a struggle to get though the gap. Turning sideways, I gingerly scraped past the wooden prop (wondering about its integrity) and spotted a pickaxe on a rock shelf nearby. Without time to collect it as a trophy, I dropped down to 30 metres and changed onto my other nitrox cylinder, since the one I was breathing was too rich in oxygen for this depth. Taking the turning to the Deep Northern Line, I was on autopilot as far as the collapse. This was the end of the survey, and I'd planned to collect more data on my traverse. But then I decided that this chore would spoil my birthday treat, and the survey work could wait until another time.

I switched to the heliair for the deep section ahead. With a clearer head, I was able to appreciate the layout of the mine and the route we'd taken around the collapse; soon I was at the connection point from the previous dive and back into familiar territory. As the depth lessened, I switched back to the 30% and then 40% nitrox mixes in order to flush the helium from my bloodstream.

Motoring down the Munitions Line, I spotted Alec coming in the opposite direction. He had been as far as the Hole in the Wall and was now off-gassing along this tunnel at a depth of 9 metres. I stopped and handed him my scooter to play with, as I was just about to start my own decompression stops. But without the scooter I was now very buoyant, and made another unplanned ascent into the roof – above my stop depth. My dive computer bleeped at me angrily as I grabbed at the wall. At least I was the right way up this time, and I was able to vent my suit before I knocked myself out on the ceiling.

Reaching my rebreather after an absence of nearly an hour, I switched its oxygen supply on, purged it and started breathing from it. Checking my dive computer, I recalculated my decompression schedule. I did not own a fancy mixed-gas dive computer, but Rick Stanton had taught me some useful rules of thumb; essentially I treated the dive as one done purely on air (the nitrox I breathed when I was shallow counteracting the heliair I breathed when I was deep) and then did half of the total time of the remaining decompression stops shown by my air computer on pure oxygen at 6 metres. Alec came by on my scooter. I indicated that I was OK and asked him to take the scooter out to save me the effort. I surfaced 20 minutes later. There was no sign of Alec – and no handline out of the mine, either.

I rested by the water's edge until Alec returned and I asked him to take a photo of me surrounded by lots of equipment (which he did with his finger over the flash). We dragged some of my gear out, and I went back to my car to change out of my drysuit before returning for the rest of the kit. On the way back to the mine entrance, we came across a couple of kids and their father with our rope. They gave it back – they'd thought it had been abandoned – and this made it much easier for us to recover the remainder of equipment.

*Moving gear in Linley Caverns (Duncan Price)*

Having established a big circuit around the mine network, I felt duty bound to survey it accurately underwater. Since we already had a plan of the workings, a simple stick map of the line layout would suffice; this is just a matter of noting the distances between changes of direction of the line (which usually occur where the line is tied off to something) and the depth and bearing of the line at these points. But in our enthusiasm for completing the loop, we'd committed the cardinal sin of using an unmarked guideline in some places. Whereas most of the guideline had tags at 5-metre increments, used to estimate distance, a large section of it in the deeper part of the mine was just an unmarked length of parachute cord marking the route. So in order to map it accurately, we made several dives to replace our original exploration line with something more substantial and better labelled.

This task kept me out of mischief for the best part of a year, until I received a phone call from Walsall Council asking me to attend their offices for a meeting with the Police and Military on 11 June 2003. Dressed in jackets and ties, Clive Westlake and I turned up at the headquarters of Walsall Borough Council Engineering Division, to be met by a couple of their engineers, two uniformed police officers and a major from the bomb disposal squad. It turned out that the police had received information that quantities of World War II ammunition had been stored in the mines and had been removed over a number of years by some of the locals. An EOD team had been called in to search the site by foot and dinghy. But they had found nothing, and they found further progress into the mine impossible, as it was underwater.

Despite our initial concerns, the meeting turned out to be very cordial, as Clive and I had come well-prepared with our maps of the workings showing the areas we'd explored. We were also able to show them extracts from a book on World War II underground facilities that mentioned the history of Linley Caverns. This confirmed that despite a local myth having grown up that the workings had been – and might still be – full of munitions, the store had never actually become operational, owing to the instability of the rock and the need to pump water out. As a result, the meeting agreed that there had never been any ammunition stored underground and that there was no record of abandoned unexploded bombs in the area. Notwithstanding this, the major showed us some Home Guard-type improvised devices that we should be on the lookout for, and advised us to report anything suspicious to the police. It turned out that the authorities had been well aware of our activities all the time, via the internet.

Having defused a tricky situation the police and military left, and we settled down for a chat with the engineers to discuss proposed remedial works to a collapse on one of the roads leading to site. A hole had appeared in Bosty Lane above part of the mine workings, and the highway had been closed. This was particularly inconvenient, as the road served the industrial estate alongside the mine, and heavy traffic had been rerouted through a residential area. Pilot borings had been made into the workings to investigate, and our information about what was below the affected area was invaluable in confirming their findings. The council intended to pump gravel down boreholes from the surface into the mine in order to create dams across the passages. Cement grouting would then be injected into the enclosed area so created, in order to stabilise it. Unfortunately the work would effectively seal off the area around the Hole in the Wall connecting to Daw End Bridge Mine and Phoenix Pit that we had explored over the past 18 months, although other parts of the workings would not be adversely affected.

With the news that we would lose access to a significant part of the mine complex, it was important for us to finish charting this area. Already the visibility was being destroyed by a fine rain of cement dust that had started entering the mine. Even after the water cleared, the floor of the mine in the vicinity of the boreholes was turned into a moonscape of white particulate, which buried our diving lines. The East Anglian Cement Company workings remained clear, however, and I made good use of another one of my homemade rebreathers to complete the mapping project. For this I used my side-mounted rebreather, dubbed the D5 or Doctor Duncan's Dodgy Diving Device. It's debatable whether my time and money would have been better spent getting the appropriate training and qualifications to buy a commercially available rebreather, but sometimes the journey is more important than the destination.

Access to the mine became problematic once more in 2006, when the owner of the woodland containing the mine entrances passed away; the area was inherited by his daughters, who became increasingly belligerent towards anyone using the woods for recreational purposes. This is a pity, because the area is a rare resource in an otherwise urban environment. Despite our attempts to negotiate access, the new owners remained intransigent, and the woodland was eventually put up for sale. From a legal point of view, the landowners have obligations under the Mines and Quarries act 1954 to secure abandoned and disused mines and quarries. Consequently, a security fence was erected around the perimeter in 2013 in an effort to keep people out. For me, the new situation was a moot point, since I had moved away from the area at the end of 2006, but it's a shame that this interesting mine is no longer open to visits by cave divers. Several other flooded stone mines in the UK may still, with the cooperation of the landowner, be visited by cave divers, and they make excellent training sites. The large circuit which we had spent time exploring was 1.4 kilometres long, and over 3 kilometres of flooded galleries have been entered and surveyed. Plenty more remains to be explored and recorded.

# 14

# A Close Shave

I'm often asked, 'What's the difference between caving and potholing?' The short answer is that they're essentially the same activity – but for those who are interested in the technical details, I've written a fuller explanation about cave formation and the consequences of regional geology in the text box.

> Caves and potholes are voids in the earth which result from the dissolution and erosion of the surrounding strata by the action of water. An exception to this is a lava tube, which is formed when the edge of a flow of molten rock cools and solidifies, forming a crust; when the remaining liquid drains away, an empty core is left behind. Most caves, however, form in a poorly soluble rock such as limestone (calcium carbonate) or occasionally gypsum (calcium sulphate). Rainwater tends to become slightly acidic from contact with carbon dioxide in the atmosphere (or leachate from organic materials), generating a dilute solution of carbonic acid ($H_2CO_3$) which solubilises limestone ($CaCO_3$) according to the equation: $H_2CO_3(aq) + CaCO_3(s) = Ca(HCO_3)_2(aq)$.
> 
> The calcium bicarbonate ($Ca(HCO3)2$) thus formed dissolves sparingly in the water and is carried away. The reaction is reversible – when bicarbonate-laden water is exposed to air, some of the carbon dioxide will come out of solution. Calcium carbonate crystals will then be deposited as calcite stalactites, stalagmites and other formations, collectively known as speleothems.
> 
> The dissolution enlarges the pores and cracks in the rock, and then mechanical erosion begins to accelerate cave development. Cave formation starts out with the voids full of water, and the rock is removed uniformly to give a circular or (since the limestone is deposited in layers known as beds) lens-shaped phreatic passages. As the water level is governed by the hydraulic gradient from the sink to the resurgence, phreatic passages

typically develop into loops following the rock strata – i.e. sumps (which are inverted siphons). Dependent on the water table, the cave may also develop in a vadose fashion (where the water runs along a canyon with an airspace in the top) and the passage cuts downwards through the rock. Over the millennia, some active streamways dry up as the water finds its way down through new routes. This leads to the creation of a network of passages. Those that are left high and dry can become blocked by sediments from intermittent floods or rock falls. The deposition of calcite formations – many of which are very beautiful – can frequently seal cave passages entirely, and most cavers are reluctant to destroy such beauty even if there is the prospect of a virgin cave passage beyond.

Limestone is a sedimentary rock formed from the shells of billions of minuscule sea creatures that lived many millennia ago in shallow seas. In the Mendip Hills, the layers of limestone have been tilted by tectonic action to lie at about 45 degrees to the horizontal. Cave development follows the steeply dipping beds to quickly reach the zone of saturation (the water table), and this provides the Mendip caver with lots of short, sporting stream caves ending at sumps. In contrast, the strata in South Wales lie in more shallowly dipping beds, and the geology is ideal for the formation of large, gently sloping tunnels. In the Yorkshire Dales and Derbyshire Peak District, the limestone frequently lies in horizontal layers, and the caves develop in a stepwise fashion, the water punching between beds in vertical shafts (pots or pitches), then flowing along the layers in meandering, large bore tunnels (known as master caves).

If a hole in the ground is predominantly horizontal it's called a cave, and if it's mostly vertical it's often called a pothole. The subtle difference between caving and potholing means that the latter frequently involves a lot of abseiling or prusiking, using a method known as Single Rope Technique (SRT). I've never been a great fan of rope work, although I did quite a lot of SRT in my youth. I'm not keen on heights either. After I had taken up cave diving, I preferred to do all of my potholing underwater, swimming along a bit of string rather than dangling in free space suspended by a fraying length of rope. Fortunately the Yorkshire Dales boasts a number of caves that are almost entirely underwater and I didn't have to do any actual caving (or potholing) to go cave diving there.

One of the most accessible sites, Hurtle Pot, is situated next to the churchyard in the quaint valley of Chapel-le-Dale. Its entrance is an impressive opening, probably a collapsed chamber, with a pool of water at the base of a steep, muddy slope. According to the local guide book it's the former residence of a mischievous boggart. In times of flood, the water level rises to overflow the lip of the pot, but under normal conditions the river remains underground, flowing through several known caves before emerging to daylight as the River Doe at God's Bridge Rising, further down the valley.

I'd already made several dives at Hurtle Pot when Gary Jones and two friends, Mark Stokes and Andy Harp, joined me for a dive there in August 1997. We were intending to dive in pairs: Gary and I would take the downstream route to Midge Hole while Andy and Mark would swim upstream. Mark was the least experienced of the group, and was diving on new or borrowed gear, including a regulator that I'd loaned him. He and Andy elected to dive together, independently of us, so that Mark could take his time and not feel under pressure to dive beyond his ability.

Gary and I dropped down through a boulder-filled rift to the left of the surface pool and into the open cave beyond. I took a wrong turn and ended up completing a short loop back to the entrance, but Gary realised I'd made a mistake and successfully navigated back to the route to Midge Hole downstream. Back at Hurtle Pot, I checked my air reserves and decided to swim upstream; I'd not gone far when I came across Andy and Mark, who appeared to be doing an air-sharing drill. I paused and unclipped my spare regulator from my necklace and offered it to Mark. Both appeared to be pre-occupied, so I thought nothing of it and swam on to surface in Jingle Hole. Regaining the entrance, I had a short decompression penalty; I cleared this and made a slow ascent to the surface where someone was holding a diving torch in the water and waving it about frantically.

'Get help quickly!' Andy shouted. Mark was sitting up, propped against a rock, looking very green, with the neck of his drysuit (the one he'd borrowed from Rick Stanton) cut into shreds.

It transpired that Andy had just resuscitated Mark. Andy had dived upstream towards Jingle Pot and had reached the vicinity of the Jingle Junction before turning back. Andy had met Mark at the base of the ramp up to Hurtle Pot and the two had exchanged greetings before Andy signalled that he was heading out. At this point Mark had used one third of his air from his right-hand cylinder, but changing to his other regulator (the one I'd loaned him) he found it hard to breathe. So swapping back to his original set, he headed out, his breathing rate beginning to rise from the stress of the equipment problem. At the next line junction, Andy looked back and saw Mark behind him; he waited for him to catch up so that the two could swim out together.

Mark then indicated to Andy that he needed to share air by holding his hand to the second stage in his mouth as if to say 'feed me'. Complying with Mark's demand, Andy handed him the regulator he was breathing from, and swopped to his other one. They were just composing themselves for a moment when I arrived and passed them. But five metres further on, Mark had more trouble breathing, so they stopped again. Andy held his breath to listen to Mark's breathing and noticed that Mark seemed to be taking sharp breaths in, but was not breathing out. Mark then broke away from Andy, spitting out the mouthpiece of Andy's donated regulator and made a dash for the surface. Andy went after him, scanning the passage for signs of Mark who was found lying on his side, unconscious, one hand tightly gripping the line and one fin entangled in it. Andy freed him, turned him on his back and dragged him the remaining distance to the surface – with difficulty, since there was no air in the cylinder feeding his drysuit. Andy administered resuscitation for about 20 cycles before Mark started breathing again.

Andy loosened Mark's harness and cut away the neck seal of his drysuit. Mark regained consciousness about 10–15 minutes later; I arrived just after he had come round. Despite Andy's request for me to fetch help, I pointed out that it would be quicker for him to go, as I was still in my gear – plus I didn't want to risk getting the bends by running up the slope so soon after decompressing. So Andy went to call an ambulance, and I kept an eye on Mark.

Mark preferred to sit up against a rock rather than lie down, and I assured him that should he keel over I would leap to his aid. Just as I had removed my diving gear, Gary joined us; he de-kitted so that we could help move Mark up to the road, as he was getting cold. But before we could do this, two paramedics arrived with Andy. Mark was walked up the slope to the ambulance and taken to Lancaster Infirmary, where he was kept in overnight. Andy, Gary and I went to see Mark in hospital later that day to check that see how he was doing; Andy told Mark he needed to shave as he'd got stubble rash from resuscitating him!

*Andy Goddard at Hurtle Pot (Duncan Price)*

A couple of days later, I revisited Hurtle Pot. With Andy Goddard (dubbed 'Alien' due to his lanky frame, which endowed him with a passing resemblance to the creature from the sci-fi franchise) navigating, the two of us made the through dive to Midge Hole that I'd failed to complete when Mark had almost died. Although Mark made a full recovery, unsurprisingly he never dived again. Andy Harp subsequently retrained as a doctor.

A little way down the valley, away from the woodland surrounding the hamlet of Chapel-le-Dale, is a dry riverbed. A pool of water at the base of a gravel slope in the side of its backs marks the entrance to Joint Hole, another access point into the underground drainage of the area. A few metres from the surface, the submerged cave passage enters the main drain. Upstream, this can be followed to a point where the route splits into the logically named Deep Route and Shallow Route, as the cave heads towards Midge Hole and other feeder systems. Although at the time of writing no physical connection has been made between the Shallow Route and the Midge Hole system, some of the water here has been proven to come from Hurtle Pot (via Midge Hole) and beyond; the limits of the explored areas are very close to each other, and a connection is likely to be made at any moment. Downstream from the Joint Hole, the route quickly becomes choked with boulders.

Seventeen metres down the valley from Joint Hole is another cave entrance, called Aquaflash Pot. This site was named after the brand of diving torch that John Cordingley (who had discovered the cave) had dropped into a small crack he'd found in the riverbed. He had to widen the hole to get it out, discovering a way into the underground watercourse downstream of the Joint Hole in the process. Andy Goddard and friends had subsequently dug their way upstream to link with Joint Hole. The connection was described as 'very tight' and it's only suitable for experienced cave divers, because the current though the narrow section is quite fierce.

Downstream from Aquaflash Pot, the water eventually emerges from God's Bridge Rising. Close to the resurgence the route becomes impassable, but a side passage nearby provides a flood overflow out of Chapman's Rising. This is situated on the corner of a bend in the normally dry river bed, where a metal grille has been placed over the entrance to protect livestock; depending on water levels, this can be a static pool or a full-blown spring in its own right. After heavy rainfall, the cave entrances of Aquaflash Pot and Joint Hole discharge water into the valley, and when the underground drainage can't cope, the whole surface river bed becomes a raging torrent.

In February 1998, I made my first dive at Chapman's Rising. The entrance was submerged and a good flow came out. I slid feet-first down a narrow rift until I reached a low, lens-shaped passage which gained the top of an underwater pothole. As I had anticipated, the guideline was broken here, so I installed a new line down the shaft into the confluence with the main drain. After an initial foray downstream, I headed in the opposite direction, towards Joint Hole. The route was low and rock-strewn, but as my cylinders rattled along I found the line in good condition. Reaching the bottom of the route up to Aquaflash Pot, I found the way on was obstructed by a few rocks. After moving these to one side, I continued

## A Close Shave

*Chapman's Rising (Rob Murgatroyd)*

to the start of the tight section only a few metres from Joint Hole. The line appeared to be broken, so as I was at the limit of my air supply I headed out.

A month later, I was back in Chapel-le-Dale with Rob Murgatroyd, intending to complete the traverse from Joint Hole downstream to Chapman's Rising. I was pretty sure that the line would be intact from Aquaflash Pot onwards, but Rob agreed to dive upstream from Chapman's Rising just to be certain. I thought that the tight connecting route between Joint Hole and the base of Aquaflash Pot had no line in it, so I carried a search reel to remedy this. Reaching the narrow gap, I found that there was in fact already a line in place, which I must have missed on my previous visit. The slot was very narrow, and I had to remove both of my 12-litre cylinders and carefully manoeuvre them ahead of me through to squeeze through. It's a common misconception that cave divers do this regularly to get through small gaps, but fortunately such extreme measures are rarely needed.

I'd just passed through the tightest section when my drysuit filled with water. I discovered that the inflator housing had been ripped out of the chest of my drysuit, leaving it open to the elements. Fortunately, I managed to reseat the inflator and plug the hole. My suit had shipped a lot of cold water, though, which saturated my underclothes, robbing me of their thermal protection. Common sense dictated that I should make an attempt to exit via Aquaflash Pot (directly above me), but I chose to continue my dive out to Chapman's Rising instead. The line was still in the shaft, and I ascended this to the low passage beyond and continued to the end of the line.

It was tied neatly around a rock.

That wasn't right: the line should go all the way to the surface! I backed up the passage a short distance and realised that the water was flowing up a narrow shaft above my head. A broken length of line fluttered in the current and I realised that this indicated the path to salvation. I tied my search reel onto the end of the line and began to make my exit that way;

although I had enough air, the prospect of retreating the way I had come did not appeal to me as I was very cold owing to my flooded drysuit. As I neared the surface, I could clearly see daylight filtering through the grille across the entrance. Surely Rob should have left it open after his dive? With some difficulty, I heaved it out of the way, emerged from my tomb and waddled ponderously overland back to the entrance of Joint Hole, several litres of water sloshing around inside my drysuit.

I met Rob at Joint Hole. He explained that he'd dived into Chapman's Rising, but had found the line broken just inside the entrance. Thinking that I wouldn't complete the traverse, he'd replaced the grille and walked back to Joint Hole, expecting to meet me back there.

On New Year's Day 2002 I went back to Chapman's Rising with Rob as surface support, having given him strict instructions not to interfere with the gate while I was diving. Reaching the top of the pothole, I discovered that the line was broken again. I replaced it, but the conditions were so poor in the main drain that I went no further.

In the next valley north of Chapel-le-Dale lies one of the most important cave diving sites in Britain, Keld Head, a major spring with a large catchment area. At least three major cave systems discharge water here: Marble Steps Pot, the West Kingsdale system (Simpson's Pot, Swinsto Hole, Rowten Pot and others) and the East Kingsdale System (King Pot and others). The first through dive was made in 1978, from the downstream sump in West Kingsdale Master Cave to Keld Head – a distance of 1.8 kilometres. This feat was the subject of a TV documentary (entitled *The Underground Eiger*), and it persuaded one of its viewers – the 18-year-old Rick Stanton – to become a cave diver. A connection with King Pot was established in 1991, and the 3-kilometre traverse between two caves was front page news. Altogether, the flooded passages radiating from Keld Head amount to over 8 kilometres, making it the longest known underwater cave system in the UK.

Rick Stanton and I had dived in the downstream sump of West Kingsdale Master Cave at the end of February 1993. Once in the water, we had taken different routes, splitting up at the first junction; Rick had taken the Original Route towards the connection with the passage from the East Kingsdale System, while I had followed the longer and more spacious Mainstream Route to the point where it rejoined the Original Route and thence to Yorrurt Revisited Airbell. Rick had passed me on my way in, having completed a loop.

Unlike the downstream sump in West Kingsdale Master Cave (which requires a modicum of caving ability to reach), Keld Head is easy to get to, being next to the road which runs up the formerly glaciated U-shaped valley. As with most caves in Britain, the land around the entrance is privately owned, and the landowner's permission must always be sought before diving there. Owing to the publicity surrounding Keld Head, the farmer is a little cautious about access – a situation not helped by an incident when one group of visitors let their dogs chase his sheep. It might have been some time ago, but the farmer has a long memory, and a familiar face stands more chance of persuading him to give permission than can a stranger.

So with the help of Martin Holroyd, I was able to get permission to dive Keld Head in August 1997; Martin, being from the area, did me a favour both by speaking to the farmer on my behalf and by helping me into my gear, before cycling home without diving. For once, the conditions were excellent, and I swam up Kingsdale Passage to the connection point with the line from Keld Head and continued, to surface briefly in Yorrurt Revisited Airbell.

Having now been to the same place from both ends of the traverse, I decided to return to Keld Head via a different route from the one I came in. This involved following an oxbow passage called The Dark Side, which leaves the main line 100 metres downstream of the connection point and rejoins Kingsdale Passage 580 metres later. The roomy flooded tunnel seemed to go on for ever, and I became concerned that I might have overcommitted myself by choosing to take the unfamiliar route out; if the guideline was broken, I could find myself having to swim back the other way. As a precaution, I started to try to conserve my air by a technique known as 'skip breathing'; some divers claim that by slowing their breathing they can extend the duration of their gas supply in an emergency. But I'm not sure if this really works, as all it does is elevate carbon dioxide levels in the body, leading to all of the problems associated with hypercapnia.

After what seemed like a lifetime, I was relieved to reach the end of the oxbow at the 450-metre line junction in the West Kingsdale Passage. I could now relax and enjoy the rest of my 2.5-kilometre odyssey in Keld Head – I'd effectively done the traverse from Kingsdale Master Cave to Keld Head, albeit by reaching the same point from both directions.

I'd never really had any ambition to attempt the through dive between Keld Head and West Kingsdale Master Cave, but John Volanthen had other ideas and convinced me to tag along. The traverse is one of the classic British cave dives, and has been completed by only a dozen or so people. As I have explained, access is a bit sensitive, but on Friday 10 January 2003 John had evidently caught the farmer in a good mood. After securing his blessing, we decided to dive that evening rather than wait until the next day, in case he changed his mind. The weather was typical for the time of the year – freezing conditions, with a clear moonlit sky illuminating a light covering of snow. There had been practically no rain for a week, and we hoped that by diving straight away we could avoid any deterioration in water clarity caused by potholers tramping in the caves upstream over the weekend. Even so, Keld Head rarely has good visibility, so we expected the worst.

A small mountain of gear was efficiently assembled at the cave entrance. I was diving on open circuit with two side-mounted 15-litre cylinders of air filled beyond their advertised working pressure, plus a couple of chest-mounted 12-litre cylinders containing nitrox-30. These should not be necessary for the dive, but I was taking no chances. John was using his chest-mounted rebreather, with a pair of 12-litre cylinders as bailout and diluent supply for his rebreather. We set off at 6:30 pm with John in the lead. Both of us had written directions for the dive on our slates to back up what we remembered from previous dives there. The visibility was poor – less than a couple of metres – but adequate for our purpose. The plan was for John to lead all the way, but for him to wait for me at junctions, where he would mark the out direction using a wooden clothes peg. In the event of one of us having to abort our dive, it was agreed that we would split up and leave the other one of us to carry on.

Things went awry at the second junction, when John followed the main line to the right but I took the longer and bigger passage ahead. At the next junction, I turned left to join the main line at the 100-metre airbell where there was a five-way junction. After going along the wrong line for a short distance, I realised my mistake, returned to the five-way junction and started up the correct line. I was soon caught up by John, who had come via a shorter but more awkward route. With John the lead again, we continued upstream. We negotiated the next few junctions without difficulty, and we soon found ourselves at a notorious restriction known as 'Dead Man's Handshake'.[3]

I had to turn on one side to fit all my cylinders through this section – the wall was covered in scratches and flecks of paint from previous divers' cylinders. This manoeuvre caused me to lose contact with John, and once in the larger passage beyond I swam up and down the line a bit to check that I was still heading upstream overall. I caught up with John at the next line junction, with its distinctive makers pointing down the parallel oxbow route of The Dark Side.

We were now swimming in a low, wide bedding plane. The line was positioned over to one side in the passage, and we had to keep our heads turned to the right to maintain visual contact with it. Our depth had gradually increased to nearly 20 metres, when we arrived at the base of an impressive shaft. Rising slowly up this, I had to be careful to dump air from my suit through the auto-dump on my wrist; it didn't help that I was wearing my slate on the same arm, which restricted the escape of air. Another awkward bedding plane followed, and eventually we reached Yorrurt Revisited Airbell, where we could pop our heads out of the water and chat. At this point I'd used one third of my air from my side-mounted tanks, but had not touched my chest-mounted ones.

Doubling back on ourselves, we followed the line heading to Kingsdale Master Cave, selecting the longer but easier Mainstream Route towards our destination. Even so, there were several low sections beneath cross-rifts which we had to pass, and with John ahead of me I was sometimes following him in zero visibility. He'd run out of clothes pegs, so at least his wake provided a signpost at junctions. After one confusing moment, we regained the thicker Original Route line for the final slog, to surface in the downstream sump in West Kingsdale Master Cave.

We'd done the 1,900 metre underwater traverse between the two caves, and our time of just over 100 minutes wasn't bad, considering the problems with route-finding and the exceptionally poor visibility. I threatened that I might just turn around and swim out again, as I'd used a little less than half of the air in my 15-litre cylinders, and my 12-litre tanks were still untouched. But John offered to give me a lift to the pub, so I decided against it. Since then, one diver has actually done the trip in both directions, to avoid carrying his gear out the hard way.

---

[3] This had been named after an incident when one of the original explorers had become unable to find his way back through a narrow vertical slot, the line having been pulled into an impenetrable crack. After he'd been stuck for some time, the diver behind him had come looking for him, and seeing his lights had reached through the hole to guide him out; the rescue diver reported later that when he'd grasped the trapped diver's hand it had felt like shaking a 'dead man's hand'.

*A Close Shave*

While removing our equipment, we met a couple of cavers *en route* from one of the potholes high above the resurgence that connects with the Master Cave and its dry exit, Valley Entrance. We were unable to persuade them to help us with our gear, so John and I cached our cylinders near the sump, with the intention of collecting them the next day. We stuffed our regulators inside a bag that I'd brought in, strapped to one of my tanks, and started making our way out. The 6-metre rope climb directly above the pool into the high-level passage leading to the surface proved difficult, as it's not easy to rock climb in a drysuit. But eventually John's height advantage got him up, and I followed. Surfacing at 10 pm, we had ample time to celebrate.

# 15

# In Search of Chamber 26

Wookey Hole Caves in Somerset is the spiritual home of British cave diving. It was here in the summer of 1935 that Graham Balcombe led the first successful dive to discover new cave passages. Balcombe and his climbing partner, Jack Shepard were telecommunications engineers based at Portishead near Bristol, who took to exploring the local Mendip caves. They had reached an impasse at Swildon's Hole (one of the feeders for the resurgence of the River Axe at Wookey Hole) where an ominous pool barred their progress. They tried to remove the sump using explosives, but unfortunately Sump 1 (as it is now known) lay directly beneath the parish church and the locals were not impressed when morning service was disturbed by the cavers' activities.

The pair approached Siebe Gorman & Co. with a view to obtaining some of the lightweight diving respirators then under development for the military. But these were considered too dangerous for civilian use, so the cavers were offered a couple of sets of cumbersome hard-hat diving suits instead (plus an instructor to teach them how to use them). These weren't suitable for the confines of Swildon's Hole, but not wishing to turn down the opportunity, Balcombe and his gang decamped to the more spacious surroundings of Wookey Hole, to make the first cave dives there. Jack Sheppard could not join in the 1935 expedition into Wookey Hole, and the honour of support diver fell to the only woman in the team, Penelope Powell. Sheppard later became the first person to pass Sump 1 in Swildon's Hole in October 1936, using a pump-fed diving suit that he'd made himself.

After World War II, Balcombe returned with members of the newly-formed Cave Diving Group to continue explorations using the aforementioned war-surplus oxygen rebreathers. This resulted in the discovery of the Ninth Chamber, in 1948. More diving discoveries were made in the 1960s and 1970s, when the final air space, Chamber 25, was reached by Martyn Farr in 1976. The cave has a long history as a tourist attraction, and at the time of writing is operated as a show cave by the circus impresario Gerry Cottle. The route of the show cave was extended to the Ninth Chamber by the construction of a tunnel in the 1970s. This has offered cave divers the dubious benefit of starting from an advance base accompanied by a sound and light show.

## In Search of Chamber 26

The naming of chambers in Wookey Hole is somewhat haphazard: beyond the show cave limits in Chamber 9, a single dive reaches Chamber 19. Chambers 10, 11, 12, 13 and 18 are small air pockets, whereas the other chambers represent previous limits of exploration. Chamber 20 is a large, off-route fossil passage leading from Chamber 19. The water flow upstream of Chamber 19 can be followed to the next major airspace, Chamber 22, again without surfacing. But here the underground river is lost, and the amphibious caver must travel overland to a deep, static pool at the far end of the chamber that is the sump which leads to Chamber 23. Muddy, arduous going through one or more (depending on water levels) short, stagnant sumps sees the diver into Chamber 24 where the River Axe is met again at Sting Corner. A brief swim and a clamber up rocks leads to a division in routes, either following the stream along a rift, or an easier way via a rope climb into a dry oxbow, where there is an underground campsite. Both passages reunite at a large lake containing another sump. A further dive gains Chamber 25 where there is a rib of rock dividing two deep pools. From here, the cave continues underwater, down a steeply descending passage to the current limit of exploration – a low, gravel-filled restriction at a depth of 67 metres, first reached by the late Rob Parker in 1985. This expedition, using lightweight composite cylinders of trimix, lasted a week, with the support team, which included the late Rob Palmer (better known for exploring the flooded caves of the Bahamas), Bill Stone and Ian Rolland, all camping underground. Despite visits by a number of divers since then (including an underwater digging campaign), the next airspace – Chamber 26 – remains elusive at the time of writing.

During 2001, when caving activities across the country had been largely suspended due to the foot-and-mouth outbreak, cave diver and film cameraman Gavin Newman had secured permission from the show cave to make a documentary telling the story of cave diving exploration at Wookey Hole. In the absence of cavers tramping the streams which feed the River Axe, Gavin and his team had enjoyed excellent diving conditions. After a few false starts, he even took a video camera to the mobile shingle slope that had defeated previous explorers. Rick Stanton saw a preview copy of the footage, and noticed that the water flow appeared to be coming out from one side of the passage rather than straight ahead. Not for the first time, Rick's knowledge of 'how caves work' led him to believe that something had been missed. He resolved to visit the place for himself, and arranged to have some cylinders of trimix taken into Wookey Hole in preparation for a dive.

But his plans were delayed by a change in insurance cover for all caving activities in the UK, and access to Wookey Hole Caves was suspended until new arrangements could be made. This gave Rick the opportunity to make a streamlined rebreather which could be worn on his side rather than his back. At the time, I was also working on my own side-mounted rebreather, and the pair of us frequented the Coventry swimming baths, testing out designs. Rick ingeniously decided to evaluate the layout of his proposed device by fashioning a carbon dioxide scrubber from an empty sweet jar. At that point the scrubber didn't actually contain any sodalime, but simply acted as a proxy to see if the buoyancy and breathing characteristics would be acceptable. Rick and I took turns with his prototype in

*Rick Stanton with sidemount rebreather at swimming pool (Duncan Price)*

the deep end of the pool. Despite having to flush the breathing loop regularly to clear the build-up of carbon dioxide, the concept showed promise.

At the end of May 2004 we were back in business. I travelled down to Somerset over the Bank Holiday weekend to do a set up trip on the Monday with John Volanthen. *En route*, I received a message to say that the show cave didn't allow cave diving at busy periods such as public holidays; we could, however, dive the next day, 1 June. John and I were joined by Nick Lewis, a specialist in polar and mountain film support,[4] Ian Pinkstone and Laura Trowbridge, to accompany Rick and a modest pile of gear into Wookey Hole as far as Chamber 24. Ian and I planned to continue to Chamber 25 to support Rick – but the line was broken at the elbow of the sump and only Rick and I had sufficient gas supplies to repair this and reach the final airspace.

From Chamber 25, I did a quick bounce dive to a depth of 50 metres before returning to the dismal chamber above to wait for Rick, who passed me in the murk as I was on my way out. An hour later, Rick surfaced to say that he'd found a low arch off to the right and had followed this down the gravel slope, through a squeeze to reach the elbow of the sump into an ongoing tunnel with an ascending rift in the roof. The arch passage bypassed the blockage encountered by Rob Parker in 1985, and the way on appeared to be wide open.

Rick and John made arrangements for a follow-up dive. However, when John and Ian took some more gear in few days later, they found that the guideline between Chamber 22 and Chamber 23 was missing. After making a temporary repair, they reached Chamber 24 – only to discover that a cylinder stored there had been emptied. This was clearly a deliberate act of sabotage. The culprit was temporarily suspended from the Cave Diving Group, as it turned out that he'd also had his sights on the end of the cave and, feeling that his project

---

4 He also helped film the 'river of chocolate' scene in *Charlie and the Chocolate Factory*, starring Johnny Depp.

## In Search of Chamber 26

was being poached by Rick, had tampered with the cylinder then tried to cover his tracks. Matters came to a head when the culprit snuck back into the cave to recover some of his equipment. This was the final straw, and resulted in his expulsion from the CDG.

Over the next two weeks, a more permanent repair to the guide line was carried out. We lugged enough equipment to Chamber 24 to allow Rick and John to pass the squeeze and explore the passage beyond. Nick, Ian and I helped the pair as far as Chamber 24; Laura had started out as well, but had dropped out in Chamber 9 due to ear clearing problems. Rick led off, followed by John who was wearing his small chest-mounted rebreather modified from an Italian wartime oxygen rebreather; although this was less streamlined than Rick's bespoke homemade unit, it was very compact and easy to manoeuvre in small spaces. They examined the roof-rift, but it appeared to close down at a depth of 48 metres. So they followed the main route ahead along a roomy tunnel, but after a couple of turns this ended in what appeared to be a pothole about 4 metres across. The floor of this was at a depth of just over 70 metres, but it was full of large angular boulders; the current seemed to emerge from one side of them. Rick and John arrived at this point together and were somewhat dismayed to find that the cave apparently ended so suddenly.

After the dive, Rick and John were a little disheartened, but they resolved to have another look at the blockage before giving up entirely. So at the beginning of July, they went back, supported by a couple of cave divers from the Somerset Section of the CDG (Andy Chell and Jon Beal), Gary Jones, Nick Lewis and me; it was make or break for the chances of further exploration. We moved a few rocks aside to gain a view of the passage floor below. Some larger boulders were still in the way, but the divers surfaced optimistic that with the right gear (i.e. a lump hammer, a crowbar and a lifting bag) they could engineer a way through.

With Rick's shift work pattern as a firefighter dictating the dates for trips, the next visit took place on a Monday. Only Andy, Jon and I were available to support Rick and John for the dive, and we patiently waited at the campsite in Chamber 24 while they were gone. An hour later, Rick came back earlier than expected, due to problems with the electronic readout for the oxygen content in his rebreathers; the display kept turning itself off at depth. (The fault was later found to be the housing which distorted at depth and affected the battery contacts.) John had continued alone, and he returned after a further hour with more promising news: he'd managed to pull the key boulder out of the end, but as he had only one pair of hands it had slipped back into place.

With John and Rick off to France for a cave diving expedition, the support team took a much-needed summer break. Then the National Union of Rebreather Porters reconvened for business at the beginning of September, with the regulars (Andy, Jon and me) joined by newcomers to the diving effort, Pete Mulholland and Jo Wisely, in support of Rick and John. Rick was delayed in Chamber 9 while making running repairs to his rebreather, but we eventually sent the divers off from Chamber 24 in good time. Rick and John managed to shift the boulder at the end of the sump, enabling John to reverse through the gap, dragging his rebreather behind him. Gaining clear water upstream of the blockage, he could see that the passage continued. But mindful of the awkward return, he turned around, and spent several worrying minutes trying to locate the route to safety; eventually he made good his escape by using Rick's diving lights as beacons to guide his way through.

For the next trip, we were joined by Gavin Newman, who had brought along his video camera in order to record the proceedings. With the latest developments in the exploration of Wookey Hole, his film (which hadn't yet gone on general release) was becoming increasingly out of date. Again, Rick had problems with the readouts from his rebreather, threatening to scupper his dive, but they were taken apart, dried out and made to function. Secretly, I felt somewhat embarrassed, as I was the designated porter of Rick's baby. Each member of the team seemed to fall into unspoken roles in support of each lead diver, and as the third in line behind Rick and John, I acted as the unelected shop steward of the merry band of helpers.

With Gavin behind the camera, Rick and John were interviewed before they set off. Then the rest of us sat down at the campsite to wait for them. Each dive was getting longer and longer, so this time I had brought along some tins of All Day Breakfast to heat up on the spirit stove, in addition to the usual fare of chocolate bars which accompanied the cups of instant coffee and tea; preparing hot food helped fill the time as well as our stomachs. Meanwhile, Gavin filmed the activities and interviewed us for posterity. Nick described the food as 'unidentified meat products' as he spoon-fed Gary a dollop of unappetising mush.

Rick and John came back after a couple of hours, cold but happy to have explored another 70 metres of passage which ascended to the lip of another pot at 59 metres depth, at which point

*Left; Gavin Newman interviews Rick Stanton and John Volanthen in Chamber 24 (Duncan Price)*

*Right: Gary Jones and Nick Lewis in Chamber 24 (Duncan Price)*

they deemed it prudent to return. Significantly, the route had briefly gone below a depth of 75 metres, meaning that they had achieved a new UK cave diving depth record.

While John and Rick were plied with hot drinks, Gavin debriefed them. Some choice comments were made about the tight squeeze that had given John so much trouble on the previous trip. Rick admitted to having 'some' trimix remaining in the diluent cylinder for his rebreather. When pressed by Gavin to expand on this, Rick replied that it was 'enough, but not plenty'– ! With the post-dive interview wrapped up, the team made a speedy exit to the usual beer (at Rick and John's expense) in the village pub where we chatted to Gerry Cottle Jr. about our achievements.

With the news of a new depth record, Wookey Hole was keen to get some publicity. A 'meet the press' event took place on 29 September at the show cave; radio and TV interviews were given in Chamber 3. Celebratory glasses of champagne were offered to the divers in their gear, accompanied by a toast to 'Chamber 26 – and beyond!' With Rick and John still being feted by the media, the support team slipped into the water for a slightly inebriated swim.

The last trip of the year took place at the end of October. A setup trip was planned for 23 October, and a push on the following day. Over the course of earlier visits, I carried in two cylinders of heliair-33 to Chamber 24 in order to do a deep dive beyond Chamber 25. I reached Chamber 24 carrying a large cylinder of nitrox-40 and a smaller one of pure oxygen. But the River Axe was in full spate, and I was knocked off of my feet in a deep pool, dropping some of my gear in the process. Thankfully, Gary Jones was on hand to help retrieve everything (apart from one of my torches). And the diving was called off.

In comparison to trips done in 2004, the continuing underwater exploration of Wookey Hole in 2005 was of a different character. Previous visits had been arranged on an ad hoc basis, and were of an Alpine style whereby the team turned up (often midweek) and took most the gear in and out on every push. But at the start of the 2005 Wookey Season, a well-planned calendar was agreed between the lead divers (Rick Stanton and John Volanthen) and their trusty band of support divers; the dives were to take place only at weekends, so that those involved need not take time off of work. This also meant that there was often an audience of non-divers, who could be persuaded to help carry equipment from the car park to the dive base in Chamber 9. Nick Lewis dropped out of the scene, as he and his wife had moved to the USA to start a family. My personal circumstances had also changed, in that I was now separated from my wife after 14 years of marriage.

It wasn't until 14 May 2005 that I got to do my dive beyond Chamber 25. John Volanthen accompanied me from Chamber 9, and we made good time to Chamber 24 where I collected the cylinders of heliair that I'd left there. I had decided to wear a wetsuit rather than a drysuit as this would make carrying my gear, with only John to help me, much easier. In addition to the pair of 7-litre side-mounted cylinders containing the helium mixture, I carried another 7-litre cylinder of nitrox-40 and a further 7-litre cylinder of oxygen. My intention was to use the nitrox to dive to Chamber 25 and drop off the oxygen cylinder at a depth of 6 metres beyond the final airspace. I would continue breathing the nitrox down to a depth of 25 metres, where I would leave this cylinder before switching to the heliair-33 to pass the squeeze at 65 metres depth.

The purpose of this dive was no longer just a whim to dive deeper in a British cave than most other people, but also to check that the route through the gravel-filled arch was still passable. I almost didn't get beyond Chamber 24, though, as I had problems clearing my ears. Fortunately I'd brought some decongestant spray with me and this fixed the problem. By the time I dropped off the cylinder of nitrox beyond Chamber 25, I was on a mission to get as far as I could. I'd carefully planned the dive using decompression software that I had written myself. This was tailored for cave diving, and allowed me to accommodate the restrictions on descent and ascent rates imposed by the profile of the cave. I wore two dive computers to provide a real-time indication of my decompression obligations, and carried three sets of handwritten decompression tables as back-up.

I'd seen Gavin Newman's footage of the old end of Wookey, with Rob Parker's line disappearing into the sand. But actually being there in person (with a clear head) was like being part of cave diving history. Just before the end of Rob's line, a thin cord snaked off to the right through a low arch and then down a mobile gravel slope. Even in my very streamlined rig, I was aware of the coarse sand running down behind me in the constricted passage as I wriggled though. After a couple of body-lengths, I emerged into little chamber at the elbow of the sump. Above my head was an ascending rift. This had been probed by Rick and John on their first dive together, but the way on lay to the right where the cave passage continued as a narrow canyon towards the boulder choke that had almost trapped John. I didn't have enough gas to dive that far and return; besides, I'd already got down to 70 metres, and in a wetsuit – my deepest cave dive in the UK! Turning around, I struggled up the loose slope to the stage cylinders above me, finally reaching Chamber 24 after only an hour's absence. I was so cold that according to John I could hardly speak. But the effort of carrying all the gear out soon warmed me up, and I had a big grin on my face all the way.

My first exploration dive of 2005 took place just over a month later. I was tasked with transporting a cylinder of oxygen to Chamber 25 for decompression. This meant that I was unable to carry gear for Rick or John, because I had to take extra cylinders to use for my onward dive from Chamber 24. Gavin Newman had also come along, with an underwater video camera to shoot John and Rick as they set off. Although the first restriction was open, there was some concern that the boulder choke beyond might have moved. But in the event this was still passable, allowing Rick and John to push on from the lip of the pot at a depth of 58 metres beyond this. The route dropped down a series of shafts to a depth of 75 metres, where the passage turned into a meandering rift as the floor fell away below them. John stopped at a depth of 78 metres, but Rick continued alone. But then, with the passage narrowing ahead of him, he was forced to descend to wider part of the rift at a depth of 90 metres for a short distance, so he prudently returned to base.

Back in Chamber 24, we were having a miserable time: the air quality was so poor that none of the lighters would work, so we couldn't have any hot drinks. Eventually, Tim

Morgan soaked the lens cloth from my camera gear in methylated spirits and managed to set it alight after drying the flint with the heat from Gavin's filming light. I don't think Tim really should have needed to have used *all* of my camera cloth, but at least we could brew up. By the time John and Rick had returned, we were all keen to leave the cave, especially as everyone had to go to work the next day.

I missed out on the next push, at the beginning of July, as I'd had a wisdom tooth extracted and had been told by my dentist not to dive until the gum had healed over. What I heard about it was the following: given the depth and distance from base, John and Rick elected to dive separately. John was going to use two rebreathers – his chest-mounted unit that he'd worn on previous dives, and his own side-mounted rebreather. Gavin was keen to get some footage of the cave beyond Parker's limit, so Rick went into the sump with the aim of filming up to the boulder choke. Martyn Farr was also present to take some still photographs, so it was all rather crowded. But John was unable to get through the first restriction with both rebreathers, and had to turn back. Rick reached the boulder choke beyond this, but on surfacing found that the camera wasn't running. So apart from the photos taken by Martyn in Chamber 24, there wasn't much to show for the trip.

A few weeks later, we were all back for another go. Technically it was now Rick's turn to dive, but John had streamlined his gear and was ready for a second attempt. Gary Jones and Gavin Newman had helped set up equipment in the cave in the middle of the week prior to the trip, and a smaller team of Jon Beal, his mate, Charlie Reid-Henry, Rick and I put John into the water for the push. Clive Westlake caught up with us in Chamber 24 to help carry out the gear. With lower water levels than in June, the sumps from Chamber 23 to Chamber 24 were largely open, and so the air quality at the campsite was better. Rick was rather bemused to find himself amongst the ranks of the support team for the first time, and was unused to the concept of sitting around for hours on end telling stories. Meanwhile, John was able to push on from Rick's limit for another 50 metres to a chamber at 90 metres depth, where the water appeared to rise through boulders in the floor. With a sense of déjà vu, John was adamant that he'd gone far enough and that it was now Rick's turn. The dive took over four hours.

After the team took its summer break, we reconvened at Wookey Hole on 17 September in preparation for another solo push – this time by Rick, who had only just returned from a cave diving trip to France. A couple of helpers turned up to assist Rick, John, Charlie and me with the setup trip to Chamber 24, but two of the team had to drop out early, and transporting all the extra gear to the end was a bit of a headache for the rest of us. The next day we were back at Wookey Hole, with Martyn Farr and Gavin Newman on hand to take photos in the show cave and get more film footage. This was going to be the final scheduled exploration of the year, and a crowd of cavers turned out to see us off. Rick was put into the water in Chamber 24, with John accompanying him to around 40 metres depth in the final sump, where he placed a backup rebreather for Rick to use in an emergency. Rick also carried a small helmet cam built by Gavin to film some of the passage *en route* to the end.

This time everything went to plan, and Rick reached John's previous limit. He was able to confirm that the route ahead was blocked by boulders. Out on a limb, beyond two psychologically committing restrictions, the prospects did not look too hopeful. However, having pulled one of the rocks aside, Rick reckoned that he might just be able to squeeze through if he took his gear off and pushed it ahead of him. This would have been quite a committing manoeuvre at such a remote spot, so he turned for home, having spent an hour beyond the 1985 limit. He had to spend another three hours and twenty minutes decompressing *en route* to Chamber 24; this exercise required two rebreathers, a heated undersuit and endless patience by the sherpas, Jon, Brian Judd (who came in behind the others on his own), Charlie, John and me. We left some of the gear behind in Chamber 24, to be recovered later.

Over the two summers spent pushing the furthest limits of the cave, 230 metres of new passage had been explored and a new British cave diving depth record established. Given the logistics involved, the distance explored for the total amount of effort is laughably miniscule (about one foot per man-hour). The depth record itself was more of an inconvenience than a prize, too, since it meant that the divers had had to spend more of their time decompressing than exploring. Gavin Newman was able to provide an up-to-date conclusion to his *Wookey Exposed* film, and in 2010 we celebrated the diamond anniversary of the early diving at the caves by publishing the book *Wookey Hole: 75 Years of Cave Diving & Exploration*. Along with my co-editors, Jim Hanwell and Richard Witcombe, we told the stories of the cavers and cave divers since the faltering first steps in 1935 – often from first-hand accounts by contributors. The final chapter, appropriately enough, concerns the events recounted here, and the book received the Tratman Award for the best speleological literature of 2010 *(see colour section)*.

*Jon Beal and Duncan Price in Chamber 9 (Martyn Farr)*

# 16

# Veteran Cave Diver

At the beginning of 2007, I left the Midlands to return to my native Somerset. I exchanged the life of an overpaid and underworked academic for a job in the semiconductor industry, dealing with the by-products from silicon chip manufacture. This might not sound that interesting, but since it involves combustion the role satisfies my obsession with fire. I'd never really imagined that I would end up living only a few miles away from where I grew up, but it means that my daily commute to work now takes me along the spine of the Mendip Hills and past many of its caves.

One of these sites lies in a copse at the rear of a dairy farm, where a small stream sinks; it is known as Wigmore Swallet, and it is unusual in having been formed in Keuper Marl and Dolomitic Conglomerate. The former is a calcerous mudstone from the Triassic period, notable for its all-pervading pink colour, which quickly turns everything that comes into contact with it the same rosy hue. A long campaign by the Bristol Exploration Club (BEC) had opened up the cave in the 1980s. The stream sinking into the entrance had been traced to emerge from the risings in Cheddar Gorge some 9.2 kilometres away and 237 metres lower. This is one of the longest water traces in the Cheddar catchment, suggesting great potential for further exploration – but unfortunately when the main river passage was discovered in August 1991, the way on was found to be barred by upstream and downstream sumps. The upstream passage had been pushed as far as a third sump, which was blocked with mud; the downstream route had been explored through nine sumps to enter a section of open streamway which ended at a boulder choke. This was named Goodbye Bob Davies in memory of a cave diving pioneer who had recently passed away when it was first reached.

The BEC recorded their exploits in a special publication which gave a blow-by-blow account of the discovery of the cave. The principal editor, Mike 'Trebor' McDonald, who had spearheaded much of the cave diving, wrote when discussing the prospects for extending the cave: 'Alternatively, some young bloods may develop the enthusiasm, stamina, resources and wherewithal to make the 20 or 30 trips necessary to dig or blow out the Wigmore terminal choke.'

I had long held an interest in going to see the end of the cave, if only to discover what Trebor had been on about. But I had been pipped to the post by more junior cave divers,

Chris Jewell and Stu Gardiner, who had picked up Trebor's gauntlet and over a number of trips had gone progressively further downstream. In the process, Chris had spotted an airbell in Sump 7, which turned out to be a major fossil route; the new passage was dubbed Young Bloods' Inlet in reference to Trebor's remarks. An attempt at radiolocating the end of this passage was going to be made at the end of February 2008, so I volunteered my services to help carry gear.

After I rendezvoused at the BEC HQ with the diving team of Chris, Stu and their slightly older sidekick, John Maneely, , they (already in wetsuits) piled into a white estate car to drive to the cave, while I followed in my black hatchback in the company of a young BEC caver, Matt Traver, who had offered to help as well, but like me had never been down the cave before. After a courtesy call at the landowner's farmhouse to ask permission to visit the cave, we sped down a muddy track, negotiating a couple of gates … it was two brown cars that pulled up next to a cowshed. A short walk across a field and down into a small wooded depression found us at the entrance shaft, which was covered by a large metal grille. A free-hanging ladder descent of this shaft led to a series of climbs and crawls deeper underground. With each of us carrying at least one bag of gear, I decided to reverse along some of the narrower parts, pulling the bag along. This plot backfired at the first flat-out section, in Christmas Crawl, where my bum got stuck. A number of doubts began to set in: firstly that I was actually too fat for this cave, and secondly that I was going to have to let the others down by going out. But after removing my belt, which had kept snagging on all the sharp rocks, I was able to continue.

*Carrying gear into Wigmore Swallet (Stuart Gardiner)*

*Matt Voysey in the approach to Butch's Arse, Wigmore Swallet (Stuart Gardiner)*

A scramble down over plastic bags containing digging spoil got us to some more crawls, which brought us to a couple of rope climbs and a descent through shored-up boulders. A short drop through a tight slot (tricky on the return because there was nowhere to put our feet to push upwards) reached a low, wet wallow. This was followed by the most awkward section of the cave, a tight vertical slot crossing a blind shaft (with a metal bar across it to balance on) and a tight U-tube leading to a 6-metre-long narrow crack. The U-tube was prosaically named Butch's Arse in reference to Alan Butcher from the Shepton Mallet Caving Club, who had famously predicted that the cave wouldn't 'go' as long as there was a hole in his arse! So after the BEC had broken into the river cave beyond, the final obstacle was named in his honour.

The narrow rift beyond Butch's Arse contained a pair of ropes – one of these was used as a haul line to ferry gear through the tight section, and the other was a safety line to attach yourself to as you squeezed along. Getting out of the rift and onto the ladder to descend the pitch required me to lunge at the chain holding the wire ladder, praying that the safety line would provide me with some protection as my feet flailed around to gain purchase on some minute ledges. At the bottom of Black Pudding Pot, another awkward crawl through boulders got me to the final pitch (Yeo Pot) where Chris, John and Stu had started to assemble their frogmen's apparatus.

While they were getting ready, Matt and I followed a short section of passage to the junction with the main streamway. The downstream sump lay almost immediately to our left, but we were able to follow the river upstream for a little way to the next sump. Once the divers had disappeared into the downstream sump, we set off to the surface. With nothing to carry, we made it out of the cave in under an hour.

We had just changed out of our caving gear when the surface team for the radiolocation exercise showed up; they had obtained a fix on the transmitter placed by the underground party beneath an aven in Young Bloods' Inlet. This was in a field between three surface depressions, and prompted much speculation about finding an easier way into the far reaches of the cave.

My offer to help carry gear was not an entirely a selfless gesture, as I was hoping to get invited to help push the cave in the future. My cunning plan worked, and I was invited along on the next trip. I'd like to believe that the lads were impressed by my caving prowess and good humour, but I think that they just wanted me along to be able to laugh at some old duffer. In any case, the trip was set for 10 May and the diving team was to be Chris, Stu and me.

Chris already had his cylinders in place, and as Wigmore Swallet was practically on my doorstep, I thought that I should do likewise. Peter Bolt (who'd been to the end in the 1990s) recommended that I use a pair of 4-litre cylinders. I had three of these in my shed: but only one was fully functional. One had a broken cylinder valve and the other was so corroded that even I dared not fill it from my compressor. I transplanted the cylinder valve from the dodgy cylinder onto the one with the broken tap after wrapping the threads with a judicious amount of PTFE tape and giving it a good torqueing up with a big spanner. My first attempt at sealing the valve resulting in a leak, but the second one held, and with the assistance of John Volanthen I left the cylinders near the sump; we were in and out in less than two hours (I'd expected it to take much longer). John had to drive home in his caving clothes as while looking for the entrance before I arrived he'd fallen into some cow slurry. His trainers and jeans were not a pretty sight!

As the date of the trip got nearer, several emails were circulated to make the final arrangements. It was rapidly becoming apparent that we were short of willing assistants to get gear into Wigmore Swallet for the dive. Eventually a begging notice was put on the UK caving internet forum, but that failed to elicit any help. It looked like we'd have to carry everything in ourselves.

Arriving at the BEC's headquarters for 9 am on the big day, I learned that Stu Gardiner was not diving, as he had an appointment with his solicitors in the afternoon concerning the sale of his house. He would, however, come to the dive base to help with the gear. An hour later, we were underground. My burden had been increased by a 3-litre cylinder of Chris's that he'd secreted into my bag.

Everything was going well until we reached the tight rift leading out onto Black Pudding Pot; I was in the lead and had clipped onto the safety line running through the rift, when my cowstail (the cord connecting me to the rope) became stuck and I could go no further. After a bit of thrashing around, I managed to undo the karabiner on my belt and swing out of the rift onto the top of the ladder, unprotected.

The next problem arose at the bottom of Yeo Pot (the dive base) where one of my regulators was giving a good impression of a machine gun. 'Game over!' I thought. 'We'll have to abort the trip.' I'd just informed the others of this, when the errant device started to deliver air on demand rather than all the time. I'd wasted quite a bit of gas, but I was confident that I'd have enough – especially as the other cylinder (the good one) had been filled to more than its working pressure. Chris and I, each carrying a bag of gear, set off into Sump 1 a couple of hours after leaving the surface; I went first so that I could see where I was going. We weren't wearing fins, but were sufficiently weighted to be able to crawl along the floor of the underwater passage.

The first four sumps were fairly easy and the intervening stream passage not unpleasant. The air-filled section of Wigmore 5 was different, for although it was only 10 metres long, it was also quite narrow and the passage continued like this underwater into Sump 5. In order to get into the sump I had to reverse in feet-first on my side. After shuffling backwards for a few body-lengths, I gained an enlargement where I was able to turn around and go head-first. Because of the twisting and turning required to get through this obstacle, the place had been named Rubik's Sump *(see colour section)*.

The going improved marginally in Wigmore 6, which was a low waterlogged tube with a series of low airspace ducks with a diving line put through them to aid navigation. Beyond Sump 6, the cave developed into a pleasant streamway with a couple of cascades to a large deep pool, Sump 7. This was the longest sump, at 65 metres and probably 8 metres deep. I dropped down a shaft and over the crest of a silt bank, where an ascending line led up to Young Bloods' Inlet. The floor dipped away again as the passage became lower and more rectangular. Algal pendants hung from the roof and line – I didn't investigate these too closely as they probably derived from the farmyard above. After what seemed like an age, I reached the end of the sump, and two shorter sumps quickly brought me to surface in Wigmore 10.

Having arrived first, I located a good spot to remove my gear close to the sump, which would guarantee me pole position on the way out again. While waiting for Chris to dive through, I noticed that there was a large aven right above the end of the sump. Although some spare diving line had been left on a ledge above the water at about head height, the rock, which looked quite friable, didn't give me the impression that it had been climbed; I had to straddle the walls a little way downstream and crawl along a slippery shelf to get onto the ledge, where I collected the spare line and looped an end over my wrist in order to tow it up with me as I climbed. I could see that reversing the route might be difficult, and the line might be useful to help me get back down again. A back-and-foot ascent of the aven gained another ledge with a large block above me. I managed to pass this with a very exposed move; a fall here would not be nice. Several holds came away, and bits of rock bombarded Chris (who had now arrived and was taking his gear off). But once I was above the boulder, I found that the passage levelled off. A small trickle of water ran down between mud banks coming from a smaller aven to one side.

During the climb, I'd managed to smear mud over my face, close to my right eye, so I carefully rinsed it away while Chris was coming up to join me. I offered the lead to Chris, but he sent me ahead as it looked like the passage closed down. We hadn't gone more than a few paces when I realised that I could hear the noise of water ahead of me. This had to be coming from upstream of Sump 7, and sounded even more impressive when I pulled back my wetsuit hood to listen more closely. We rounded a corner and I looked out into a black hole with a rope hanging down it; on closer inspection, I could see a bolt hanger in the wall at the end of the passage. Chris was able to confirm that we were overlooking Aven 2 in Young Bloods' Inlet, which he had climbed on his last trip. He'd put an anchor in the wall at the end of the passage, but had not swung into it. This was a very exciting discovery; not only had we bypassed three sumps but – given the results of the radiolocation exercise – maybe there could be a dry way all the way to the end of the cave. We resolved to visit Young Bloods' Inlet on the way out so that a rope could be rigged into the balcony.

Back at the downstream end of Sump 9, I went ahead, leaving Chris to hang a proper climbing rope down the pitch. I used the dive line that I'd hauled up to steady myself, but I still had to jump down the final section to the water. I tied on a bag of climbing gear for Chris to pull up, and set off downstream to explore. I passed a couple of avens; then a sharp left-hand bend in the passage indicated a possible inlet up a muddy climb. Sure enough, a steeply sloping rift went off to the south-east. It didn't look like this had been tackled before, and there appeared to be a strong chance that I could end up falling down into a tight bit of the rift and not be able to get back out. So I collected another length of spare dive line to use as a handline, and I took a chocolate bar, which I left at the junction to show Chris where I'd gone.

I used a convenient rock as a chock stone to fasten the line onto. I'd just done this when Chris joined me. Deliberately sliding down to the base of the rift, I followed it for a few metres to a blockage, then I struggled back up the tight passage to a higher level, where it was possible to go on. But I didn't fancy this, so after traversing back to the start of the rift I passed the lead to Chris. He went on to look at 30–40 metres of uninspiring passage which closed down. We later learned that this had been visited by the original explorers and was drawn on the survey. The lack of marks on the muddy walls suggested that water must back up to a considerable depth during floods.

Continuing downstream via a couple of cascades, we came to the top of a short climb, where Chris had left a rope and ladder on an earlier visit. We climbed down to where the stream disappeared through boulders, and a body-sized hole nearby brought us to the top of the aptly named Slime Rift. Chris rigged the ladder amid a maelstrom of water which at least washed the mud from us. At the bottom of the cataract, we picked our way through a boulder choke, entering Goodbye Bob Davies, which ended at another wall of boulders which was, as mentioned above, the termination of the original exploration. We scrambled up a slippery mud slope to one side, in a vain attempt to find a way around the obstacle. Both of us tried digging away the mud with our only tool, a short crowbar. Although it wasn't a very satisfactory implement, we soon cleared away some infill below a large block; it was apparent that we'd need to break this up to be able to get into a promising-looking open space beyond.

We had become very muddy from digging, but by the time we'd climbed back up the waterfall we were clean again. Back at the sump, we had something to eat; it turned out that Chris hadn't brought any food, so I gave him one of the chocolate bars that I'd brought. He didn't have a watch, either, and had no idea of the time. Once we had donned our diving gear, I got to dive out first.

But halfway through Sump 7, I realised that I was making easier progress than expected. The bag I'd clipped to my harness was no longer there. I turned around and met Chris coming towards me near the downstream end of the sump. He followed me back and we held a conference in the little airspace between Sumps 7 and 8. Fortunately, Chris was carrying the bag with the drill and climbing gear, whereas my bag had only contained the remaining food. While Chris went on, I dived back through Sump 8 and found my bag, by touch, about halfway through Sump 9. By the time I reached the branch line up to Young Bloods' Inlet the visibility was seriously compromised, so I had to double-check the route. I surfaced in a large pool, perhaps 3–4 metres across, Chris having scored the prime changing spot this time.

I was just removing my gear, when my mask strap broke. I muttered a few choice words and sent Chris on ahead while I made a repair. Fortunately there was enough slack in the remains of the strap for me to feed some more through, although the mask now felt little lopsided and tight. One of my cylinder taps was leaking as well, but the leak stopped when the valve was closed, so I reconciled myself to the fact of losing a little air when I was actually diving. At least I'd passed the longest sump already.

I caught up with Chris in a large chamber with a tall aven in the roof. He was almost ready to climb up the rope left there from his previous visit, and I got ready to lifeline him. Chris prusiked to the top of the rope and continued upwards, placing bolts and standing on an etrier to gain height. Eventually he informed me that he was in a safe position and no longer on the rope. I relaxed while he went off to explore a horizontal passage to a small chamber with a tight vertical rift continuing upwards. Then Chris set about rigging a rope into the other end of the sump bypass we'd found earlier. We shared the last of my food before diving out. This time as I was the first to be ready, I got to be in the lead.

By 9 pm we were back at the base of Yeo Pot and on the last leg of our journey out. Passing the tight rift at the top of Black Pudding Pot was a major ordeal. I couldn't turn at the end of it, and once I'd pulled the loads though I had to reverse through the tight U-tube beyond it. Chris's bag was particularly bulky and jammed constantly. I split my load into two (Chris's cylinder and my bag) rather than one heavy and awkward single unit.

We surfaced after 13 hours underground and drove back to BEC HQ where there were a handful of occupants. On the journey out I had regaled Chris with various 'war stories'; it transpired that I'd started diving before he was born, so we decided to name the passage we'd discovered The Generation Game.

We were quite keen to go back, and we arranged a trip with Stu Gardiner and John Maneely for the beginning of June. Our trip coincided with a Mendip caving jamboree, and since we had a lot of gear to take with us, we advertised for helpers by saying that a presentation on Wigmore Swallet was going to be delivered as a practical session involving the transport of diving paraphernalia down the cave. But even with the help of two gullible sherpas, we each had a large bag to carry. Because we would be using The Generation Game to avoid the last three sumps, we needed less air for the dives, and in advance of the trip I took the opportunity to exchange my depleted 4-litre cylinders for a pair of 3-litre ones. We planned to use some explosives to break up the boulder in the final choke, but since none of us held a valid explosives licence (mine had long since expired) we had to resort to using electrically detonated snappers. These are a bit like oversized fireworks that can be set off remotely and don't require a licence to acquire or use. They're supposed to be used to break up concrete, but we were going to apply them to limestone.

Arriving at BEC HQ at 9 am, I found the others busy sorting their gear. The snappers had been individually sealed into condoms to keep them dry, and there was much innuendo about the nature of our banging at the end of the cave. We made a tamping rod out of an old car aerial and packed it in with the drill. Stu was also taking a set of camera gear. My bag was deemed too light, so I acquired an additional cylinder to carry, and once our helpers had arrived we headed off in convoy to the farm.

We went underground at 11 am and made good time to the dive base, with no major dramas. John set off first with the bag of camera gear (which was quite buoyant) and I followed with a ladder for The Generation Game. John and I had been waiting in Young Bloods' Inlet for some time before Chris and Stu popped up together. Apparently Stu had been diving close behind me, but had encountered problems with the line in Sump 7; he was just on his way out when Chris caught up and showed him the correct route. We divided the gear between a photography team (Stu and John) and a rigging team (Chris and I) who were to sort out the climbs.

Once at Aven 2, Chris prusiked up into The Generation Game and hung a ladder for me to follow. I took a second ladder for the climb back down into Wigmore 10 above the downstream end of Sump 9. But the ladder turned out to be too short, and in order for it to reach the bottom I had to hang it out over the drop via an exposed traverse. Landing on the ledge above the sump pool, I tried a direct descent of the overhanging shelf rather than skirting around to one side, but I slipped and fell ungracefully into the deep sump pool *(see colour section)*.

## Veteran Cave Diver

Reaching the end of the cave, I set about clearing mud from around the boulder at the end with an entrenching tool. While Chris prepared the drill, John attacked the face and reckoned that some of the right-hand wall looked loose. I applied a crowbar to this and enlarged the gap before the drill was passed up to me. I made a hole in the rock and inserted the snapper (still in its sheath) into the hole, then tamped the charge with a mixture of duct tape and mud. We all retired to a safe distance to set it off. Chris fired the snapper by simply connecting the end of the wires across the terminals of the drill battery. The noise was a little disappointing – a sharp crack like a starting pistol – but the pall of smoke produced by the explosion soon reduced visibility to the point where I had to use the firing cable as a guideline to find my way back to the dig face. The fumes are supposed to be non-toxic *(see colour section)*.

It appeared that we'd not removed enough rock and that another shot would be in order. But just when we were about to start drilling again, I decided to have another go myself – and passed the squeeze cleanly. In the fog It was really difficult to see what was going on, but I made a body-length of progress to another hole, which would also need enlarging. As the conditions were so terrible, we decided to retreat and get some photographs on the way out. I was last up Slime Rift and had to de-rig the ladder. I managed to overtake the photography team at the climb up into the Generation Game and so I reached the diving gear ahead of the others *(see colour section)*.

We carried as much of the equipment out of the cave as we could, and reached the surface after 10 hours underground. As it was still a reasonable hour, I drove Stu and Chris over to Priddy Village Hall (John having travelled independently) where I was encouraged to linger with the promise of some barbecue leftovers and a free pint. Quite a few hangers-on remained from the festivities, and there was a live band striking up in the hall. We didn't have much new passage to show for our efforts, but at least Stu had taken some nice photographs.

*John Maneely, Stuart Gardiner, Chris Jewell and Duncan celebrate after a trip (Helen Brooke)*

A visit in July to exchange some cylinders found that the diving gear had been scattered widely by floods, and my pair of 3-litre cylinders was nowhere to be found. We collected what we could, and hoped that my tanks were not already in Cheddar. Fortunately my tanks were recovered at the end of the month from the start of Sump 1 when John Maneely undertook an ambitious solo trip to the end. He wrote:

> I had another trip back to the end on Saturday (26th), our previous bang job was passed no problem (well if Duncan fitted I was pretty sure I would …). It

leads to a small open section, a climb leads up 5–6 m to a roof jammed solid with large boulders. I spent 45 mins or so digging out a boulder at the same level as our previous obstacle to gain 5 ft in the downstream direction. This heads down to more open passage below. To make it passable there was a pinch between boulders that needed opening out. I drilled and banged the offending article and returned for a look-see. The gap is now big enough to get down but bells out below so returning maybe tricky. I drilled and placed a bolt for a hand line but didn't have any rope. A return is required to check it out. Might just be the short section of standing passage I can see but might prove prosperous.

I helped John recover the gear the next day, and we made plans for another assault at the beginning of August. But in the event we had to cancel it due to bad weather, and the following weekend was equally wet. Finally, John and I managed to arrange a trip later in the month and we beat the rain clouds.

In the meantime, Tony (J'rat) Jarratt and fellow cave digger, Dave (Tuska) Morrison, had concocted a plan to make a dry way into Young Bloods' Inlet from the surface, using a Hymac digger to excavate one of the three depressions which had been radiolocated over this part of the cave. Tony was quite a character in the local caving scene, and had devoted much of his energy to digging various caves, but by then he was seriously ill with terminal cancer.

By overlaying aerial photographs of the area on the cave survey, I estimated that the middle depression was situated directly above the cave (100 metres below) and suggested that they dig there. On the day after my birthday, John and I turned up to find that work had already started and the dig was looking good. Arriving at the end of Wigmore Swallet, John put a handline down the rift and had a look below. There was a tight descending slot, blocked by a boulder jammed across the passage. I joined him in a rather cosy spot and jumped up and down on the obstruction to loosen it; then, while I made a difficult escape back up the rift, John dived in head first and was able to rotate the rock through 90 degrees. I passed down the drill; he put an expansion bolt into the boulder and tied the rope to it. Together, we lifted the rock out. Then John managed to get down to waist level in the continuing passage before it became too tight, but there seemed to be an enlargement below and we could hear the stream.

With no battery power left, we headed out. I had an epic struggle at the upstream end of Sump 5, where I lost my weight belt in the battle to escape. Back on the surface, the digger had exposed an open rift, and 10 metres of concrete pipe were put in to maintain access so that the hole could be made safe, before the soil and rocks were replaced.

The next trip took place soon after this. Chris and John went underground without me, but I caught up with them later in the pub. They'd opened up the squeeze and regained the stream, although they were still in the boulder choke. They had found about 10 metres of passage: half of this was walking-sized. They had drilled and popped a rock blocking the way on towards Cheddar, though no-one had gone back to inspect the damage.

Tony Jarratt died just after midnight in the early hours of 31 August. He had played a pivotal role in the caving scene and had shown great personal interest in our activities in

Wigmore Swallet. His exploits were an example to everyone – not always a good example, but certainly someone who embodied the motto of the BEC: 'Everything to excess!'

Another blow to the team was the death of John Maneely during a cave dive in the Source du Doubs, France, on 28 September 2008. His body was found wedged under a lip in a vertical shaft above a tight section. He must have encountered difficulties returning through that section at depth, causing him to remove much of his gear underwater and manoeuvre it by hand through the restriction. There was a cylinder lying below him unattached to his body, so evidently he had been unable to replace his gear and had made an uncontrolled ascent holding a single cylinder which he had ultimately dropped.

So in the space of a few weeks, we attended another funeral service. I found myself explaining the circumstances of John's demise to his girlfriend over lunch in the Hunters' Lodge Inn.[5] John had worked hard and played hard, and his list of interests on his user profile at the Yorkshire Divers web forum illustrated this: 'Caves, wrecks, fast bikes, wheelies, booze, not all together.'

When a misfortune like this occurs, people react in different ways. Stu Gardiner gave up cave diving. Chris Jewell and I, however, 'got straight back onto the horse' and made another trip to the end of Wigmore Swallet in October. We cleared the debris from the last session and spent a couple hours digging before firing another snapper. I found my weight belt in Sump 5 and left it at the dive base with my part-used cylinders.

A month later, Chris and I went back to see the results of our handiwork. Another young cave diver, Dave Garman, came along on his first visit to the end of the cave. Also with us was a portion of Tony Jarratt's ashes which were to be scattered there; Tony had been central to the discovery of Wigmore Swallet, and a celebration of his life was being held that day, with several events taking place. At the dig site we found that the obstructing block had been broken up, allowing us a view of a body-sized gap into the passage beyond. But this was still too tight to pass safely, so we drilled two holes in the surrounding rock and put snappers in them. We scattered Tony's ashes in the final section of streamway and saw them off with a bang.

My last visit to the end of the cave took place in April 2009 with Chris Jewell and Claire Cohen. Claire hadn't dived in Wigmore Swallet before, so I was persuaded to provide moral support by accompanying them to the end. A digging trip had taken place in the interim, but as the snapper had failed to go off I took a multimeter to check the wire. After struggling down the cave with all of our gear, diving through several squalid sumps and climbing up and down numerous pitches, we all reached the dig, successfully fired a new charge and struggled all the way out again. A lot of effort for 30 minutes work!

After that, my diving cylinders remained underground until early 2011 when I went back to retrieve them. Time had taken its toll, and everything in the cave was in a very sorry state; for example one of the wire ladders that had been left *in situ* snapped when someone

---

5 It was an in-joke amongst the team that John Maneely (32), Stu Gardiner (30) and Chris Jewell (26) were all brothers, and that I (then 44, 'so OLD' as Stu put it) was their dad – we had even managed to convince a mourner at Tony Jarratt's funeral that this was the case.

was climbing it a few months later, but fortunately no one was injured. Heavy rain then caused complete closure of the cave due to slumping of spoil heaps in the entrance series.

Meanwhile, the dig at Home Close Hole (above Young Bloods' Inlet) is making steady progress. Siege tactics are being employed, with a motorised winch and winding frame over the piped shaft to remove rocks and mud. A small crack is being followed down a tortuous route, with occasional enlargements and a promising draught of air; the known cave is not far away...

*Adam Strawbridge and Duncan aged 11, snorkelling in Wembury Bay, Devon (Derek Price).*

*Norton-Radstock BSAC Branch attends the Wess-Fed snorkel event at Bristol docks (1981) (Derek Price)*

*Above: James Magregor, Howard Price and Mark Sewards at Keld Head (Duncan Price)*

*Left: Mike Wright rigging the entrance to Gaping Gill (Duncan Price)*

*Opposite page: 300 metres into Sump 2 in the Emergence de Crégols, near the start of the passage discovered by Rick Stanton in 2002 (Liz Rogers)*

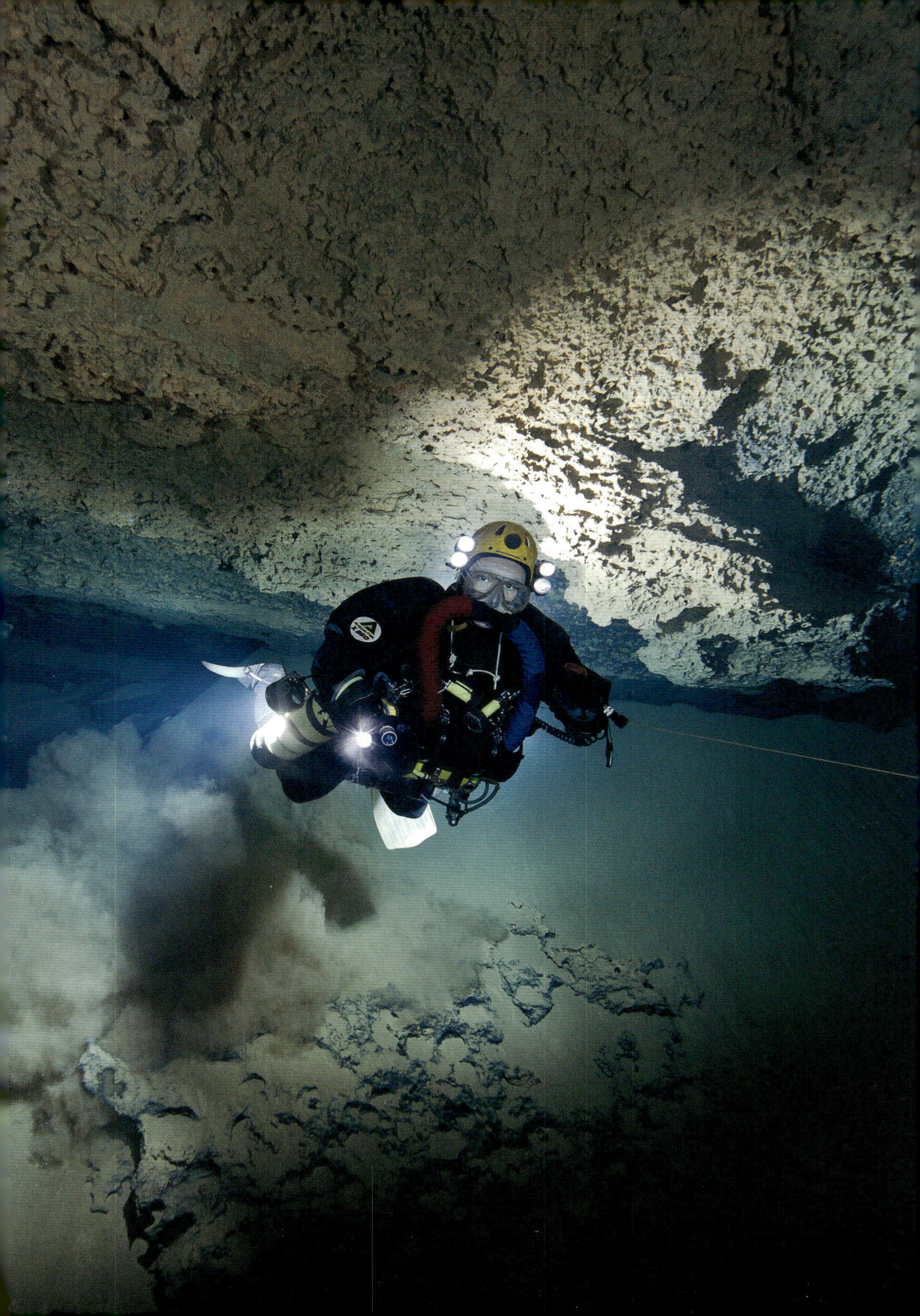

*Above: Spanners, John Hunt (trying to unlock the gate) and Steve Tooms at the entrance to Agen Allwedd, photo (Duncan Price)*

*Left: Duncan, Steve Tooms, Spanners, Rob Murgatroyd, Jim Arundale and John Hunt, 'Absent Friends' Rift' (Duncan Price)*

*Spanners at the breakthrough point into High Traverse Passage (Duncan Price)*

*Mike Wright in the Snowboat dig (Duncan Price)*

*Rob Murgatroyd and Simon Abbott enter the river passage of Maytime in January 1988 (Duncan Price)*

*Left: Rick Stanton at the upstream end of the Gloom Room Sump (Duncan Price)*

*Right: Rick Stanton in the San Agustin Way (Duncan Price)*

*Opposite page: The Shallow Route in the Emergence du Ressel (Liz Rogers)*

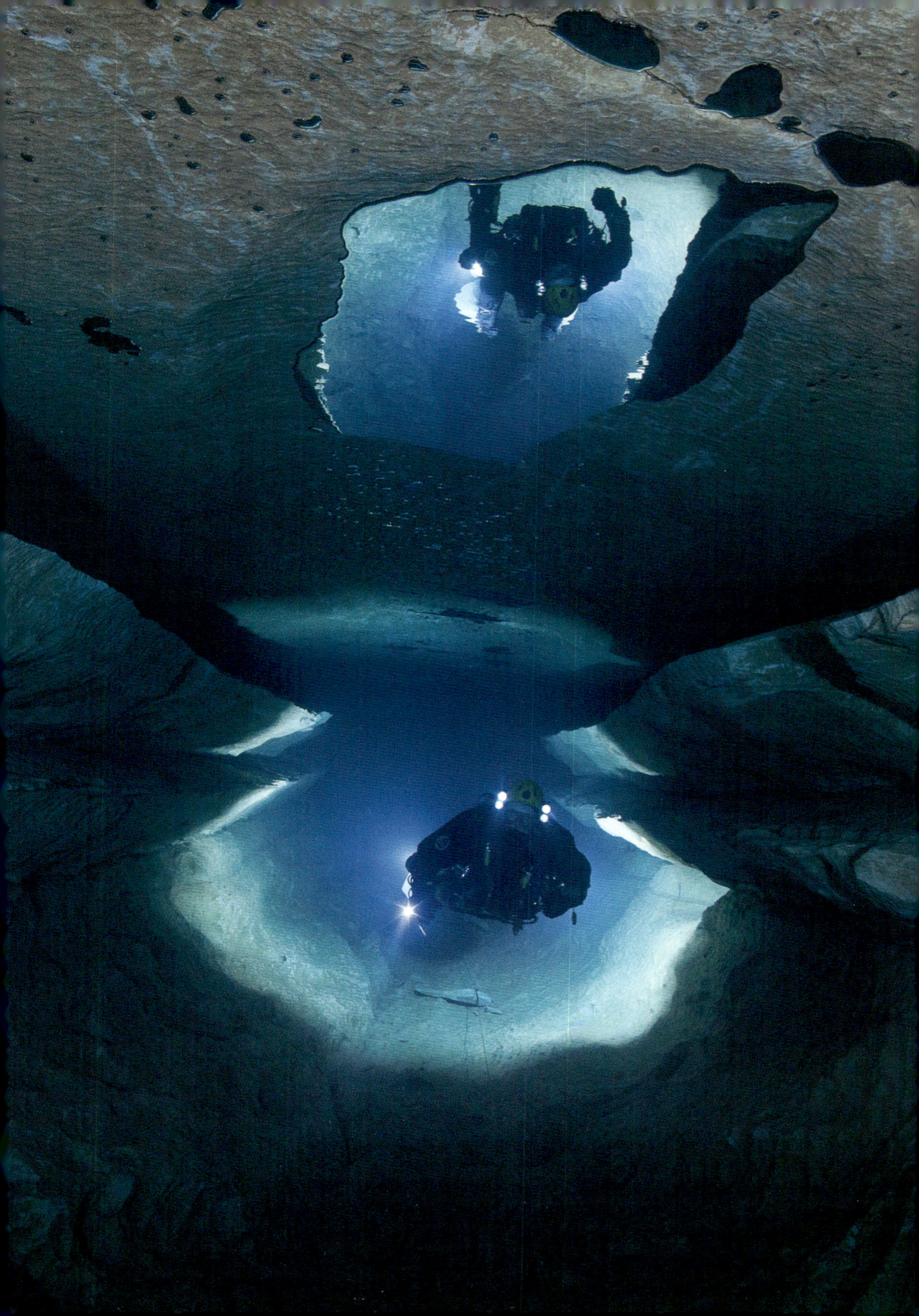

*Above: Tom Morris entering Silver Glen Spring (Cindy Butler)*

*Right: Duncan decompressing in Eagles Nest (Jon Bojar)*

*Left: Jon Bojar models Rick Stanton's rebreather (Duncan Price)*

*Below: Pwll-y-Cwm in the snow (Duncan Price)*

*John Volanthen at Telford Spring (Duncan Price)*

*Rick Stanton poses for the cover photograph of the Wookey Hole book (Gavin Newman)*

*Left: A sign on the wall underwater in Linley Caverns (Will Smith)*

*Below: The awkward upstream end of Sump 5 in Wigmore Swallet (Stuart Gardiner)*

Left: The climb up into The Generation Game from Wigmore 10 (Stuart Gardiner)

Right: The end of Wigmore Swallet (Stuart Gardiner)

Exiting from Slime Rift (Stuart Gardiner)

*Above: Perte de Thémines (Clive Westlake)*

*Right: Duncan's 40th birthday dive at Pwll-y-Cwm (Nick Lewis)*

*The final surveying dive in Pwll-y-Cwm, April 2011 (Martyn Farr)*

*Rob Harper at the sump in Dingley Dell,, Reservoir Hole (Peter Glanville)*

*Source du Marchepied*
*(Liz Rogers)*

# 17

# 'And then the Donkey Stood on my Foot!'

My caving and cave diving career has not been limited to Britain and North America. France offers the British cave diver a welcome respite from the privations of domestic sumps and the opportunity to do some 'resurgence flopping' in good visibility with fine phreatic scenery. Caving is something of a national pastime in France, and the French are less dismissive of those who practise the sport. The French have also given the caving world various terms used to describe parts of caves and caving techniques; for example the word 'aven' is borrowed from the name for a pothole in the Grand Causses (rich in Jurassic limestone) the Midi-Pyrenees and Languedoc-Roussillon, which will feature in the following pages.

But first let's go to Franche-Comté: specifically the *département* of Doubs, where Rob Murgatroyd, Kate and I spent a week in June 1992. We'd gone out in Rob's car, and being short of space had only taken wetsuits and modest-sized cylinders. After a couple of dives using this gear, I was lucky enough to be able to secure the loan of a drysuit (which fitted me after a fashion) and a pair of 12-litre cylinders for a dive in the Source Doubs. This is a major resurgence, and the origin of the river that gives the area its name. The spring is fed by glacial snow melt from the Jura Mountains, and even in June the water was freezing. I should have realised that the dive would not be without interest when one of my regulators started free-flowing on account of the cold water even before I'd set off; I hit it against a rock at the entrance until it stopped leaking – and then I headed into the cave.

The first sump is a roomy, shallow tunnel. The force of the river coming out of the resurgence had torn the thin French guideline into shreds, but the exceptional clarity of the water let me follow its remains to the next airspace at the head of an underwater shaft. This descends to around 50 metres before leading through a tight section into the cave beyond. As I fell into the abyss, the regulator that I was breathing from started to free-flow, so I shut it down and changed to my other one. I should have started my ascent immediately, but since I thought I could see the floor a little way below me, I decided to continue. But no sooner had I touched down on the bottom than my other regulator malfunctioned. No air! I had no choice but to open the pillar valve on my cylinder manually in order to snatch a breath as needed, then turn it off again; this is a technique that British cave divers learn

*Source Doubs (Kate Price)*

as part of their training and one that has come to my rescue on a number of occasions. I repeated this cycle until I was in shallow enough water for the load on the regulator to be reduced enough for it to work properly again.

One of the more amusing aspects of the trip was the ongoing practical joke played out on Neil Rushton. He is particularly well-nourished, and rejoices in the nickname 'Fat Neil'. He and Geoff Ward had travelled out to France in Neil's estate car, and Geoff (who worked in the motor trade) had substituted the car's number plate with a more personalised version. No-one knew for sure whether Neil had noticed the exchange, but as the day of our departure loomed I was keen to obtain a photograph of the stunt, so I fed Neil the line that I was trying to use up the film in my camera by taking pictures of the campsite before we left, and instructed him to stand between his tent and his car 'just for the record'. Apparently Neil had wised up to the joke quite quickly, but played dumb anyhow, enjoying the ruse. But things came to a head when he and Geoff reached Calais to board the ferry to England; Geoff was getting visibly agitated about being allowed to enter the country in a car with the registration FATNE1L. Finally, Neil confronted him and asked him to replace the legitimate plates before they were due to sail.

A few months later I was back in France as part of a team of British cave divers who had come out to the *département* of Isère to continue the exploration of the Grotte Du Guiers

## 'And then the Donkey Stood on my Foot!'

Vif. This cave lies near the top of the cliffs of the Cirque de St. Méme at the head of the valley above the village of St. Pierre d'Entremont. The cirque is a quite a tourist attraction, with ample parking, an ice cream shop and a picnic area populated by droves of French families who come to sit by the river, which emerges from the cave entrance some 300 metres higher via a series of picturesque cascades. A footpath from the car park leads up through the woods to the second cascade, whereupon it takes a near-vertical ascent to the cave entrance, a large tunnel leading into the hillside. The first part of the cave requires no caving gear apart from a head torch, and 200 metres of walking reaches a large ramp down to the first sump. The Guiers Vif drains a significant area, and very few of its surface feeders have been explored.

*Entrance to Grotte du Guiers Vif (Duncan Price)*

Sump 1 and beyond had been explored by a French diver, Fred Poggia, who passed 200 metres of clear and spacious passage to surface at the foot of a waterfall. At the top of this, further short, shallow sumps followed in quick succession, to a final 210-metre sump, ending up at a dry section with a number of leads accessible only by climbing. Rick Stanton had attempted one of these in 1983, and Andy Goddard and another Leeds-based cave diver, Phil Murphy made a further assault four years later. It was not until 1991 that Andy and Phil (joined by more Northern CDG members, Dave Brock and Paul Atkinson), gained a series of high-level passages which intercepted the main streamway beyond its previously explored limit upstream, and ended at an undescended pitch (The Tower of Power) in the other direction. It was the intention of this year's expedition to follow up these leads and hopefully make a connection to the plateau.

At the end of July 1992, I travelled out to France with Rick Stanton to join the others. Rick and I would operate as a pair, as we were self-sufficient with our own compressor and had brought our own sherpas in the form of non-divers: Steve Joyce, Rick's girlfriend, Angela, and my wife, Kate. We even had underground camping gear should the need arise. After we had done the first of many gruelling slogs up to the cave, Rick and I were ready to go. Meanwhile, Phil and Paul dived to the end of Sump 6 to check the condition of the guidelines.

For our first trip, Dave and Andy were to investigate the Tower of Power area, while Rick and I were to work in the lower levels beyond the end of Sump 6. Wearing two side-mounted 7-litre bottles and a chest-mounted 12-litre tank, I was last to enter Sump 1. But 60 metres into the dive, I experienced multiple regulator failures, when two out of three of my valves free-flowed; luckily, I was able to limp home on the remaining cylinder.

Back at dive base, I removed my cylinders and packed up my regulators for fettling back at the campsite. Leaving the cave still in my wetsuit, I was lucky enough to bump into a gang of Leeds University cavers; they kindly helped me out of my neoprene prison and took me on a caving trip to explore some of the oxbows in the entrance series. Meanwhile, Rick gave up waiting for me, and joined the others to descend the Tower of Power. This dropped into the underground river between Sump 3 and Sump 4. Rick, Dave and Andy then set out from the Tower of Power to explore another route (called Golden Shower Passage) as far as a deep pool which looked tricky to cross, so they left for it another time.

I spent the day after my aborted trip at camp, servicing gear and filling cylinders before going to the swimming pool in St Pierre de Chartreuse – where I showed off my free-diving ability by covering four widths of the crowded pool without surfacing. Certain members of the expedition remarked that considering the reliability of my diving gear it was just as well that I could hold my breath so long. While we made another carry up to the cave, another team pushed upstream to reach a sump. They climbed above this into a higher level, which terminated in a large chamber with an undescended pitch.

My next dive was more successful: I surfaced beneath the waterfall at the upstream end of Sump 1, discarded one cylinder and hauled myself up a climb wearing the rest of my diving gear. Rick followed me and led off through the next two sumps. Having left one tank behind, I was now underweighted, and bumped off the roof of the underwater passage all the way. At the end of Sump 3 we exchanged our diving gear for SRT kit, to climb up the rope into the Tower of Power. Our first target was to continue the exploration of Golden Shower Passage beyond the pool. This turned out to be only waist deep, and brought us to a T-junction with a major passage. Rick took the right-hand lead down a calcite slope directly to a sump pool, while I explored the gradually ascending passage to a duck decorated with calcite straws in the roof.

Returning to collect Rick, we surveyed as far as the duck. Having wallowed through it, I was encouraged to find myself in a handsome continuation. When I reported this, Rick followed reluctantly (since he wasn't wearing a wetsuit jacket). Then the passage stopped abruptly, overlooking a large trunk route. The place looked familiar to Rick and we scrambled down, to discover that we'd come out through the end of Cardiac Passage. This had been explored as far as the duck last year and had been named in dubious taste after someone at the campsite had had a heart attack on the team's last night there. We returned downstream to the Tower of Power, where I was dispatched back through the duck to collect our climbing gear which we had left at the start of Golden Shower Passage.

After a food stop, we set off to explore upstream where a series of climbs brought us level with a cascade which represented the limit of exploration in 1991. We passed the waterfall via a traverse and a little further on noted an inlet on the left, which we vowed to look at it on our return. We enjoyed some fine caving following the stream until we reached a sump in a deep rift. An obvious climb up to the right gained entry into a dry high-level passage called The Aorta. Collecting various bits of climbing equipment, we went to the furthest point of exploration – a rubble slope overlooking an overhanging drop into a chamber. Rick rigged a rope and abseiled down. In order to save time I followed by simply wrapping the rope around me and sliding down it. The chamber was floored with boulders cemented together by calcite. We thought we could hear the sound of a large river through gaps between the rocks, but there was no way through short of a major excavation. I located a promising hole emitting a strong draught of air, and optimistically scratched the instruction 'DIG HERE' nearby.

A little disappointed, we left some gear for a future party to use, and returned downstream. Reaching the inlet we'd seen earlier, I squeezed along a rift and summoned Rick to follow. Suddenly the passage opened out at the base of an enormous aven 10 metres wide and 40 metres long, rising to an indiscernible height. Drips of water fell from the roof, giving the impression that we had stepped outside at night during a shower of rain. This cathedral appeared to be divided in two by a rock fall, and continued along a fault line before closing down. The chamber was pretty awesome and was subsequently christened Secret Aven, although on our survey notes we had initially labelled it simply 'BIG'.

With our spirits lifted by this discovery, Rick and I headed out, checking a few more side leads *en route*. Each of us carried an empty cylinder down the hill for re-filling, and we arrived back at the campsite just before midnight.

Meanwhile, Fred Poggia had rolled up for a trip with Dave and Andy (who were both suffering from food poisoning). Angela and I encountered him striding through the entrance series when we were up at the cave delivering some more gear, and he made the point of shaking our hands and wishing us good day in broken English before going to join the others. Now in his forties, Fred was slightly eccentric, bloody tough and a very talented diver.

Dave, Andy and Fred spent over four hours digging through Cholesterol Choke (which Rick and I had found on our previous trip) to discover that the sound of the river was just the noise of a strong draught of air. Thinking that they were into new territory, they then found that they were not the first cavers to enter the passage: they had thus managed to connect the Guiers Vif with a side gallery in the Trou des Flammes, a cave first explored by an English team in the 1970s and later extended to a 10-kilometre system by a secretive consortium of three local cavers.

Naturally, although this development did take the edge off of our expedition, we were all very pleased; Fred Poggia was over the moon and went around shaking even more hands with great gusto, promising to bring a crate of champagne for the team. Unfortunately we had to depart before he could return, so we would miss his celebrations.

Rick and I made one more trip into the cave, to tackle the high-level sump we'd discovered at the end of Golden Shower Passage. Setting off with a pair of cylinders, Rick disappeared into the water. Ten minutes later he returned to say that he'd surfaced after 25 metres and the passage continued above water. We split the bottles between us, and using one cylinder each traversed the shallow, murky sump. We explored a gently descending dry streambed, enticed onwards by the sound of a river in the distance. Rounding a corner, we were halted by a 10-metre drop to a familiar-looking section of passage. Rick climbed down to confirm that we'd arrived at the downstream end of Sump 2, not far from the waterfall into Sump 1. We surveyed the path back to our discarded diving gear and checked that we hadn't missed anything.

Our last day in the area was spent collecting our remaining equipment. Unfortunately after we left, the skies opened and it rained incessantly for several days; Sump 1 rose by around 20 metres, submerging the diving gear left nearby. With the end of the expedition looming and with lots of expensive gear still in the cave, Dave and Andy managed to get through the sumps to attempt an exchange trip with a party in the Trou des Flammes. Although the other group got lost and failed to meet them, at least Dave and Andy were able to recover the kit that had been left behind.

In the summer of 1987 Kate and I drove to the commune of Gramat in the *département* of Lot in the Midi-Pyrénées. We had gone out a few days ahead of Rick and Angela in order to do some sightseeing before the house we had rented would be overrun by cave divers. Before leaving the UK, I had purchased a backplate and wing buoyancy compensator in order to try continental-style backmount diving using large cylinders. But after a couple of tense dives in this rig, I found that I was more comfortable employing the configuration that I used at home – indeed, the French refer to sidemount diving as *plongée à l'anglaise* (English-style diving).

The highlight of the holiday was the opportunity for me to do some long and deep cave dives in clear water. I visited such classic sites as the Trou Madame and the Emergence Ressel. The latter is a well-known site, with its entrance in the bed of the River Célé. Rick had teamed up with Jason Mallinson, with whom he would go on to forge a very successful cave diving partnership; at this point the pair were just building up to some extremely bold diving here, which resulted in significant extensions to the cave. I helped Rick by lending him some of my cylinders to use as stage tanks. In return for this favour, Rick loaned me his new scooter, an Oceanic Mako model, to take for a dive in the Source de Saint Sauveur. At the time, the spring was not officially open to cave diving, and we'd heard rumours of the police turning up and confiscating divers' gear. Because of this, Martin Holroyd and I made an early start and were in the water before 9 am. This suited our purposes nicely, as we'd both been accompanied to France by our partners, and it meant that we could avoid domestic discord by spending the afternoon with them … if only we'd thought of that sooner!

With strict instructions from its owner not to take the scooter deeper than 55 metres, I set off into the cave. The Source de Saint Sauveur descends rapidly down an underwater gravel scree slope for over 70 metres, and I monitored my depth closely as I was propelled along. Then, as if to remind me, just as I reached 55 metres my computer went *Bleep!* and the display went blank. This left me in a bit of a fix, so I turned around and motored back to the entrance area, in sight of daylight, to a depth (which I reckoned would be around 15 metres. Here I handed the scooter to Martin and wrote a message on my slate along the lines of 'My computer is broken: I'll wait here for a while'. I contemplated the leeches which inhabited the cavern zone as I swam in circles while Martin enjoyed a ride on the scooter. Then a buzzing sound indicated his return and I sidled up to him underwater to sneak a look at his dive computer. Like me, he'd just done a bounce dive and so had no decompression obligation, so with some relief we surfaced together.

In 2000, I made another visit to the Lot area with a group of friends from the Welsh section of the Cave Diving Group. We were joined by Clive Westlake, who was older and more sensible than us youngsters. Two of his friends, Brian Hague and his girlfriend Liz (now his wife) turned up later. Brian acted as team mechanic – fixing the borrowed compressors which we repeatedly broke – and when Liz wasn't helping Brian put his gear on she acted as mother hen to keep the boys in check. Unlike the rest of the group, Brian had not adopted the convenient American sidemount configuration, so after putting his cylinders on he had to be pulled to his feet.

There was a certain amount of friendly rivalry within the team, particularly between Ian Pinkstone and myself, about who could do the 'best' dives; Ian worked in the City of London, and consequently had a lot of nice shiny gear as opposed to our unreliable tat. We were fortunate with the weather, so the water in many of the caves was unusually clear. At the Gouffre Cabouy, I was able to make a through dive to the Gouffre de Pou Meyssen (some 800 metres) on my first dive there. I surfaced to meet Gary Jones, who had driven to the Pou Meyssen end, and went for a short dive with him in the upstream continuation of the cave, then I returned overland to the Cabouy with my gear. I had walked halfway there when I regretted not having asked Gary to undo my shoulder entry drysuit zip … I couldn't get out unaided, nor could I hold on any longer. This subsequently left Ian with the dubious privilege of letting me out of my smelly drysuit.

Our headquarters for the fortnight was a campsite just outside Gramat, opposite a safari park. There was a small swimming pool to relax in, and a communal area which hosted various entertainments. Out of deference to our fellow holidaymakers, we found a secluded layby about a mile away from the campsite to run our noisy portable compressors. We would take turns to fill our cylinders while the others lounged by the pool. We didn't realise that behind the double chain link fences next to our temporary air station was the Centre d'Études de Gramat – a military base dedicated to studying the resilience of weapon systems to nuclear and conventional attack …

We had only just set up our three compressors and started filling cylinders when the local Gendarmerie pulled up, nervously (we outnumbered them) fingering their side arms. 'Nous sommes spéléo plongeurs Anglais,' we declared and showed them a rag-tag collection of documents in support of our claim. Once we had convinced the authorities that we presented no threat to the Fifth Republic, they departed – although it then became common for the police to drive by whenever we were there, and wave to us.

*Filling cylinders beside the road (Duncan Price)*

Having found the Gouffre Cabouy in good condition, Gary and I decided to attempt to traverse the sump upstream from Gouffre de Pou Meyssen into the large cave passage beyond. This is a dive of 1,250 metres with a maximum depth of 24 metres. Using the goodwill of other team members, we borrowed the necessary cylinders, and employed the services of Brian Hague and his off-road motorbike to ferry our gear to the entrance. Both of us wore a pair of 15-litre cylinders and another pair of 12-litre cylinders. But then Gary had to turn back early due to buoyancy problems. Surfacing beyond the sump in a little over an hour, I continued to swim for some distance to the end of a deep-water canal, where I found a suitable spot to remove my gear. I wished Gary had been with me, as I needed to empty my bladder again and I was once again trapped in a neoprene prison. Once I'd made myself (un)comfortable I continued up a majestic river passage to Sump 2 where I found the line was broken, before I undertook the long (and damp) dive out.

As well as visiting the mainly flooded caves of the area, we did a photographic trip with Clive down one of the dry caves, the Perte de Thémines (one of the sources of the River Ouysse that we had been swimming in further downstream). Our visit was notable for a modification that we made to the entrance pitch, when the boulder that I was standing on at the top of the entrance shaft decided that it would prefer to be elsewhere. I deftly leapt to one side as it went from under my feet. Martin Groves had just stepped off the bottom of the ladder and I shouted a warning to him. Fortunately the rock jammed across the shaft halfway down, turning the descent into an easy free climb – just as well, since the rock fall had sliced through the wire ladder. We were lucky that no one had been hurt or trapped *(see colour section)*.

In 2001, we staged another invasion of the French phreas. This time we had a two-site holiday, spending the first week in the Languedoc area before relocating to Gramat. Languedoc includes the three *départments* of Aveyron, Gard and Hérault; the last is the one that British cave divers usually refer to when talking about this part of France. Languedoc is further from the Channel ports than the Lot, and much hillier, and its most attractive cave diving sites can be some distance from the highway.

## 'And then the Donkey Stood on my Foot!'

Jon Bojar flew over from Florida to join me for the trip. I was recovering from a biopsy on the lymph nodes in my neck and was under strict instructions to keep the wound dry. I had insured Jon to drive my right-hand drive SUV, but when he told me that he'd left his driver's licence at home, I thought the better of it and did the 14-hour drive to our campsite singlehanded.

Jon proved to be a bad influence on me, as we did a number of deep air dives both in the Hérault and later in the Lot. On one occasion, he and I visited the Résurgence de Gourneyrou where, when we were 380 metres into the cave, we reached a depth of 70 metres. Jon and I had not intended to dive so deep; at a depth of 60 metres I had tried to turn around by putting air into my drysuit – but I continued to plummet down the underwater shaft I was in, until I came to equilibrium. I felt fine until I started to swim up the shaft, at which point the cave seemed to spin around me. So taking a firm grip on the line, I added more air to my drysuit to let my buoyancy do the work for me until I was in shallower water.

Clive had used his network of contacts to arrange a dive in the Source L'Esperelle near La Roque-Sainte-Marguerite; the source is a public water supply, so permission to visit the site is difficult to secure. It seemed as if the population of the whole village had turned up for a communal picnic to observe our antics. Avoiding the crowds and the danger of being swept through the sluice gate at the entrance, we set off. Tim Morgan, Jon and I arrived at the bottom the shaft at a depth of 60 metres, whereupon Jon disappeared down a tight rift towards the end of the line while I waited, somewhat concerned, as Tim followed him. Clive, the last to enter the water, didn't get to see much of the cave.

Despite being more mature than the rest of us, Clive outdid Jon and me by diving to 74 metres in the St Sauveur (in the Lot) using trimix. We weren't far behind, breathing air, but we were out of the water before Clive owing to our more cavalier approach to decompression. During our time in Hérault, we had adopted the +1 metre decompression stop in the nearest bar as a matter of course before driving over the high ridges between valleys back to our base. So when Clive surfaced, Jon and I were busy rehydrating on French beer which we'd chilled in the entrance pool.

*Tim, Duncan and Gary in an airbell in the Emergence du Ressel (Jon Bojar)*

At the end of April 2002, I returned to the Lot area with Rick Stanton, Jason Mallinson and Rich Hudson; Rich effectively acted as Jason's assistant, filling the same role that I had adopted with Rick. At the time, Rick and Jason were preoccupied with exploring the further reaches of the Fontaine St Georges near Montvalent. This is the resurgence for the spectacular show cave of the Gouffre de Padirac, and a year later Rick was successful in connecting the two caves. In 2002, Rick and Jason were just starting out on this venture, but already tensions were developing in their partnership owing to differences in personality; Jason's autocratic approach did not mesh well with Rick's more relaxed attitude. At one point the pair weren't speaking to one another, leaving Rich and me to act as go-betweens.

I'd recently bought Rick's Mako scooter from him, and in three dives I took it to the limits of its capabilities. I also employed mixed-gas diving techniques to minimise decompression and reduce narcosis. In the Source de Landenouse and the Emergence de Ressel, I took the little scooter to the limit of its depth and distance rating; its batteries were dying as I returned to the entrance of the Ressel, as I was wearing a lot of gear and had towed Rich back from 650 metres to the base of the shaft 400 metres in. Rich was very grateful for this, because his dive computer had thrown a wobbly and now indicated a substantial decompression penalty. At the entrance, I passed Rich the oxygen cylinder from my homemade rebreather so that he could complete his final stop.

*Jason Mallinson at the Fontaine St Georges (Duncan Price)*

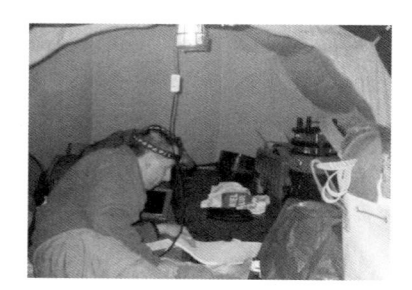

The day after my dive in the Ressel, I parked my scooter 900 metres from the entrance of the Fontaine St Georges, and continued down to the elbow of Sump 2 at a depth of 78 metres using an assortment of gases. I did the oxygen decompression necessary for the dive out while scootering along the shallow section of Sump 2; I did this by removing my dive computer from my wrist and strapping it to the top of my scooter so that I could keep an eye on it to hold my depth at a constant 6 metres. During our holiday, we had frequently bumped into a group of divers who had adopted a unified team diving approach known as 'Doing It Right' (DIR). Their philosophy (which had originated in Florida) was that all divers should use the same gear for every cave dive – an approach which fostered good cooperation and dive planning. In contrast, our continuously changing equipment configuration and self-sufficient mentality appeared to an outsider somewhat anarchic; however, our highly adaptable approach of tailoring the gear to suit each cave dive generally saw us go in further than the DIR divers did.

*Rick Stanton plans a dive using my laptop (Duncan Price)*

As if to reinforce our cavalier approach to cave diving, two days later Rick and I undertook a reconnaissance into the Emergence de Crégols. We had just visited the Source de Lacaunhe, where I had been cajoled into diving the miserable Sump 4 after an exhausting traverse of the carbon dioxide-laden approach passages. The underwater cave passage in the terminal sump was sufficiently notable for its small size and disgusting mud that for it I coined the word Clogwynesque (after Ogof Clogwyn in the Clydach Gorge, where I'd explored a similarly uninspiring passage). Rich and Jason had helped us at the Lacaunhe, but were leaving for England, so didn't accompany us to the Crégols.

After surfacing amongst boulders at the end of Sump 1, an easy climb gained a section of spacious river cave which ended at what Rick described at the time as the 'best sump in France'. We dropped down a roomy shaft and peered into the horizontal continuation from the bottom at a depth of 25 metres. This is as far as we could go, as both of us were diving on single cylinders: I was on one of the partially used 7-litre cylinders that I had taken into Lacaunhe, and Rick was using a 4-litre oxygen cylinder from his rebreather which he had topped up with some air. Neither us was wearing fins, and we both admitted to thinking 'is this wise?' before we scrambled up the mobile gravel slope at the base of the shaft and climbed, hand over hand up the thick rope that hung down from the airspace above.

We returned the next day, wearing drysuits and with ample breathing supplies. Rick carried his KISS rebreather in a bag through Sump 1 with his bailout tanks side-mounted. I wore a pair of 15-litre cylinders of air and had to remove one to get through the sump. Rick rebuilt his rebreather at the start of Sump 2 and followed the fragmentary line for 290 metres to the base of an ascending ramp which rises from 43 metres to surface amongst boulders. Being cave-savvy, Rick noticed an undercut to the right and decided to investigate. Since he expected the route to be an oxbow to the main tunnel, he did not lay a guideline as the visibility was so good.

*Rick Stanton reassembles his rebreather at the start of Sump 2 in the Emergence de Crégols (Duncan Price)*

But instead of it re-joining the main passage, Rick discovered that he was in a separate trunk route upstream. He ascended a shaft to a depth of 20 metres before laying what meagre supplies of line he carried. The cave continued wide open. Aware that he was well past the end of the main line, up an unknown and unmarked side tunnel, he decided to turn around, and caught up with me when I was decompressing at the start of Sump 2. Meanwhile I had continued along the original line for 370 metres, almost to the end of the sump, but I had not noticed the newly found continuation. We travelled back to England a few days later and Rick swore me to secrecy until he would be able to return to France to continue exploration there.

I took an extended break from cave diving in France and did not return until August 2009. My girlfriend Antoinette and I spent 10 days at our friends' holiday home in Saint-Privat, Hérault. We had driven out in Antoinette's 4x4 which I had filled with a large quantity of diving gear including my portable electrically powered compressor. But after I made my first dive (in the Source du Durzon), I discovered that the rating of the domestic supply could not cope with the starting current of my pump. The only way around this was to leave the compressor in the car overnight so that it stayed warm and was easier to turn over.

Being able to fill my cylinders became irrelevant when I came down with gastroenteritis. Once I had stopped being spectacularly ill from every orifice, I decided to make a dive in the Emergence de Gourneyras. This is located in the Vis Valley, and the cave is approached by driving down a forestry track from the main road. We had instructions (in French) how to find the place, and as I had been to the neighbouring cave (Emergence de Gourneyrou) in 2001, I knew the way. So Antoinette drove while I navigated.

We left the highway on a bend in the road and set off down a narrow rocky track with a substantial drop through trees down to the valley floor on one side and a vertical cliff on the other. Between the track and the cliff, there was culvert carrying water. After driving as far as a rickety bridge (which I remembered from last time) I was on the lookout for a '*Grande Randonnée*' sign which was supposed to be opposite the path down to the cave. We passed a disused house whereupon the terrain became more difficult. As the passenger, I could see that the culvert was awfully close as we edged through the undergrowth. Meanwhile Antoinette was concerned that the car's offside wheels would slip over the edge. I couldn't remember any of this from last time, but I kept my mouth shut as I didn't want to unnerve her.

Eventually we arrived at a clearing on a bend with ample room to turn around. We stopped the car and got out to hold a full and frank discussion. Considering that she was already on the verge of a nervous breakdown, Antoinette took my admission that we'd overshot the path (by some considerable distance) with remarkable composure. To calm her down, I helpfully said that I would drive back up to the main road. Just then, we heard voices from further down the track shouting, 'Allez! Allez!' So we walked around the corner to investigate.

A French family of four were on a donkey trekking excursion. They had hired a pair of animals and one of them was refusing to cross a slippery section of the track where water from the culvert was seeping out and flowing over the precipice. To be honest, I don't blame it. As they had got the other donkey across, we offered to help. But after I'd made overtures to the stubborn beast in order to gain its confidence, it still refused to budge. I loaned the father of family my mobile phone in order to call the donkey hire company, as their phone had no reception. We were advised to hobble the creature by lifting up one of its front legs and holding it bent at the knee – once the donkey lost four-hoof drive, it would be easier to manoeuvre, so we were told.

I volunteered for the task and grabbed the donkey's right front hoof ready to get it across the stream. Even minus one leg, the animal stubbornly resisted. We were just beginning to make progress, when I slipped on the wet rocks … and then the donkey stood on my foot!

I didn't take much notice at first as I was wearing sandals and my feet were soaked in the cold stream. We tried again, but failed. Then I realised that my right foot had a painful swelling the size of a grapefruit developing on the top of the outer arch. Antoinette took one look at it and decreed that I ought to go to hospital. I didn't think it was broken, but under the circumstances, I decided to comply. The mother of the family kindly donated an elasticated bandage with which I could strap up the injury, and we scraped our way back to the public highway.

We stopped at the nearest village to ask for directions to the nearest hospital. This turned out to be miles away from where we were staying, so we opted to head in the opposite direction, towards Lodève, where we knew there was an A&E department. Expecting to have to wait to be seen, we stopped at our holiday cottage for provisions *en route*; I had promise to stay in the car as Antoinette was sure that if I got inside the house I would emulate the donkey and refuse to leave.

Once we reached Lodève, we found the hospital and went into the main entrance. The place was deserted except for an old lady dressed in her nightgown. She was obviously an inmate and immediately latched onto us. I left Antoinette to deal with her while I hopped around to the A&E department next door.

I didn't have to wait very long to be seen by a nurse, and was ushered into a consulting room. Fortunately Antoinette had escaped from the clutches of the mad women and was able to join me.

Nurse: Ce qui s'est passé?
Duncan: Un âne a marché sur mon pied droit!
Nurse: Un âne?
Duncan: Oui! Un âne!
Nurse: Un âne?
Duncan: Un âne … comme un cheval.

At which point I gave a passable imitation of a donkey by making some ears on my head with both hands and producing a braying noise. A smile of understanding spread across the nurse's face as she repeated the French word for donkey with no perceptible difference in pronunciation from the way I'd said it.

She left the room and a few minutes later a doctor appeared. I had to rehearse my performance, including the donkey impression, before he got the message and summoned the radiographer. Once more, I staged the pantomime for her and finally for another hospital employee, before I was wheeled into the X-ray suite. Fortunately no bones were broken and I was discharged with a prescription for anti-inflammatories and strong painkillers. As we were leaving the hospital, I'm sure we spotted the final visitor to the treatment room pushing a broom around. I strongly suspect that we were just providing entertainment for the cleaner.

# 18

# An Unfortunate Series of Events

By the summer of 2004, the exploration of the sumps in Daren Cilau was largely complete and I started work on the survey of the route through the main sump between Pwll-y-Cwm and Daren Cilau. This took place at a leisurely pace, dependent on my inclination and the weather conditions. A large party of divers converged on Pwll-y-Cwm in August 2004 to celebrate my 40th birthday, when I was able to progress the survey to 200 metres from the choke using my homemade side-mounted rebreather. On subsequent trips, I dived on open circuit, often with extra cylinders carried specifically for the survey work *(see colour section)*.

I took measurements of distance, depth and forward bearing at every line belay where the guideline changed direction, and recorded this information in pencil on a diver's slate of waterproof paper. During one trip I lost contact with the guideline while taking notes, but I had the presence of mind to use the survey data in order to navigate back to the guideline by dead reckoning. The long dives were fairly chilly affairs, as I was swimming slowly when collecting data; I had to abandon one session when I was so cold that I could no longer read my depth gauge accurately. But by the end of March 2007, the job was done and we had a basic centreline map of the underwater passage. All that remained was to tie the upstream end of the sump survey into the dry cave survey.

Another task was to replace the guideline from the sump in Elm Hole so that we could measure this section accurately. Somewhat ambitiously, I decided to do the latter on the evening of Saturday 7 April 2007, after spending most of the day moving house. Because I wanted to have the numbered tags on the line incrementing from airspace in Elm Hole, I decided to go into the cave and lay the line towards Pwll-y-Cwm from there. With no one around to help, it took me nearly two hours to cover the 60 metres from daylight to the dive base before I was ready to go. Wearing a wetsuit and with the bag I'd used to transport my gear into the cave neatly rolled up and strapped to me, I set off into the sump. My 7-litre cylinders weren't full, and each contained an unknown nitrox mix left over from some other diving project. I reasoned that it would only be a short trip through to Pwll-y-Cwm (which I had dived the previous weekend so knew to be open). What could possibly go wrong?

## An Unfortunate Series of Events

Reversing down the constricted passage, I placed the new line parallel to the old one from the surface as far as The Window. At this point I became caught up by my fins. Clearing the mess, I fell out into the main passage, my only point of reference now being the reel that I was still holding containing the replacement line. I crawled along the floor, severely overweighted, desperately hoping to locate the permanent line and the route to Pwll-y-Cwm. After several fraught moments, I found myself on the main upstream line, and I ditched the reel and headed out around the loop and through the choke. But then there was no line in place to the surface, so I just had to follow the walls upwards from memory. Tim Morgan was on the surface, waiting for me. He had ordered me a steak in the pub, thinking I'd be hungry. I was more relieved just to be alive.

The next day, Tim and I dived into Daren Cilau. We took a tape measure, compass and clinometer tucked inside our drysuits, and used these to tie the diving survey into the 'dry cave' survey. Finding the end of the latter proved a challenge, as the final station had been marked as a cross on the floor of the passage at a T-junction, and over the years countless cavers had obscured the spot with muddy bootprints. Fortunately Tim had bought a 'pirate's map' consisting of bearings taken from the final survey point to various points in the passage. Using this information we were able to triangulate on the place where we thought the mark should be – and there it was, faintly inscribed in the floor like some *Here Be Treasure* X.

On the way out, I dived around the loop route to Elm Hole and collected my discarded reel from the previous day's adventure. Reaching The Window, I found that my line entanglement had broken both of the lines leading to safety from that point. It had been a close call.

With the conclusion of surveying work, our explorations in Daren Cilau effectively came to a halt. The diving route into the bottom of the cave became a means of ferrying stores to the underground camp at Hard Rock Café, particularly heavy and crushproof items such as paraffin or booze, which could be carried in without needing waterproofing. Likewise, divers could help bring out any discarded items of camp gear such as old sleeping bags or other rubbish, since it didn't matter if they got wet.

Although we had a perfectly good line drawing of the sump, it remained to be fleshed out with the passage width and height. Given that the visibility underwater was typically less than a couple of metres, it seemed unlikely that this could be done without a great deal of effort and exceptionally good weather. However, in the spring of 2011, I bought a waterproof hand-held sonar wand and practised with it at Wookey Hole. The concept of using such a device for underwater cave surveying was hardly new, since Mike Barnes and Pete Mulholland had used one to map a large underwater chamber in Pridhamsleigh Cavern, Devon, some 20 years before – but I was planning to take this to new levels of detail.

Armed with my magic wand and a homemade chest-mounted rebreather, I then made a series of dives in Pwll-y-Cwm, methodically recording the distances of the walls, roof and floor from the permanent line at every marker – that is at 5-metre intervals. At each station

I recorded the number on the tag, the depth and the distance to the left and right walls, roof and floor. Using a rebreather gave me ample time in the water and kept me warm. In two 90-minute dives I covered the first 350 metres of the sump. I used a supply run to the campsite in Daren Cilau to survey the shallower part of the sump from the Daren Cilau end to the 500 metre mark; I did this on open circuit breathing from three 12-litre cylinders. Only 150 metres remained, and I should be able to cover this in one mission.

My final surveying trip took place on Easter Saturday 23rd April 2011. I had planned to do this on my rebreather with a pair of 12-litre side-mounted cylinders. On previous closed-circuit dives I had used a pair of 7-litre cylinders, but this time I felt that these might not provide enough bailout gas should I have a problem at the far point of my dive. Martyn Farr was keen to come along to take some underwater photos of me at the bottom of Pwll-y-Cwm, and had brought Bonnie Cotier along to hold the backlighting flash; she was an American citizen who had come to live in the UK on account of her husband's job with the military. I had first met her at the Cave Diving Group's AGM & dinner in the Yorkshire Dales the previous weekend. Bonnie had initially learned to cave dive in the USA using typical Floridian techniques and equipment. Then she and her husband had undergone training in the UK with Martyn Farr, to become accustomed to British methods. She had got on well in Yorkshire on her own, using sidemounts, so it was agreed that once the photography was done I would go off to finish the survey while the she and Martyn would dive independently. I'd installed a line from the surface down to the choke on a checkout dive two days before. This was still in place, but there was no fixed line through the restriction to the start of the permanent line; the mobile nature of the gravel slope meant that any line here would become buried or broken and could be more of a hazard than a help. Bonnie had never dived Pwll-y-Cwm before, so Martyn Farr was going to put a jump line though the restriction after the photography was done, and was then going to remove it (at my request) when both of them were out *(see colour section)*.

Despite the extra equipment I had, I was ready to dive first. There was no rush, so I floated idly in the surface pool while Martyn fiddled with his camera and Bonnie made the final adjustments to her gear. At the bottom of the entrance shaft, Martyn went ahead through the archway without a line while I waited for him to get into position before coming through into the lowest part to pose for him. Bonnie stayed behind with the slave flash to illuminate me from the rear. About 15 minutes into the dive, Martyn signalled that he was done and that I could go. The visibility was quite good (about 3–4 metres) and I completed the task of surveying the final section of the sump without incident, returning to the choke area after an absence of just over an hour and a half. There was no line though the restriction, although I found a small finger spool (commonly used as a search or gap reel) on the boulder slope beside the permanent line. Suspecting that this belonged to Bonnie or Martyn, and that there might be a modest reward for its return, I picked it up and carried it out, removing the line up the shaft in the process.

I surfaced to meet Martyn, who waiting at the edge of the surface pool. 'Are you OK?' he inquired anxiously. 'Sure,' I replied nonchalantly, adding, 'Where's Bonnie?'

## An Unfortunate Series of Events

'She's still down there!' was the reply. The look on Martyn's face said it all – if Bonnie was still underwater there was no chance that she was alive, as she would have run out of air by now. We obviously had to go back in to look for her. I removed my chest-mounted rebreather and got ready to dive just with my bailout tanks. Martyn's partner (now his wife), Helen, appeared with a couple of fresh cylinders for him to use. I waited for Martyn to kit up and we re-entered the water together, with me in front laying a line down to the bottom of the shaft. Once through the choke, I set off on my own up the route to Elm Hole.

The Elm Hole line was the obvious place to search. During my surveying dive I had followed the main line to Daren Cilau and hadn't seen Bonnie. So there was a chance that she had negotiated the awkward and tight passage to reach the airspace in the dry part of the cave beyond. Reaching The Window leading to Elm Hole, I instinctively continued upstream on the line to The Corner. This route forms part of a small circuit around a large flake which divides the main passage. But then, 5 metres further on, I saw stationary lights in the passage, and I closed in on Bonnie's body hanging vertically in the water just below the line. I swam down to her and checked the contents of her cylinders; both were empty and there was a short length of white cord around her, probably from a search reel. Then I reached around the back of her harness and grabbed her by the base of the shoulder straps. As part of my training of new divers, I had many times made them simulate moving a dead diver underwater – but I had never expected to have to do it in anger.

Bonnie was heavy in the water to start with, but as we reached the restriction, the air in her suit began to expand so I reached around to the dump valve on her drysuit to vent as much as possible. I tried to push her body ahead of me through the tight section, but thought better of it and we managed to pass through the low, wide archway side by side. I tried to expel more air from her suit before lifting her to the surface; she was negatively buoyant at the bottom, but as we ascended she began to rise like a balloon, and I struggled to prevent us from being trapped beneath an overhang near the surface. Then a few metres from daylight, we were in clear water, so I let her go and bobbed up next to her. A policeman crossed the river to us and promptly slipped on the wet rock, joining me in the surface pool.

Bonnie's body was taken across the river and resuscitation started. I caught the eye of one of the paramedics involved and shook my head. He responded with a shrug as if to suggest that he knew the attempt to revive her would be futile, but they had to try. I turned my back on their activities and took my gear off. I left my cylinders in the gorge and walked up carrying my rebreather and fins. Reaching my car, I got changed as more people turned up to help. My phone had a missed call from one of the cave rescue wardens. I called him back to tell him that I had just taken part in the body recovery. Martyn, Helen and I were then asked to go to the police station in Abergavenny and (since my car was blocked in by a waiting ambulance) I travelled with them. I made a couple of calls to family and close friends to advise them that there had been an incident and that I was OK. I was concerned that something might appear in the news and although I couldn't go into detail I didn't want anyone to worry over my own safety.

Martyn gave a statement to the police while we waited for the rest of our gear to turn up. My account was recorded the next day. Bonnie's husband, Steve, was working in Belgium and there was a delay while the US Embassy tracked him down. Steve was finally told the bad news at 11 pm – he was a little concerned that he'd not heard from Bonnie, but had put this down to Bonnie having a good time and a poor mobile phone signal. He caught the Eurostar to London and continued by rail to Newport, where the police met him.

Martyn told the police how he had left the camera gear at the bottom of the entrance shaft and tied on a line reel to the metal I-beam where the line to the surface was belayed. Martyn had installed his line through the restriction and attached it to the permanent line on the other side. Both he and Bonnie had set off along the main line upstream with Martyn in the lead. Martyn had looked back periodically to see Bonnie's bright primary light behind him. She was still following him at the 80-metre mark, but when he had turned around at the 100-metre tag there was no sign of her. Martyn had used a third of his air from the pair of 5-litre cylinders he was wearing, and although Bonnie had larger cylinders it would not have been unreasonable to expect her to turn around before him, since it was her first dive there and she was less experienced. Until that point, everything was going to plan, as it had been agreed that we would all be diving independently of one another.

Martyn now swam towards the exit. As he neared the point where his line had been tied off, he saw Bonnie's lights moving to the right, indicating that she was ahead of him and seemingly about to enter the restriction. Martyn continued to his reel, disconnected it from the permanent line and slowly began to wind it in. At the base of the entrance shaft, he untied the line from the I-beam, collected his camera equipment and made a slow ascent to the surface, following the line that I had left in place. But once out of the water, there was no sign of Bonnie. He stood up to see if she had crossed to the far river bank. She hadn't. Evidently she was still somewhere below.

Martyn immediately descended with his line reel. He reconnected this to the I-beam and went back through the restriction to conduct a search. After following the left-hand wall for a short distance, he crossed to the other side of the passage. There he found Bonnie, who reached out to take hold of him. Martyn dropped the reel and, as she appeared negatively buoyant, grabbed her harness at the shoulders and began guiding her in the direction of the restriction. His right-hand cylinder ran out at this point, so he swapped onto the other one. Knowing that he had very limited air remaining, Martyn once more caught hold of Bonnie and moved her towards the low section. But suddenly she broke away and turned back into the cave. Martyn consulted his contents gauges for the first time; the needle was well into the red on the cylinder he was breathing from. He decided to stay exactly where he was, to act as a beacon. A minute or two passed, and he moved to the upper side of the restriction, where again he took station. But eventually, with one completely empty cylinder and just 20 bar in the other, he had no choice but to surface. He de-kitted quickly and ran back to his car to alert Helen. She was asked to bring spare cylinders to the scene straight away and call the emergency services *en route*. Helen arrived about 15 minutes later. Martyn returned to Pwll-y-Cwm, where he met me.

Bonnie's funeral was held in St Neots, Cambridgeshire, two weeks later, and a memorial service was held in the United States. Although I had not planned to draw up the cave survey immediately, it now became part of the evidence that was submitted to the coroner, in addition to our witness statements. Although I wasn't specifically requested to attend the inquest held the following September, I went along anyway, both as a gesture of support and to get some form of closure on the whole episode. Evidence of Bonnie's diving experience was heard, as well as a statement from a police diving specialist concerning Bonnie's equipment, and the pathologist's report. The coroner had not expected me to be there and was going to read out my statement, but since I had turned up, I was asked to give evidence under oath. The conclusions were that although every precaution had been taken, Bonnie had become disoriented and subsequently drowned. The coroner stressed that she had died doing an activity she enjoyed and wanted to do. Steve had already stated that he'd had no concerns about Bonnie cave diving that day – he'd been more worried about her driving there safely.

# 19

# Deepest Mendip

The Golden Age of British cave diving was over by the time I came on the scene. During the 1970s, most sumps had received some form of cursory examination and all of the easy pickings had been pushed to a conclusion. I had initially taken up cave diving as a means of reaching the dry parts of caves that lay beyond sumps; what original underwater exploration I have done in the UK has resulted from improvements in methods and equipment, plus a lot of hard graft. For example, when Rick Stanton, Barry Suddell and I began diving in the Clydach Gorge in 1990, underwater digging was uncommon. Also, hardly anyone took a drysuit down underground to put on, let alone take it off again beyond a long sump in order to go caving again. I owe a lot to my contemporaries for introducing me to such techniques, which we turned into commonplace activities.

If you're a newcomer keen to explore sumps in the UK, I advise you to do your research thoroughly before going underground. I have edited the current Cave Diving Group Sump Indexes for Wales and Somerset. As a consequence, and I have a hit list of places which might 'go' with a bit more effort. But some of these are out of bounds due to problems with landowner access. However, if you are prepared to play a waiting game, or invest in a little diplomacy, then this can pay dividends.

Another way of finding sites to explore is to wait for someone else to do it for you; this worked well for me in Ogof Carno and Ogof Draenen. Closer to my home on the Mendip Hills, cavers have spent years trying to open up new holes or extend known ones by digging. Then occasionally they find a sump and need the services of their friendly neighbourhood cave diver. This happened to me in December 2010 when I received a telephone call from one Ali Moody, inviting me to dive the terminal sump in Charterhouse Cave during the 'open season' in the following year.

For many years, Ali and her friends had been carefully working their way down through a boulder choke, following a breeze of fresh air that indicated that more cave lay beyond. They finally broke through in 2008 and quickly explored a fine stream passage to reach a sump at the end of 100 Fathom Passage. The underwater continuation was examined by Ali's husband, Pete, and then Phil Short, but it became too tight. As Phil is one of the hardest and thinnest cave divers I know, it was clear that the sump could be written off. I visited the cave on a tourist trip in August of that year when I extracted his line reel from the sump where it had become stuck in the low underwater passage at the further point of his dive. By pulling very hard on the line from dry land, I was able to free the reel and return it to its rightful owner. The sump did not inspire me!

A little way upstream from the sump was a calcite flow down one wall called The Frozen Cascade. A tarpaulin had been hung down this, in order to protect the crystalline floor. At the head of the Frozen Cascade was an abandoned high-level passage, The Time Line. This also ended in a sump, dubbed Portal Pool. But this was also too constricted to dive, so Ali and company built a hand pump out of bits of drain pipe and sheet rubber, lowering the water level and thus being able to explore the dry cave beyond. In 2010 they reached another sump; this lay at the deepest point of the cave, 220 metres below the entrance.

But before my planned assault on the terminal sump, I was offered a place on a tourist trip to the far reaches of the cave at the end of April 2011. No one had been beyond Portal Pool since the previous summer, and Ali was keen to see how the cave had fared over the winter months. I met Pete Buckley, JC and Ali at the Wessex Cave Club HQ, where I told them I had brought a lightweight set of diving gear to make a reconnaissance of the sump. They had no objection, and we headed over to the cave entrance in Ali's car.

We drew up in a farmyard, where it was safer to leave the car rather than at the side of the public highway. Cavers' vehicles are frequently the targets for car thieves because the passengers are often gone for some time and are likely to have left their valuables behind. Pete, JC and Ali had changed into wetsuits back at the caving hut, but I decided put my thin surfing wetsuit on at the farm and over it wore a nylon oversuit to protect it from abrasion. We walked over to the cave through some fields full of bluebells in the crisp spring sunshine.

The first part of Charterhouse Cave has a tight squeeze where a gate used to be, and I wondered if I'd put on any weight since my previous visit when I'd ripped a hole in the backside of my coveralls getting through. I didn't have a problem this time, but Pete, who was behind me, guessed that I was left-handed as I seemed to be tackling each obstacle in the opposite fashion to him. We left some food and drink for the journey at the bottom of The Frozen Cascade before continuing to Portal Pool. There was airspace through this, and I was glad; given the size of the route through, I wouldn't like to have to dive it.

As we progressed into parts of the cave that were new to me, it was difficult to believe that anyone had ever been there before; the winter floods had removed all evidence of previous visitors and it felt like we were exploring virgin territory.

The next obstacle was Diesel Duck, named after the smell of a fuel leak from the farm above that had seeped into the cave. Like Portal Pool, Diesel Duck can flood completely, and the previous explorers had put a diving line through as a precaution. Reaching a large chamber (The Hall of Time), we climbed up into the roof and made a slippery traverse across to a boulder choke. A series of contortions beneath a roof of doubtful stability brought us out into the floor of a major trunk route, High Time, completely out of character with the rest of the cave and anything else I had seen under the Mendips. It was more reminiscent of Welsh caves, tall and wide with a mud and boulder floor. Rather than lay strips of striped plastic flagging tape to define a route along the passage (and protect the rest of the floor from damage), the discoverers had placed reflective markers, which shone brightly in our lights, to indicate the path.

We continued to Zebra Junction, whose walls had noticeable stripes of calcite in the rock, and turned right into a large canyon passage with abandoned plunge pools. The cave changed character again at the base of Jet Pitch, where the mud took over. As we headed downstream, we were careful not step in the small stream which had joined us, so as not to cloud the water which I would shortly be diving in. Eventually, our way was barred by a roomy sump pool – the aptly named Hippo's Delight.

I emptied my bag of gear and donned a wetsuit hood, mask, neoprene gloves, compass and knife. The bottle I had brought was a 0.9-litre aluminium tank. This had begun life as a paintball gun cylinder but I'd fitted it with a DIN valve so that I could breathe from it using a diving regulator. The day before our trip, the tank had been filled with oxygen, but I had vented some of this and refilled it with air. I hadn't bothered to check its oxygen content, but I reckoned that it would be unlikely to be too rich for the depth I was likely to achieve. Instead of a conventional line reel, I had brought a 15-metre tape measure to act as my safety line. With one end of it threatening to fall off my wrist I plunged in, with JC patiently feeding my makeshift safety line out to me.

I was still very buoyant in my wetsuit as we'd only been able to find one block of lead *en route*; according to JC, I went in for 8 metres along the roof of the sump. At the furthest point I was able to view a handsome passage gently sloping off into the depths. I turned back, wondering if my tugs on the tape measure would be understood at base, then emerged from the water in obvious excitement and with a few words along the lines that I was going to need more serious gear next time.

The slog out was hard work, as we were now far below the surface and nearly 2 kilometres from the entrance. I experienced several agonising bouts of cramp in my thighs which were only relieved when we reached our food dump at The Frozen Cascade. Luckily JC had some salted cashew nuts, and plied me with these until my symptoms abated. We surfaced after 7 hours underground, a long trip by Mendip standards – and I'd dived the sump that lay at the deepest point below the Mendip Hills!

I was keen to go back and push the sump properly. There was little, if any, height difference between the water level at Hippo's Delight and the altitude of the resurgence near Gough's Cave in Cheddar Gorge, so the cave passage could be flooded all the way to where the water entered Gough's Cave through a boulder choke at the end of the third upstream sump. I reckoned there must be inlets, too, from other caves which drain to Cheddar (such as Wigmore Swallet), making the sump one of the best cave diving leads in the region.

But I had not factored in the level of control that the original explorers exercised over who did what in the cave and when. Charterhouse Cave was gated and locked at the request of the landowner. A strict leader system operated to protect the cave features from damage. The digging team had drawn criticism for installing a second gate in the cave at the start of their dig to keep others out of it. Yet this gate had remained in place long after the extensions that

## Deepest Mendip

they had found had been opened up. En route to The Frozen Cascade there was a pitch which required a ladder to descend; the digging team hung theirs up by the drop, neatly coiled and padlocked, so visitors had to bring their own. Even the parts of the hand pump used to drain Portal Pool were removed and hidden from sight to prevent others from using it.

I had no choice but to let the original explorers complete their aven climbing programme before I had a chance to dive. This was somewhat frustrating, given that the weather was very favourable at the time, but the delay did at least allow me to acquire some old 6-litre cylinders from Clive Westlake and make them look good enough to take underground. Andrew Atkinson and my girlfriend Naomi cached the cylinders were cached just beyond The Frozen Cascade in early June 2011, then they were moved to the top of Jet Pitch by Adrian Hall, Ali, Naomi and me a few weeks later. I also cached a bag containing my harness, buoyancy jacket, fins and a line reel. We scheduled the dive for 23 July and Ali nominated a team to support me. Then it rained …

A couple of days before we were due to go, it was apparent that even getting past Diesel Duck would be questionable, so we cancelled the trip. Andrew Atkinson went down the cave anyway, and found the duck had sumped. With good weather forecast for the following week, we rescheduled the dive for 30 July. Steve Sharp from my own caving club; Stu Gardiner, my youngest 'son', and Naomi were conscripted to assist; Steve and Stu were both leaders for the cave, although Steve had not been into the 2008–09 extensions before.

We all met up at the Wessex Cave Club HQ before setting off in the company of the digging team who were going in ahead of us to work on a bypass to The Frozen Cascade. They had already opened up a crack through into The Timeline from a blasted tunnel, and were going to make it caver-sized. I travelled into the cave empty-handed in order to be fresh for the dive – but in the event this made hardly any difference, as I was wearing my diving wetsuit long johns which severely restricted my mobility. I might as well have been wearing a suit of armour.

We left the diggers at work and continued to Zebra Junction. Here I removed the oversuit I'd worn over my wetsuit long johns, and donned my wetsuit jacket. To make the final preparations easier, I put on my harness and buoyancy compensator at the bottom of Jet Pitch. At Hippo's Delight I drove a length of plastic pipe into the jelly-like mud to act as belay for the dive line, then I balanced on the bags that we had brought the diving gear in to try to stay clean while Naomi acted as dresser and helped me attach my cylinders without getting too muddy. Three hours after leaving the surface I was ready to dive.

*The Charterhouse Cave dive team, July 2011 (Ali Moody)*

Entering the water, it was apparent that the silt cloud that I'd stirred up getting into the sump was rolling ahead of me. Quickly, I went in for 10 metres, and jammed another length of plastic pipe into a mud bank on the right-hand wall to act as a secondary belay. But while I was securing the line to it, one of my fins became caught up, so I had to stop to free myself before pressing on. The passage ahead swung to the left and then back to the right as it developed into a rift.

At 30 metres from base and a depth of 9 metres the route narrowed in; the only way on was a horizontal slot at floor level to one side. I tried to reverse into this over the mud floor, but I only managed to get in up to my knees before it became impassable. I made a belay for the line from some more plastic pipe carried expressly for that purpose, tied the line to it and cut the reel free. I returned to dive base in zero visibility – and I wrote the survey notes from memory much later. Eleven minutes after setting off, I surfaced and was helped out of my gear.

The trip out was a slow one with as much equipment as possible being taken with us. We deposited the reel (still with lots of line left on it) and two blocks of lead at Zebra Junction. Steve got lost in The Hall of Time, and we spent 20 minutes looking for him When we reached The Time Line, we found that the diggers had opened up the hole they'd been working on when we went in, so we were able to crawl through into 100 Fathom Passage without crossing The Frozen Cascade. Then we stopped for a picnic . On again! The thinner members of the party cursed me for giving them the bags containing my diving gear (particularly the one with my fins in them) to manoeuvre through the tighter sections of the cave on the way out, but we made good progress and surfaced at 7:30 pm.

The sump had not lived up to its promise, but the explored part of Charterhouse Cave was now 229 metres deep, and the end of the sump was the deepest known point in any cave beneath the Mendip Hills.

The water from Charterhouse Cave, Wigmore Swallet and other sinks emerges from a number of springs in Cheddar Gorge near the popular tourist attraction of Gough's Cave. This is operated as show cave by its owners, Longleat Estates, and about the same time as my diving in Charterhouse Cave, I became involved with a project to produce a new, high quality survey of the place. The University of Bristol Spelæological Society were mapping the dry cave, and asked me to survey the underwater parts and what lay beyond them.

Until 1985, Gough's Cave held little attraction to cave divers, but an insignificant puddle at the bottom of a shaft in an oxbow to the show cave turned out to be the way into the flooded river passage that lay directly below the tourist trail. The entrance was tight and awkward, so it was called Dire Straits. Upstream from this, a large tunnel surfaced in a lake chamber known as Lloyd Hall; a dry route was later forged into this from the show cave, bypassing the privations of the Dire Straits. Beyond Lloyd Hall, the underwater passage continued, to reach an enormous chamber called Bishop's Palace. At its far end, Sump 2 gained a short section of streamway before reaching Sump 3. The final sump dropped down a shaft, to a depth of around 50 metres; the late Rob Palmer had explored this as far as an underwater boulder choke. Then in 2002 Rick Stanton found a way through this, to surface amongst boulders in a rift airbell with no apparent way on.

In 2007 John Volanthen and I had dived Sump 1a downstream from Lloyd Hall. We had continued to the end of the cave at a narrow vertical shaft (Persecution Pot), that rose from a depth of 33 metres to about 10 metres. As I'd managed to source accurate survey data for the cave upstream of Lloyd Hall to the start of Sump 3, the main thrust of my work was to measure the downstream section. Despite its moniker, Dire Straits did not seem so bad after all – it was close the entrance and with care I could get there in my drysuit. My first dive took place just before Christmas 2010, when I installed a new line from Dire Straits upstream to Lloyd Hall and surveyed the route back to base.

My next visit took me downstream from Dire Straits, where the sump continued to deepen from 20 metres at the point of entry to over 30 metres at the bottom of Persecution Pot, some 150 metres distant. I had told my helpers that my dive would be about an hour. This was true – but I hadn't counted on accruing a further 45 minutes' decompression penalty in the confines of Dire Straits. Fortunately, the sporadic bubbles from my exhaled breath convinced my assistants that I was still alive and they guessed that I'd had to wait until my stops had cleared before I could surface.

Having acquired a centreline survey of the sump, I needed to measure its dimensions. I used my handheld sonar wand for this, and I covered the 160 metres of passage up to Lloyd Hall in one go. For my next dive, I went downstream from Dire Straits, looking for the point of entry of a flooded shaft close to the entrance of the show cave known as Skeleton Pit. This derives its name from the remains of a 9,000-year-old male that had been found there. The survey indicated that the shaft probably connected with the main drain 75 metres downstream of Dire Straits on a prominent corner. Sure enough, there was a rift in the roof of the passage at this point, but the walls of the cave were coated with goethite so I wasn't inclined to investigate.

Since I had plenty of air left, I continued downstream to the 100-metre point, then returned to base recording the passage dimensions every 5 metres using my magic wand. I reached the start of Dire Straits to discover that I needed to carry out 30 minutes of decompression before I could surface. But once I was in the tight passage leading to the surface, I found that I could no longer read my instruments in the poor visibility. Fortunately, I had marked the positions of the decompression stops at 6 and 3 metres' depth – but I couldn't see my watch, either. So I did some quick calculations based upon my surface air consumption and the tidal volume of my lungs. I estimated that I did 10 breathing cycles a minute at rest, so I counted these until I was able to clear my stops.

As part of my survey work, I wanted to get passage dimensions for Sump 1b upstream from Lloyd Hall and also conduct an overland survey of Bishop's Palace. The first 90 metres of Sump 1b had been covered in April 2011 when Chris Jewell and John Volanthen went through to Bishop's Palace to stage some gear for a dive in Sump 3. This time, we all set off from Lloyd Hall together and I was still underwater by the time they had returned from dropping off their gear. Then when we returned a month later we surveyed the final part of the sump. I had used a tape measure to gauge the distance through the sump and had attached it to the guide line with cable ties. I came out ahead of the rest of the party cutting the cable ties off as I went. But I also sliced through the tape measure that kept me in contact with the line out. Finding myself off route and in very poor visibility did not concern me greatly – I had lots of air and knew that the other divers were close behind me. So I dropped to the floor of the sump to await rescue – but fortunately I landed on the guide line and so was able to find my way out unaided.

*Bishop's Palace, Gough's Cave (Clive Westlake)*

During this outing, I also surveyed Bishop's Palace overland from Sump 1 to Sump 2 while Chris and John were using rebreathers to get to the end of Sump 3. They did not find a way on, but John had brought along his Lazy Boy underwater cave mapper. This is an ingenious device comprising a digital electronic compass and pressure gauge which logs the direction and depth of travel as the diver swims through the sump. A propeller attached to the casing spins in the current, and the number of turns it makes can be used to establish the distance covered. So now we had a line survey of Sump 3 as well.

I made my final surveying dive at the beginning of October 2011, when I completed measuring the sump downstream of Dire Straits as far as Persecution Pot. Initially I had planned to do this on my birthday in August 2011, but I'd managed to stick my foot through the leg of my drysuit in the process of putting it on, so I'd had to console myself with an ice cream in the sunshine instead. Now, having brought an old drysuit out of retirement to complete the work, I was helped into the water by Naomi and two of her friends from university, Ben Heaney and Annie Turner (now married). Getting my gear on at the start of the sump required an assistant to stand above me, wedged in the passage, passing me items to put on one at a time. In order not to spend ages decompressing, I'd filled my cylinders with some nitrox-36. The mix would be a bit 'hot' at the maximum depth of the sump, but I considered that I wouldn't be there long and would not be exerting myself, as I would only be surveying.

The others watched anxiously as I worked my way into the sump and slid out of view. Initially my exhaust bubbles came up in discrete pulses and then the flow became continuous as they merged into a single stream. Then the bubbles stopped. This was because I'd moved away from the shaft, but it can be quite unnerving for spectators (particularly, in this case, for my girlfriend, Naomi) as for all intents and purposes they don't know if I'm alive or dead – or like Schrödinger's cat, both alive *and* dead. Naomi decided it was time for an ice cream, so they went out to enjoy the autumn sunshine while I was beneath them completing the survey. The choice of gas mix was just right, and I surfaced after a no-stop dive just when my helpers returned to check up on me.

A little way up Cheddar Gorge from Gough's Cave, there is an area for open-top buses carrying tourists to turn around in. Next to this is a covered reservoir, and in the base of the cliff behind it, the gated entrance to Reservoir Hole. The cave had initially been explored by the redoubtable Dr Willie Stanton, Mendip's master cave digger and cave conservationist. He would think nothing of constructing walls and laying out pathways to prevent visitors from damaging vulnerable cave formations. Willie and his team spent many years extending the Reservoir Hole via protracted excavations, frequently working their way upwards through unstable boulder chokes which they stabilised with cement as they went. Digging could be quite exciting at times, and he records that after they had softened up the face with explosives they did the initial clearance of the debris with the aid of 'an agile bachelor'.

Willie Stanton passed away in 2010, and his work in Reservoir Hole was continued by a team of cavers who, since most of them were retired, dug in the cave on weekdays. They achieved success in 2012 by breaking through into an enormous chamber, The Frozen Deep, which gained fame for being the largest known underground chamber (in terms of ground plan) in Britain. Only the Main Chamber of Gaping Gill in Yorkshire (said to be able to accommodate St Paul's Cathedral) can rival it in size.

In one corner of this void, a tortuous route down through boulders led to a sump. Several of the digging team were cave divers, and the site was dived first by Peter Glanville (a retired GP) and then by Rob Harper (a vet). Rob wanted another crack at the site before handing it over to someone else, and put out a request for help with portage for his last attempt there. Seeing this as an opportunity to get involved, I volunteered my services along with a couple of fellow cave divers, Claire Cohen and Connor Roe, as well as Naomi. To complete the party, Nick Chipchase a designated leader for the cave, came along; he was one of the regulars to the digging team, and had helped discover the sump in the first place.

But a few days before the dive, Rob said that he had a cold and couldn't dive. This was the second time that this had happened. But at least he was still able to cave and, not wishing to cancel the trip again, offered me the chance to have a go instead. Some of the digging team had other ideas, as after Rob had given up they had promised the site to John Volanthen. So I called him, and he said that he didn't mind if I had a crack at it. In retrospect, this was a wise decision on John's part *(see colour section)*.

On Sunday 5 May 2013 we met up in the parking area opposite the reservoir and changed into our gear. I had not slept very well as I'd developed an ear infection, but I was determined to dive and had dosed up on a cocktail of drugs. I hoped that the sump would 'go' and against Rob's advice had brought my trusty pair of 6-litre cylinders to dive with. Along with a container holding my regulators and mask, there were four loads split between the six of us.

We made steady progress to The Frozen Deep, where Nick proudly pointed out the 5-metre-tall stalactite pillars that went from the floor to the roof. The ceiling soared out of sight – in some places, over 30 metres above us – and the chamber appeared to be divided by a natural rock arch 40 metres across. I barely had time to appreciate the scenery as I was keen to get to the sump. I hadn't expected the carry to be too difficult, as the cave had been explored by a bunch of pensioners – but things changed when we started to worm our way down into the approach to the dive site in the innocuously named Dingley Dell.

To start with, neither Rob nor Nick could find the right route, but eventually the gear was lowered down on a rope between dangerously poised rocks. Nick elected to remain in The Frozen Deep with his sandwiches and camera gear; he had been to the sump before and was not a cave diver. As I slipped down through a particularly alarming section, I remember turning around and looking up at what was behind me. Wondering what I'd let myself in for, I made the comment that the boulders appeared to be held up 'by the force of habit'.

But then, having done the worst part, we reached an eye-hole at the approach to the sump. The floor was in knee-deep mud, and the narrow crevice that we had to pass through was at head height. The shorter members of the party required help to get into position, and we used a variety of tactics to get though the squeeze, including the 'bum wedge' and the less successful 'one leg before the other'. The latter manoeuvre simply resulted in me becoming stuck astride a sharp rock, but fortunately my wetsuit provided plenty of padding.

Rob had fixed a wire ladder down the other side of the slot to facilitate the return, and elegantly launched himself head first through the opening while holding the top of the ladder, to land with a somersault. The rest of the ladder was laid out down the mud slope to the water, and I was helped into my gear by Naomi. According to Rob, the water level was 2–3 metres lower than it had been during his previous dives. These had taken place in the winter months and the ladder now hung short of the water, so I had to lower myself by my arms down the steep bank into the sump.

Once underwater, I backed down a low muddy passage in poor visibility until the route enlarged sufficiently for me to be able to turn around. The visibility improved at this point, as I emerged into a clean-washed rift with a mud floor. A depression in the floor indicated a possible way on down to the right, and I attached a spare block of lead to the line to weigh it down in the widest part of the approach passage. I reversed into the low descending tunnel for just over a body-length before it became too tight at a depth of 10 metres; had I been wearing boots instead of fins, I might have been able to kick the mud away and go further. But the water remained clear, so this passage must be an outlet.

Moving further along the rift, the source of the water was marked by a boil of coarse sand being kicked up from under the left-hand wall. The rift closed in beyond this and I tried sticking my fins into the place where the water emerged. Changing over regulators, I got a mouthful of gravel that had lodged on the mesh protecting the second stage from debris. I spat it out, and started to make my way out. I was exactly 30 metres from base and I wound in the line, but left the drop weight still attached to it in order to determine the position of the outflow passage.

I surfaced to be greeted by Naomi, and handed her the reel with instructions to leave it as it was. But, the message didn't reach Claire, who thought that she'd be helpful and detach the weight from the line while I was taking my gear off. My right ear really hurt as a consequence of diving under the effects of a cold, and I suspected that I had caused some serious damage to my ear drum as I was partially deaf. In pain from this and annoyed that my request had been ignored, I had a total sense of humour failure with Claire, and threatened to go back into the sump to relocate the outlet until I was persuaded otherwise.

We packed up all of the equipment, including the line reel, for removal although we left the lead weights at the approach to the sump, then forming a human chain, we passed the gear ahead to the bottom of the final climb up into The Frozen Deep. Here we met Nick, who had come down to assist us. He had rigged a ladder to make it easier to get up the awkward narrow rift. Rob, Claire and Connor went up first and hauled the diving gear up into the chamber above. But Naomi was just climbing the ladder when there was a deafening rumble as the pitch head collapsed above her. Claire later described it as sounding 'like a skip full of rubble being emptied'.

I was at the back of the group behind Nick and saw Naomi fall, accompanied by a couple of enormous rocks. I didn't get a clear view of what happened as Nick was in my way, but I remember witnessing her drop like a rag doll and disappear behind a boulder that jammed across the passage. The next thing that I heard was Nick shrieking 'Oh my hand! Oh my hand!'

Naomi was silent until Rob shouted down to us, concerned about what had happened. She calmly reported that she was pinned by a rock and bleeding from her face. From my point of view it looked like she was upright and trapped from the chest down. I thought that her chances of making it out of the cave alive must be slim, and felt numb. Nick, on the other hand, remained agitated: his left hand was trapped behind the boulder blocking the rift. Unknown to me, Naomi had landed in a sitting position with a large rock on her lap and she was able to extract herself unaided; she had been struck in the head as she fell and was bleeding profusely from cuts near her right eye.

After telling Nick not to worry and that we'd get him out, Naomi scaled the remains of the ladder to join the others. A shower of stones fell down as she departed, and I cowered under what shelter I could find, whereas Nick had no choice but to remain when he was. Naomi and Connor went to get help, and despite Naomi's entreaties to Connor to go on ahead, he stayed with her until they reached the surface. There was no mobile phone signal by the cave entrance so still in their muddy caving gear they jumped into my car, reversed over Connor's caving helmet, then drove down to Gough's Cave to call out the cave rescue team.

Meanwhile, I was getting concerned about Nick, whose fingers were sticking out between a 1-tonne boulder and the cave wall. I could envisage a '127 hours' scenario developing, as I feared that we wouldn't be able to free him without surgery. I felt around Nick's hand to assess the situation: it appeared that only his ring finger was caught. Rob came down to the top of the climb in order to pass down a rope, but I was nervous about letting him come any further as I feared that another collapse would occur. The nearest digging tools were at a site in the cave called Skyfall, but they might as well have been on the moon. After asking Nick's permission to climb over the boulder pinning his finger, I looped an end of rope around one side of it. 'Don't worry, Nick,' I reassured him, explaining, 'I'm a doctor!' There was a glimmer of hope in his eyes, which I quickly dismissed by adding, 'of Chemistry!'

The first attempt to shift the rock didn't work, and I privately considered the options. After all, Rob was a vet and I had my diving knife with me. Then Nick positioned his right shoulder under the point where I'd attached the rope and we tried again. Success! Nick pulled his bloodied finger out – he couldn't straighten it but he was free to leave the cave. Claire was sent out as a runner to pass on the news that we were making our way out. While Rob helped Nick across The Frozen Deep, I packed up a bag full of gear to carry out, but most of my kit was left behind to be recovered later.

Rob, Nick and I made good progress out of the cave. I had trouble keeping up with them, and Rob came back to help me with my load. We emerged into bright sunshine to be greeted by six police cars, three fire engines and four paramedic teams waiting for us, along with a gaggle of Bank Holiday weekend tourists. Mendip Cave Rescue had already been stood down by Claire, who was waiting for us with Connor. Naomi had been taken by ambulance to Weston-super-Mare Hospital to be patched up. Nick was driven by one of the paramedics to Taunton for treatment. I got changed and, after covering up the muddy seats in my car with towels, drove to the hospital to collect Naomi. Her cuts have healed well, but Naomi says that her scar hurts whenever she sees loose rocks. Nick took longer to recover due to tendon damage, but went back caving again – only to break his arm down Reservoir Hole when someone dropped a rock on him! Nick must rank as the most accident-prone caver in the country …

# 20

# No Picnic at Ilam Park

I considered leaving the next anecdote out of this book because it did not fit well into the narrative. But I have given it a standalone chapter in its own right. It is appropriate to record it here, since this brief adventure came the closest to being my last, and it matches my disclaimer at the start.

Near Ashbourne in Derbyshire is the National Trust property of Ilam Park. The estate straddles the River Hamps just upstream of its confluence with the River Dove on the Staffordshire side of the county boundary, and the principal building (Ilam Hall) is operated as a youth hostel. Several springs boil up on the north bank of the river at the edge of a picnic area, and the local amenities (i.e. the tea room) make this an ideal cave diving venue if you like squirming through tight underwater passages followed by scoffing a slice of chocolate cake.

Ilam Main Rising is the primary cave diving site, and is situated in the middle of the group of springs. A substantial flow of water comes out of several openings and no caving is required to get to the entrance. It is possible to carry your equipment from the National Trust car park, change discreetly into diving gear in the public toilets and go for a dive; if you don't tarry, you can complete the entire operation in time to pay only the minimum parking fee.

Ilam Main Rising had previously been explored for a distance of 267 metres to a depth of 53 metres, where the way on was lost. The underwater passage is notoriously tight in places, and progress along it has to be slow and deliberate. A fatality had occurred here in 1977, when local cave diver, Mike Nelson, had drowned. His body was been found wedged beyond the end of the guideline 40 metres into the sump, and it took several dives to cut his gear away and bring his body to the surface. The passage was so tight that several rock flakes had to be hammered off to ease the process. At the conclusion of the recovery operation, boulders at the entrance moved causing a partial collapse, and this left gear trapped underground until the rock fall could be cleared.

A few metres downstream of the Main Rising, a smaller spring discharges into the River Hamps. This is called Ripple Rising (the tiny Raspberry Rising lies nearby) and this had been connected via a side passage to Main Rising in July 2001. A bypass to the tight, original route through the first 50 metres of Main Rising had been discovered at the same time. I made several dives in Ripple Rising in September 2001 while I was being treated for cancer – it was only an hour's drive from where I lived, and my consultant hadn't told me not to go cave diving. Ripple Rising continued beyond the link with Main Rising, and I reached the end of the explored passage on my third dive there, noting its potential for further exploration if a little underwater digging was carried out.

*Gary Jones and Tim Morgan at Ilam Main Rising (Duncan Price)*

The diving season at Ilam Risings is only during the summer months when the flow drops and the water clarity improves. The earliest that I had ever dived there was in March, but the conditions then were pretty grim. The best time was in August and September although this involved interacting with tourists who were curious about our activities; Gary Jones was once asked 'Does your mother know you're here?' Generally, the sightseers were friendly, sometimes to the extent of offering us food from their picnics, but at busy periods it was useful to leave someone stationed on the surface to act as crowd control.

By the following year, my attention had switched to the end of Main Rising. I had discovered that a dye test had been carried out which showed that water from the deep section at the end of Main Rising came out at all of the springs (including Ripple Rising), so there was little point in pushing these, as they were all distributaries to the Main Rising. Rick Stanton had been to the end of Main Rising using trimix, and had tipped me off to where a possible way on might lie. At the time I' had been doing a lot of mixed gas diving in Linley Caverns and was highly motivated to take up the challenge.

On Tuesday 27 August 2002, I bunked off from work and went to Ilam on my own. I ferried several diving cylinders over to the springs and changed into my drysuit. The ivy that had grown around the risings had been cut back, depriving me of somewhere to hide my car keys so I tucked it under the bumper of my 4x4. There was hardly a soul around, and I don't think I'd told anyone my plans, as I was supposed to be elsewhere.

The first obstacle was a narrow shaft just inside the entrance, which dropped down to a depth of 6 metres where I left a small cylinder of oxygen at the apex of a mobile slope of sand. I took the roomier bypass route to a squeeze 50 metres from daylight breathing a chest-mounted 12-litre cylinder of a weak nitrox mix containing 25% oxygen. Beyond this I used two high-pressure 300 bar, 7-litre side-mounted cylinders of heliair-20 (20% helium, the balance air). By the time I reached the end of the line at a depth of 53 metres, I'd used up a third of the gas in one of these cylinders.

I changed over to the unused cylinder and picked up the line reel that had been left there since this point had first been reached in 1994. Ahead of me lay a low arch, and I forced myself down into a flat-out bedding plane for about 5 metres. The way on seemed to be over a rock rib to the right, where the flow of water appeared to come from – it was difficult to tell, though, as I could hardly turn my head in the constricted space. I tied off the line, intending to back out. But found myself stuck fast by my cylinders, which had splayed out behind me, wedging me in.

I tried to relax … focus … think … remember my training … I methodically moved one hand down my body to locate a clip on my harness whilst using the other to moor myself to a rock. This enabled me to remove one cylinder and pull myself forward, using all of my strength, and turn around. I've no idea how I managed to do it: I think I practically folded my fins in half to make the manoeuvre. Then I squeezed back out into the larger approach passage, only to find that my thrashing around had broken the line and I was lost in the murk I'd stirred up while making my escape. I re-attached the cylinder that I had unclipped and considered what to do: there was no time to deploy a search reel to recover the line, so I followed the particulates suspended in the water hoping that the current would lead me in the right direction. At the next squeeze I found the line to safety. I consulted my contents gauges: I'd gone in with a full cylinder, but only 40 bar of gas remained in it. I was still over 250 metres from the surface and at 47 metres depth.

There was no point in worrying – it would only raise my breathing rate – so I swopped back to the first cylinder which I knew to be one third depleted. A regulator failure would be fatal right now, but fortunately nothing had been damaged during my struggle. I resolved not to look at my pressure gauges again as it didn't really matter. I had whatever gas remained and this would have to do.

My chances of escape improved when I reached the stage cylinder that I'd left on the way in, and I breathed from this as far as the bottom of the entrance pot, where I switched over to the oxygen. But I'd been gone for 55 minutes and I faced another 35 minutes of decompression. Quite remarkably, I managed to eke out my little oxygen cylinder for that time, a miracle in itself. It ran out just at the moment when I was clear to go to the surface. My report to the Cave Diving Group Newsletter was more concise; merely ending with the statement 'Max depth 54 metres'.

Anyone remotely 'normal' might have decided to take up a less risky hobby; not me! Three days later I'd refilled my cylinders and I went back for another go. More wisely this time, I had Clive Westlake follow in my wake (quite literally). He went to a depth of 31 metres, where he met me returning from the final chamber before the terminal restriction. This time I had set off down the pot with five cylinders: a 3-litre cylinder of oxygen, a 12-litre stage of nitrox-40 (left at a depth of 30 metres), a 7-litre cylinder of air (which was breathed as far as the squeeze into the final chamber at a depth of 47 metres where I'd relocated the line on my previous dive) and two high-pressure tanks of heliair-30 which I used to examine the end of the cave. With the benefit of a clearer head owing to the higher helium content of the deep mix, I decided that although the flow definitely came out of the bedding plane, I wasn't following it. I examined the rest of the chamber but noted no other leads. On the way back I stayed on the helium mixture until I collected the nitrox. Once we were both out, Clive and I adjourned to the National Trust café for tea and flapjacks – how civilised!

I did my final dive at Ilam in November 2006. It was a bit late in the year to be diving there and conditions were not optimal. I had visited a nearby company on business and had turned down the offer of a free lunch in order to go to Ilam. I should really have gone back to work, and was there on my own, unsupported and anonymous. It felt good to be back, but I knew that I was about to move away from the area so it was unlikely that I would get the chance to make this dive again. I was doing this for myself – I shunned recognition and simply recorded:

> The purpose of the dive was to try out a new drysuit/undersuit and use up some Heliair-20 left over from Wookey dives. A 12 L stage tank of air was breathed to a depth of 25 m and the diver continued on two 7 L tanks. A line break at -45 m was patched using some string from the diver's search reel but this cannot be seen to be a permanent repair. The end of the line (27-08-2002) was viewed from the final chamber but under today's high flow conditions did not appear to emit much current. Total dive time 90 minutes including 30 minutes decompression.

That's the end of the cave as far as I'm concerned. Although Ilam Risings continues, I stop here.

# Acknowledgements

I have relied on a number of sources to construct these reminiscences of my misspent life. Most of my early exploits are recorded in my personal caving logbooks. But once I owned a washing machine, these fell into disuse, as it was while I was waiting in the laundrette for my smalls to dry that I normally updated my diaries. I have instead used articles and reports I had submitted to the newsletters of the Chelsea Speleological Society Newsletter and the Cave Diving Group to refresh my memory of events. It has been a challenge to reinterpret these often terse, impersonal and understated accounts in order to turn them into more rounded stories to fill these pages and I appreciate the help of my copy-editor, Caroline Petherick in achieving this.

This book would not have appeared without the influence of diving author Rod Macdonald, who provided the spark which ignited my publisher's interest. I also value the indulgence of Dr Keith Whittles and the staff at Whittles Publishing for supporting this venture.

Numerous other people have helped me write this book and I would like to express my gratitude to a selection of them in approximate order of appearance:

Firstly, I would like to thank my long-suffering parents, Derek and Valerie Price, who have blessed me with their unconditional love and support over the past 50 years. Should you read this manuscript, I hope that you'll forgive me for being economical with the truth about my activities – it really was for your own good.

Dr Michael Wright introduced me to caving and made some useful comments after reviewing an early version of what became the first two chapters of this book. I hope that my storytelling has lived up to your expectations.

Three of my longest-standing friends, Professor John Hunt, Rob Murgatroyd and John 'Spanners' Stevens, were responsible for encouraging my interest in underground exploration.

Martyn Farr's classic book, *The Darkness Beckons*, was a major factor in motivating me to take up cave diving, and I'm honoured that he has written the foreword to my memoirs.

Rick Stanton MBE deserves special mention, not only for participating in so many of my adventures, but also for providing me with endless opportunities to make jokes at his expense. It has been difficult to get this far in the text without a reference to the size of Rick's nose, but I think I've done pretty well.

For many years, Gary Jones, Tim Morgan and John Volanthen and I operated as the Llangatwg Section of the Cave Diving Group (even though John doesn't have a Welsh surname). I could not have had better companions.

I owe Jon Bojar a great deal for letting me take up residence in his spare bedroom and also for breaking an ornament in his apartment – I've absolutely no idea how it happened!

Clive Westlake deserves a lot of credit for tolerating my youthful enthusiasm and disrespect over many years.

I would also like to acknowledge my adopted 'sons' – Stuart Gardiner and Chris Jewell – for being able to keep up with me.

Steve Hubin kindly reviewed Chapter 18, and provided me with a fuller picture of the events of that fateful spring day from his perspective.

The cave plans have been compiled and redrawn from from work by numerous organisations: Bristol Exploration Club, Brymawr Caving Club, Cave Diving Group, Chelsea Speleological Society, Grwp Ogoffiedd Craig a Ffynnon, Mendip Nature Research Committee & the University of Bristol Spelæological Society in addition to records from the British Geological Survey - it goes without saying that these schematic diagrams should not be used for underground navigation!

Finally, thank you Naomi, for sharing Chapter 19 with me, and for being my closest counsel during the preparation of this manuscript.

I will close by passing on some words of wisdom from two of the biggest influences in my cave diving career. Rick Stanton believes that a cave diver's biggest assets are strength of character and lack of imagination. This is not to say cave divers are not creative; in reality the opposite is true. But we don't let fear be our master. Rick explained to me that the secret to his success is: 'The more you do it, the luckier you get!' There may be some truth to that, but (despite the evidence presented here) I still prefer to follow the caution given to me by Martyn Farr when I first started out: 'Mind how you go ...'

# Glossary

| | |
|---|---|
| ABLJ | Adjustable Buoyancy Life Jacket; it is worn around the neck, and its prime purpose is to help the diver maintain **NEUTRAL BUOYANCY**. To do this, the diver can add air to it either from an inflator connected by a hose to the wearer's **REGULATOR** or from a dedicated mini-cylinder, and can also dump air. In an emergency it is possible to breathe from the rancid air trapped in the jacket to sustain life. It has been around for a few decades and has mostly been superseded by the **STAB JACKET** and more recently the **WING**. |
| abseil | Sliding down a rope using friction to slow a caver's descent. In its simplest and most uncomfortable form this can be achieved by wrapping the rope around the body. A more controlled method is to employ a **DESCENDER** attached to a body harness to provide a braking action. |
| adit | An artificial horizontal tunnel driven by miners to intercept ore (or, in the case of Carno Adit, a source of water). |
| airbell | An enclosed space in the roof of a sump filled with air of variable ability to support life. |
| ascender | See **PRUSIK**. |
| at thirds | See **THIRDS**. |
| aven | An upwards shaft entered from its base. The term is borrowed from a regional French word for 'pothole'. |
| back and foot ascent | Method of climbing a narrow passage by pressing your back against one wall and your feet on the other and shuffling upwards; also known as 'chimneying' after the technique used by small boys employed to clean flues in Victorian times. |
| bang(ing) | Explosives (use thereof) to judiciously break up rock. Practitioners require supervised training and a police licence to use, acquire and |

| | |
|---|---|
| | store explosives. Also known as 'Dr Nobel's Linctus' – after Alfred Nobel, who invented dynamite. |
| bailout | In the context of **REBREATHER** diving, a term meaning to come off the **BREATHING LOOP** and return to the surface using open-circuit cylinders (or a secondary back-up rebreather) carried specifically for that purpose. |
| base-fed line | A safety line paid out from the surface (dive base) rather by the diver. Rope signals (tugs on the line) are often used to communicate with the person paying out the line, so this method cannot be used over long distances as the line might snag. |
| bedding plane | A low, wide passage formed between the layers (beds) of limestone. |
| bends, the | See **DECOMPRESSION SICKNESS**. |
| blind | dead-end. |
| bottom time | The time spent at the deepest part of the dive. |
| bounce dive | Simple down-up dive profile with minimal **BOTTOM TIME** and thus a limited **DECOMPRESSION PENALTY**. |
| breathing loop | In the context of a **REBREATHER**; the path through which the diver's breath is circulated from the mouthpiece, counterlung(s), carbon dioxide absorber (scrubber) and back to the mouthpiece. |
| BSAC | British Sub-Aqua Club – the second oldest diving club in Britain. The Cave Diving Group, formed in 1946, is the oldest diving organisation still in existence in the world. |
| buddy check | To confirm with your dive partner(s) that your diving equipment is functional and does not have any leaks or other defects. |
| cenote | A natural pit, resulting from the collapse of limestone bedrock that exposes an opening into an underwater cave. As commonly used in the Yucatán peninsula of Mexico, the term, deriving from the Mayan *ts'onot*, refers to any location with accessible groundwater. |
| centreline map/survey | A basic plan of a cave that only includes the length and direction of passages, with no details regarding their width, height and other features; a 'stick model' of the layout of the cave. |
| chert | A fine-grained silica-rich sedimentary rock. Also known as flint, it varies in colour from white to black. |
| choke | A blockage in a cave passage, usually caused by a rockfall. |
| clear a stop | Complete one level of a staged decompression profile, and thus be able to ascend to a shallower depth or, if it was the last stop, to the surface. |

## Glossary

| | |
|---|---|
| clinometer | A device for measuring the slope of a survey leg. Combined with the direction (using a magnetic compass) and distance (from a tape measure stretched between the two stations at the ends of the leg), this information defines a vector in three dimensions which is used to construct the centreline of a cave survey. |
| close down | A point where a cave passage becomes too narrow for further progress unless digging techniques such as banging are used. |
| crawl(way) | (n) Used to describe a cave passage that is low and must be crawled through. |
| deco bottle | 1 A cylinder of compressed gas left at a specific depth underwater for the purpose of breathing during decompression. 2 A bottle of beer left in the water to cool at the surface for consumption after the dive whilst removing one's gear. |
| decompression penalty | The 'extra time' accrued during a deep dive in order to decompress on the way back to the surface. |
| decompression sickness | Physiological symptoms brought about by the formation of bubbles of inert gas which have come out of solution in the blood due to a too-rapid reduction in pressure. Often typified by a skin rash, pain in the joints (hence the term 'bends'), neurological problems – loss of feeling, changes in behaviour, etc. Treatment involves being placed in a hyperbaric chamber so that the gas is re-dissolved in the body, and then slowly reducing the pressure. Divers have been permanently paralysed, or have even died, from decompression sickness. |
| descender | Device attached to one's harness through which rope is threaded in such a way as to slow it down whilst abseiling. |
| diluent | Make-up gas added to the breathing loop of a closed circuit rebreather in order to dilute its oxygen concentration to acceptable levels, thus avoiding toxing. |
| dive line | String laid underwater to provide a trail to follow. |
| Doing It Right (DIR) | A holistic style of diving that originated in the Florida pan handle which employs a highly standardised equipment configuration (e.g. a back-mounted manifolded twinset with regulators – one of those having an extra-long hose connecting the first and second stages so that divers can share air, the donating diver using his backup regulator). There is a strong emphasis on diving as a team and solo diving is frowned upon. |
| dolomitic conglomerate | A conglomerate is a type of rock comprising large, round fragments cemented together within a fine-grained matrix. Dolomitic conglomerate is a rock found on the flanks of the Mendip Hills, formed in the Triassic period (250–200 million years ago) from |

| | |
|---|---|
| | weathered limestone, whereby its calcium content has been partially replaced by magnesium to form calcium magnesium carbonate (or 'dolomite'). |
| draught(ing) | Air movement caused by a barometric pressure difference between the air inside a cave and the outside air on the surface. A boulder choke with a draught going through it is a good indicator of an open passage beyond – an exciting prospect! |
| duck | A section of the cave almost entirely full of water. You can pass it only by pinning your head against the roof to breathe in the limited airspace. |
| entrance series | The part of the cave communicating between the outside and the major part of the cave. |
| etrier | A short length of rope ladder. |
| exchange trip | A traverse between two cave entrances achieved by teams travelling in opposite directions from each end, typically sharing equipment (ropes, ladders etc.) which is installed by one party and removed by the other. |
| fettle | To service, repair or improve equipment – an absorbing pastime in its own right. |
| flake | 1 Rib of rock sticking out of the sides of a cave passage. Useful for holding or tying onto. 2 A chocolate bar whose friable nature makes it unsuitable for cave food. |
| fossil passage | Formerly active cave passage which no longer contains a stream and thus is not being enlarged by erosion. |
| free-dive | Diving without scuba equipment by simply holding one's breath. Just requires big lungs and balls of steel. |
| goethite | A fragile dark iron oxide compound which coats the walls of underwater caves – especially in Florida. It is considered bad practice to dislodge it, thus leaving a permanent mark. |
| head spring | A resurgence which forms the principal source of a river rather than a one which flows into the side of a river. |
| heliair | A mixture of helium and air – a 'poor man's trimix' – made by filling an empty diving cylinder with some helium and topping it up with air. |
| jump reel | Small reel of dive line which is used to traverse gaps in the guideline. It's often set up to help divers enter a side passage whose line has been deliberately separated from the main-route line to avoid most divers being side-tracked. |

*Glossary*

| | |
|---|---|
| karabiner | A metal loop with a spring-loaded gate used to quickly and reversibly connect things together. From Karabinerhaken, German for 'spring hook'. |
| karst | A landscape formed from the dissolution of soluble rocks (e.g. limestone) where there no or few surface streams and rivers, the majority of the drainage being underground, in caves. The term certainly dates back to 1177 and the Slovene word Grast, referring to the Karst Plateau across the border of southwestern Slovenia and northeastern Italy (where the first research on this type of landform was carried out), although the roots of the word are much older. |
| karst window | An opening into the underground drainage of the area – typically the result of an earlier collapse and often leading to a river cave. |
| lead | 1 A (possible) way on. 2 What diving weights are made out of. |
| line arrow | An isosceles triangle of plastic with slots cut into the opposing long sides such that it can be attached to a dive line, clearly pointing to the nearest exit. It was developed by the elder statesman of US sump diving, Forrest Wilson; at the time when it was conceived, it was thought that only a few hundred would be needed to mark the lines in Florida's caves. But now nearly every cave diver carries several, and the characteristic shape has become a well-known symbol in the technical diving community: |

*Line Arrow of Agnes Milowka (Christopher Milowka)*

| | |
|---|---|
| manifold | See twinset. |
| mung | Slowly decomposing organic matter found on the floor of an underwater cave, typically composed of leaves, twigs etc. |
| neutral buoyancy | One of the delights of scuba-diving; a state of physical enlightenment in which your body neither sinks nor rises, but floats in blissful equilibrium mid-water, apparently free of the grinding gravity suffered by surface dwellers. Sometimes, though, it is easier in a cave to be positively or negatively buoyant and crawl along the roof or floor. |
| nitrox | A mixture of oxygen and nitrogen made by blending air with oxygen. Used for shallow diving to reduce decompression penalties since it contains less nitrogen than air and also in deco bottles to expedite decompression on deeper dives. By virtue of its elevated oxygen |

| | |
|---|---|
| | content the maximum depth to which a nitrox mixture may be breathed is limited by the need to avoid oxygen toxicity (see toxing). |
| no-mount zone | A section of cave so tight that a diver's cylinders must be removed and pushed ahead for the diver to get through. |
| no-stop dive | A (short, or shallow, or both) dive that does not involve a decompression penalty. |
| no-stop time | Maximum amount of time that may be spent underwater at any particular depth without incurring a decompression penalty. |
| off-gas | 1 Decompress. 2 Fart. |
| oxbow | A meandering side passage that rejoins the main route at its other end. Similar in form, but not necessarily in function, to the loops of old road formed when a new, straighter, section of road is built. |
| pee valve | Condom catheter attached to the penis to allow urine to flow down a pipe and be discharged outside a drysuit. (There is a female equivalent, but I'd rather not go into detail …) |
| phreas | That part of the rock strata that is completely underwater, forming an aquifer (reservoir of water). |
| phreatic | Cave passage formed underwater, typically of circular or lens-shaped cross-section, due to the absence of the down-cutting of the floor that is a feature of the passages which have air in them (termed 'vadose'). If the water level drops a lot, then the passage may become dry but still retain its shape. But many cave passages, where the water level has fallen gradually, are both phreatic and vadose, with a key-hole cross-section. |
| pillar valve | The tap that lets gas out of a diving cylinder, to which the first stage of a scuba regulator is attached. |
| pitch | Vertical or near-vertical drop which usually requires a wire ladder or srt to pass. Doing so without equipment is known as 'free climbing'. |
| prusik | The reverse of abseil. Prusiking makes use of two or more ascenders, mechanical devices which slide up a rope and lock onto it, thus allowing the wearer to climb it like an inchworm. The technique is named after Austrian mountaineer Karl Prusik, who devised a knot which would move freely when not under tension but grip when loaded. Modern cavers use cam-operated devices to achieve the same goal – but being able to tie a prusik knot in a rope can get you out of trouble if you drop an ascender down a pitch (it happens …). |
| purge | Clear a diver's regulator of water by blowing air through it. |
| push | An attempt to extend a cave to see if it will 'go'. |

## Glossary

| | |
|---|---|
| rebreather | A device which recirculates the wearer's expired breathe, removing carbon dioxide and replacing it with more oxygen thus allowing greater economy of gas consumption. The French term for rebreather is recycleur as a consequence. |
| regulator | A device for taking a supply of high-pressure air (or other breathing mixture) from a diving cylinder and delivering it to one's mouth at a pressure which is comfortable to breathe. Modern diving regulators (or 'regs') consist of two parts: a 'first stage', screwed onto the cylinder outlet or pillar valve, which reduces the pressure to around 10 bar (or atmospheres) above the ambient pressure, and a second stage, which meters the gas, according to demand, into the mouth. Expelled air then exhausts into the water through a non-return valve fitted in the second stage. |
| | Jacques Cousteau gets the credit for inventing the diving regulator, but – like the history of the light bulb or telephone – it was developed by different people at different times; his colleague Gagnin, a plumber, was the brains. |
| resurgence | A place where water emerges from a cave into daylight. Used interchangeably with the term rising. American cave divers use the equivalent word 'spring' more frequently than British ones. |
| resurgence flopping | Slightly derogatory term for the act of cave diving in underwater caves which require no caving ability to reach the water. Thus you can 'flop' into the resurgence directly from your car. American cave divers term this 'spring' diving as opposed to 'sump' diving, which implies all the unpleasantness involved in 'spelunking' (caving). |
| rift | A vertical fissure or slot. |
| rig | To install ropes and/or ladders on a pitch. If the pitch is already equipped with such aids, then it is termed 'rigged'. The removal of such tackle is called 'de-rigging' – this is unfortunate if you happen to become stranded at the bottom. |
| rising(s) | See resurgence. |
| roof tube | A round passage in the roof of a cave passage. Frequently of phreatic origin, roof tubes often form oxbows. |
| second stage | The part of your regulator that goes in your mouth. |
| shale | A fine-grained sedimentary rock with a thinly layered structure comprising a mixture of clay with tiny particles of other minerals such as quartz or calcite. Shale bands often overlay limestone and frequently form the roofs of some cave passages, making them unstable and liable to collapse. |

| | |
|---|---|
| shake hole | A depression on the surface caused by collapse into a cave passage lying beneath, therefore potentially providing a way into it if excavated. |
| shotline | Vertical dive line down an underwater drop. Useful for hanging onto during decompression stops, particularly if one's trim is poor. |
| sidemount | A method of attaching (usually) a pair of diving cylinders to the wearer's side in order to reduce the diver's profile in the water and enable low cave passages to be passed. Also popular with divers who wish to explore the insides of shipwrecks for a similar reason, sidemount diving is increasingly becoming adopted by the wider diving community as a bit of a fad. |
| silt monster | A diver whose poor trim results in their kicking up a lot of silt from the floor, thus destroying the visibility, especially for those following. |
| silt screws | Lengths of plastic pipe that act like telegraph poles, keeping the guideline off the floor, or forming a belay point in a sump that is mud- or silt-floored. |
| Single Rope Technique | Using a rope to descend and/or ascend one or more pitches in a cave. See also abseil and prusik. |
| sink(hole) | An opening in the surface where water disappears underground. |
| snoopy loops | Strong elastic bands made from car inner tubes. They have numerous applications for cave diving as well as a myriad other uses. |
| sporting | Describing a section of river cave that is challenging to traverse as a consequence of being full of a raging torrent of water. |
| stab jacket | An evolved form of the ablj which looks like a waistcoat. It too can be filled with air to varying degrees, to control a diver's buoyancy. |
| stage cylinder | A cylinder that is breathed for part of the dive and then left for collection (and re-use) on exit. |
| SRT | single rope technique; using a rope to descend and/or ascend one or more pitches in a cave. See also abseil and prusik. |
| stream passage | A cave passage carrying water with an airspace above it. |
| sump | A section of the cave entirely underwater. Also used as a verb when describing a passage, e.g. 'the cave sumps after 20 metres'. |
| thirds (rule) | The principle of reserving one third of one's air supply for an emergency. Thus a cave diver using two identically-sized cylinders would use one third of the air in each on the inwards dive and then exit breathing from each cylinder equally on the way out. The thinking being that if at the furthest limit of the dive one set became unusable, then there should be enough air in the other to reach the surface. |

# Glossary

| | |
|---|---|
| toxing | Experiencing the symptoms of oxygen toxicity usually associated with short term exposure to high partial pressures of oxygen. Effects include tunnel vision, tinnitus, nausea and muscle spasms which can ultimately lead to convulsions – and to death by drowning due to loss of the second stage from the victim's mouth. Longer-term exposure to lower levels of oxygen can be damaging to the lungs and are a factor to consider during decompression diving – particularly involving breathing pure oxygen or nitrox to accelerate the elimination of dissolved gases from the bloodstream. |
| trim | Looking cool in the water by being able to float, neutrally buoyant, with your body completely horizontal when stationary in the water. |
| trimix | A mixture of three gases – oxygen, nitrogen and helium – intended for deep diving. |
| trunk route | A major passage in a cave; other side passages may be inlets to this. |
| twinset | A pair of cylinders worn side by side on the diver's back. Frequently the cylinders are connected by a manifold or rigid pipe (often with a tap to isolate individual cylinders and outlets for two regulators). This arrangement allows both cylinders to be breathed from, using either one of a pair of regulators attached to each outlet, thus providing an extra degree of safety. The bulk of a twinset is a disadvantage for diving in narrow caves, where a sidemounted configuration is more practical. |
| undercut | Recess in wall of a cave passage, usually at its base. This be a potential problem for cave divers if the guideline becomes pulled into it, especially on a corner, making it unable to be followed (forming a 'line trap'). |
| vertical caving | Caving that involves a lot of pitches, tackled almost exclusively by SRT. |
| wing | Doughnut-shaped buoyancy compensator worn under a twinset that when inflated rides up around the cylinders, supporting them like the wings of an aircraft. |

# Great dive books

... Another cracking book by Rod and one which will become the divers' bible for Truk diving in the future. Gordon Mackie, **Scottish Diver**

... It's a rich and hugely detailed work that is interesting enough for this reader when he was sat on a British sofa. For anybody planning to travel halfway round the world and see what lies beneath Truk lagoon for themselves, it's pretty much a must-read. **British Diver**

...is laced with glorious black & white photographs. ...contemporary photographs and explanatory maps. ... it's the text that captures the spirit of the moment. ... I thoroughly recommend reading this book... ...it makes for a fascinating read. **Divernet**

...this publication would be of particular use to maritime historians, divers and students alike, simply in terms of the detail and wealth of information Macdonald has included about the wrecks and their wartime context. **The Great Circle**

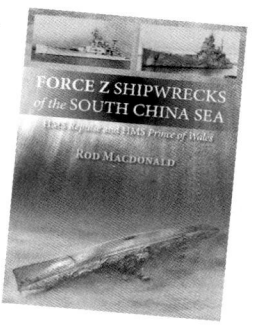

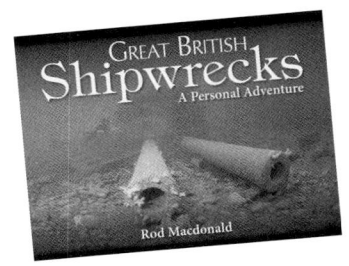

... is a gripping coffee table read in its own right... His accounts of diving the *Justicia*, HMS *Audacious* and *Empire Heritage* off Ireland's north east coast can't fail to deliver schoolboy-like excitement. ...the book is excellent. **British Diver**

... contains a spellbinding account of his journey to the heart of the Corryvrekan whirlpool. **The Scotsman**

...It truly is an excellent and informative read and a book you'll find yourself returning to repeatedly for another fix. ...is like a fusion of the most exciting presentations I've watched on National Geographic or Discovery; and reminiscent of the pioneering explorations of Cousteau. ...the late great Monsieur Cousteau may have been your idol Rod, but you're equally trail-blazing an awe-inspiring path yourself. **DiversInc**

available from
www.whittlespublishing.com